RAF
MARHAM

As part of our ongoing market research, we are always pleased to receive comments about our books, suggestions for new titles, or requests for catalogues. Please write to: The Editorial Director, Patrick Stephens Limited, Sparkford, Near Yeovil, Somerset, BA22 7JJ.

RAF
MARHAM

The operational history of Britain's front-line base from 1916 to the present day

KEN DELVE

Patrick Stephens Limited

First published in 1995

British Library Cataloguing in Publication data
A catalogue record of this book is available
from the British Library.

ISBN 1 85260 506 5

Library of Congress catalog card no. 95 77386

Patrick Stephens Limited is an imprint of
Haynes Publishing,
Sparkford, Nr Yeovil, Somerset, BA22 7JJ.

Designed & typeset by G&M, Raunds, Northamptonshire
Printed in Great Britain by Butler & Tanner Ltd, London and Frome

CONTENTS

CHAPTER 1

ZEPPELIN FIGHTERS

The outbreak of the First World War in 1914 found the British armed forces with only a nascent air service. The Royal Flying Corps (RFC) had been formed in 1912 with Military and Naval Wings to provide air support for the army and the navy, the Naval Wing officially becoming the Royal Naval Air Service (RNAS) on 1 July 1914. Official backing was still very low key, as few senior officers of the cavalry and battleship variety had any time for the new-fangled concept of air power.

Initial thoughts on the employment of aircraft had been restricted to their use as an extension of the light cavalry scout or the frigate; for reconnaissance. Early experiments by a few far-sighted individuals, often at their personal expense, had proved the value of the aircraft in such operations. However, other nations, and Italy and Germany in particular, saw greater prospects for aircraft as a military asset. The Italians pioneered the use of 'bombers' in colonial action as early as 1911. Meanwhile, in Germany the thoughts of some had turned to the strategic application of a new air arm capable of flying over ground forces and reaching long-distance targets – including England. The Channel would no longer be a barrier protected by the might of the Royal Navy; suddenly, England was open to attack. It was with the concept of the dirigible that the Germans were to perfect this principle.

When the fledgling RFC deployed its small force to the Continent in support of the British Expeditionary Force, the air defence of the United Kingdom was left in the hands of the Admiralty, with a number of RNAS stations around the east coast and gun and searchlight cordons around specific areas, particularly London.

In November 1914 the only military airfield in Norfolk was the RNAS station at South Denes, near Great Yarmouth. The primary responsibility of this coastal air station was fleet defence, whenever the fleet was operating in its area; overland air defence was very much a secondary consideration. At first it appeared that there would be no problem with this arrangement.

On the night of 19/20 January 1915 two German airships, LZ3 (Kapitanleutnant Hans Fritz) and LZ4 (Kapitan Magnus von Platen-Hallermund) cruised over Norfolk. A third, LZ6, turned back with engine trouble. Snow showers and poor visibility made navigation difficult for the airships, and they bombed towns and villages at random. LZ3 attacked Yarmouth, causing one death, while LZ4 flew a course Bacton–Cromer–Sheringham–Beeston–Thornham–Brancaster–Hunstanton–Snettisham–King's Lynn, scattering bombs along the way. Those that fell on King's Lynn killed four people and caused £7,740-worth of damage; barely significant, but sufficient to cause severe shock to a nation which had previously been beyond the range of European wars. The German press was jubilant, and the British press was furious and wanted to know what the Government was going to do about this scandal. In the short term the answer was nothing; it was deemed best to wait and see how matters developed. Moreover, at this stage little could be done in the face of shortages of both aircraft and pilots. The airship problem remained an unknown quantity. This was to change as soon as the Zeppelins began to attack London.

The City received its first major raid on 31 May 1915, when Hauptmann Linnarz in LZ38 dropped incendiary bombs and grenades, killing seven people and causing £18,596-worth of damage. The casualties and damage were again light, but this attack, seemingly mounted with impunity against the centre of British government and economy by a single airship, held the threat of worse to follow should a co-ordinated campaign be launched by the entire German Naval and Army airship forces. While debates raged as to what action should be taken, further attacks on London took place. It seemed that only an aircraft defence force would provide the answer. Although an aircraft had already destroyed a Zeppelin, LZ37 having been brought down over Belgium in June 1915 by Sub-Lieutenant Warneford, the Zeppelin commanders saw no great threat from aeroplanes. 'As to an aeroplane corps for the defence of London, it must be remembered that it takes some time for an aeroplane to screw itself up as high as a Zeppelin, and by the time it gets there the airship would be gone. Then, too, it is most difficult for an aeroplane to land at night.' So said Heinrich Mathy, one of the greatest Zeppelin commanders, and in large measure he was to be proved right in the early years.

The early raids had prompted a rethink on the existing defence pattern throughout East Anglia, one of the favoured approach routes for the Zeppelins, as they could follow the coast until they reached the Wash and then fly down it towards London. East Anglia, and particularly Norfolk, was to prove a critical part of the defensive scheme. New Emergency Landing Grounds (ELGs) were created and provided with the most rudimentary of night landing aids; usually no more than a searchlight that could be pointed along the ground. Narborough was amongst these early developments. This station opened as a Night Landing Ground (NLG) for RNAS Great Yarmouth in August 1915.

February 1916 brought an agreement that the RFC would relieve the Navy of responsibility for an aeroplane force to defend London, and this was confirmed by the War Committee's approval of the formation of specialist Home Defence Squadrons. One of these early squadrons, formed by amalgamating control of a number of dispersed flights, was 39 Squadron. This unit was to achieve an outstanding record in the next nine months, becoming known throughout England as the 'Zeppelin destroyers'.

Meanwhile, developments were taking place in East Anglia. In April 1916 the field at Narborough was transferred to RFC control and in late May the first operational unit, 35 Squadron, arrived with its Vickers F.B.5, Royal Aircraft Factory B.E.2c and B.E.2e, and Armstrong Whitworth F.K.3 aircraft to undertake training as a Corps Reconnaissance squadron.

Marham itself opened as a Home Defence station within No. 6 Brigade in September 1916 and became the home of the HQ and 'C' Flight of 51 Squadron. The other two Flights were at Tydd St Mary and Mattishall.

In common with many Home Defence squadrons, the unit had a variety of types on charge, including the F.E.2b, B.E.12b, Avro 504K, Sopwith Camel, and Martinsyde G.100. The pri-

The fragile-looking Royal Aircraft Factory F.E.2b was one of the primary Home Defence types.

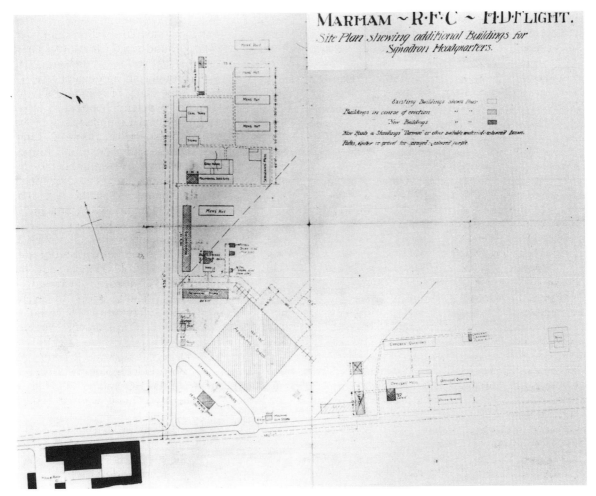

The site plan of Marham as a Home Defence airfield.

mary operational types as far as night operations against the airships were concerned were the F.E.2b and B.E.12b. The latter was essentially a single-seat version of the tried and tested B.E.2c, fitted with a 200 hp Hispano-Suiza engine in an attempt to provide the extra power needed to reach airship operating heights. The F.E.2b, however, had its origins as a two-seat fighter for the Western Front. A pusher powered by a Beardmore engine, it had a top speed of just 81 mph and a notional ceiling of only 11,000 ft, both of which made it quite unsuitable for Zeppelin chasing. General HQ Home Forces suggested that each F.E.2b should have a standard armament for night fighting of four high-explosive (HE) bombs or one box of Ranken darts, plus a Lewis gun with seven drums of ammunition for the observer. However, as in all Home Defence units the

pilots and mechanics of 51 Squadron introduced various 'home-made' modifications to give their machines better performance and, they considered, more appropriate armament.

Success came to the Home Defence forces on the night of 2/3 September 1916, when 2nd Lt William Leefe Robinson of 39 Squadron shot down the wooden Schütte-Lanz airship SL11. The airship's plunge was witnessed by thousands of Londoners and was heartily cheered. Pressure was brought to bear, and the triumphant pilot was awarded the Victoria Cross. It had been a magnificent achievement, as Robinson had to struggle with his underpowered B.E.2c to achieve the interception. Before the end of the month this same squadron had scored another victory, Lt Fred Sowrey bringing down the Zeppelin LZ32. On the same night another 39 Squadron pilot had shared in the destruction of LZ33. These victories greatly encouraged the Home Defence squadrons and made them keen to emulate the success of the 'Zeppelin killers'. However, 39 Squadron again scored the next victory, 2nd Lt Wulfstan Tempest destroying LZ31 on the night of 1/2 October. It was very frustrating for the other squadrons, with long periods of waiting for the message to take off, and cold, lonely periods of 'stooging' up and down a set patrol line waiting for something to happen.

For 51 Squadron at Marham it seems to have been a quiet time as far as operations were concerned. A moderate-sized force of ten airships left their bases on the night of 27 November to raid the Midlands. The defences were now reasonably well organized, and against this first attack since the October disaster (for the Zeppelins), the RFC mounted 30 sorties and the RNAS a further 10. Among the former were two from Marham. The first aircraft, an F.E.2b, was airborne at 03:32 but no further details are recorded. Lieutenant W.R. Gaynor took off at 04:30 on the 28th in F.E.2b 7680 to patrol the north Norfolk coast. Having found no 'trade' he abandoned the patrol, but on returning crashed fatally at Tibbenham. However, it was another bad night for the Germans, who lost two airships (L34 and L21), inflicted only small amounts of damage (£12,482), and killed four civilians.

The first half of 1917 saw very few night attacks on the UK. Up to the end of May the Zeppelins appeared on only three nights. A single airship is thought to have dropped bombs in the Kent area on 16/17 February, a force of five airships attempted to attack London on 16/17 March and, finally, six airships appeared on the night of 23/24 May. It appears that the plan for this night called for an attack on London, but that poor navigation, adverse weather, and a growing appreciation of the threat posed by the British defences turned this into an ineffectual and scattered raid. The first Zeppelins were reported off the east coast at 21:45 by the Yarmouth station, but none appeared overland until 01:18, when L40 appeared south of Lowestoft. The airships cruised around East Anglia looking for targets, and dropped the occasional bomb. The defences were alert, and the RFC sent up 39 aircraft, while the RNAS, in its biggest effort for some time, despatched 37 machines. All in all they were unlucky not to come across any of the German vessels. As part of the total, the various flights of 51 Squadron flew 13 sorties, and 'C' Flight at Marham contributed three F.E.2b sorties. The first of these was airborne at 00:50, 2nd Lt Duncan and Aircraft Mechanic Bishop getting aloft in A5520 for a 2 hr 10 min search of Norfolk's night skies. They landed at Harling Road at 03:00. Meanwhile, 4890 was airborne at 00:55 with 2nd Lt Bean and Sgt Bastable, who spent more than three frustrating hours cruising around in the hope that the searchlights would latch on to a Zeppelin and allow them to get into a firing position. The third aircraft up was 7676, Capt Barnes being airborne between 03:35 and 05:15.

A major reorganization of the Home Defence network in August brought Marham under the control of Southern Wing, Home Defence Brigade.

F.E.2bs of 51 Squadron, probably at Marham.

The Germans raided England by night on 16/17 June and 21/22 August, but Marham was not called upon to respond. September brought a major offensive, with German operations on eight nights, seven being by aeroplanes. The only Marham reaction was on the night of 24/25th, against the airship attack. Eleven airships were tasked to attack targets in the Midlands and North East England, and bombs were dropped on Rotherham and Hull. Five of the Zeppelins coasted in between King's Lynn and Bridlington in the early hours of the 25th, at estimated heights of 16,000–18,000 ft, well above that of most of the nightfighters. As part of the defensive response of 32 RFC and four RNAS sorties, 51 Squadron flew eight operations. Marham sent up 7021 piloted by Lt T. Gladstone at 00:38, although he returned within 30 min with engine trouble, and A5548 with Lt D. Montgomery at 01:12. This pilot stayed up for over 2 hours but had nothing to report. Once again the raid caused few casualties and little damage, but the same could not be said of the increasing number of attacks being made by the Gothas and, from 28/29 September, Giant bombers.

London was the usual focus of these aeroplane raids, which began to cause quite significant amounts of damage. Although the anti-aircraft guns claimed a Gotha on one of the early raids, the bombers were proving immune from the existing Home Defence aircraft. The jubilation following the success of the 'Zeppelin killers' in late 1916 had now evaporated amidst renewed calls for something to be done. One of the additional tasks allotted to 51 Squadron was to act as a trials unit for various potential night fighting machines, an example being the de Havilland D.H.10. Unfortunately, the records for this period are very poor, and such snippets of the station's history are mostly found by chance.

One of the new pilot arrivals was Lt Golding, who joined 51 Squadron in late September 1917. He recalls his arrival: 'On 25 September I arrived at Narborough railway station and was met by a tender for the journey to Marham. I reported to the Flight Commander, Captain Collinson, the next day. It was the 27th before I had my first flip. I went up in the evening for a joyride lasting about half an hour.' He says that most flying consisted of short (15–30 min) sorties in the local area, either training or air tests, plus a fair number of forced landings, after which the pilot would obtain local help to fix the machine and

then fly back to base. There was a reasonable amount of night flying, as appropriate for a Home Defence unit, plus bombing and navigation exercises. Typical of the latter was that on 9 October, with a take-off at 07:15 to fly the route Swaffham–Thetford–Bury–Sudbury–Chelmsford–Chatham–Ashford–Lympne, landing at 09:25. This also provided a good opportunity to take the train to London and see a show at the theatre before flying home the next day. Golding was with 'C' Flight for only a few weeks before he joined 'B' Flight at Tydd, and it is worth looking at a few more extracts from his log book and diary:

27.9   30 minute flight in evening.
28.9   Morning messed about doing nothing. Afternoon did a bit of bombing from 500 feet. Evening went on two recons, one halfway to King's Lynn, other to Sedgeford and Rudham, about 2 hours flying.
30.9   Quiet day so walked to Narborough aerodrome and had tea there.
3.10   Afternoon had forced landing near Narborough, started up bus ourselves and came home.
20.10 Afternoon did a little flying. Evening a Zepp raid. They dropped bombs a mile from us at Marham. Could hear whistle of bomb as it passed through the air.

The Zeppelins had returned in force on 19/20 October, after two more aeroplane attacks earlier in the month. This time the target was Northern England, and bombs eventually fell on a number of towns and cities, including Birmingham, Bedford, and Northampton. Eleven airships were involved, and inflicted the greatest level of damage achieved by the airship forces for some considerable time – £54,346-worth of damage and 36 killed. It was, however, to cost them dear. Poor weather, especially winds higher than forecast, scattered the raiders from London to Birmingham, making the task for the defences much harder. The first warnings were issued at 16:00, and Marham despatched its first defensive sortie at 19:42, Lt A. Nock getting airborne in A5723. He flew one of the longest such patrols yet mounted, not landing until 00:15, by which time he was suffering from extreme cold and had to be helped from his cockpit, not an uncommon occurrence. The only other Marham sortie was flown by 2nd Lt T. Gladstone, who was airborne in A5724 from 20:07 to 23:55. Although Marham's aircraft had no luck, it turned out to be a reasonable night for the

An aerial view of Narborough aerodrome in November 1918. This was one of the major training bases in England.

defences, with L44 being claimed by the guns and three other airships, L45, L49, and L50, crashing for a variety of reasons.

Throughout 1917 Narborough had continued its training role, various units coming and going, often *en route* to France. December 1917 saw the arrival of 83 Squadron to work up as a night bomber squadron, this unit departing for France the following March.

The units at Marham had been increased in December with the formation of 191 (Depot) Squadron, although this was soon renumbered 191 (Night) Training Squadron (NTS) to act as a night operations training unit. Equipped with a range of types including the B.E.2d, B.E.2e, D.H.6 and F.E.2b, the squadron was commanded by Major Arthur T. Harris, destined to achieve fame as Bomber Command's chief in the Second World War. Arriving, on promotion, from 39 Squadron at Joyce Green, Harris put his experience and enthusiasm into action. It was, however, a short-lived period, as he soon moved on to take command of 44 Squadron. The NTS continued to provide its invaluable training until it moved to Upwood in July 1918.

Using its long-range bombers, the German Army pursued its offensive against London, and more such raids were made throughout the rest of 1917. The airships, however, did not return. At last the defenders were receiving new aircraft types, 39 Squadron operating Bristol Fighters (the first such mission being flown on 5/6 December) and other units acquiring the Sopwith Camel. It was with the latter type that the first night victory over a bomber was achieved, Capt G. Murlis Green downing a Gotha on the night of 18/19 December. While the other HD units, such as 51 Squadron, were happy that the enemy were being countered, they were also very frustrated as they soldiered on with the older types that allowed them very little chance of scoring any victories. This frustration was voiced by the Brigadier General of 6 Brigade: 'There is no doubt that if machines with a performance equal to, say, the Bristol Fighter, had been available, two Zeppelins would have been brought down.' He was referring to the problems encountered during the airship raid of April 12/13 1918, when five of the most modern Zeppelins attacked the Midlands. These new airships were harder to detect and much harder to intercept, and the defences flew only 27 sorties, nine of which came

The only surviving period building of RFC Narborough is now used as an agricultural store. This photograph was taken in December 1994.

from 51 Squadron. Marham mounted three:

22:00–00:47; A5724, 2nd Lt J.R. Smith.
22:07–23:38; A6465, 2nd Lt S.W. Smith.
23:02–01:42; Lt T.H. Gladstone.

The enemy crossed the coast from 21:20 onwards, L62 moving in over Cromer and dropping a few bombs in the neighbourhood of 51 Squadron's 'B' Flight base at Tydd St Mary. None of the Marham pilots even saw a Zeppelin.

The continuing failure to achieve reasonable results led to another break in the airship campaign. The bombers returned to London on the night of 19/20 May, 28 Gothas and three Giants causing damage set at £177,317 and 49 fatalities, though three Gothas were shot down. The last raid of the war to involve Marham operationally took place on 5/6 August, when five airships attacked the Midlands. Once again, strong winds caused problems, scattering the airships but also making life difficult for the fighters. At Marham, 'C' Flight put up two sorties. Lieutenant H. Steele was airborne at 21:41 in A5724, but returned an hour later with a troublesome engine. Captain T. Martyn took off at the same time and made for his

patrol line. He managed to reach the very respectable height of 19,300 ft and proceeded to scan the night skies for any sign of the enemy. At least once he caught a brief glimpse of an airship but was unable to give chase. Just after midnight he decided to return to base, and descended towards the west to try and fix his position. Reaching 500 ft and expecting to be over land, he lit his underwing Holt flares and was amazed to see nothing but sea. He reduced power to half throttle to conserve petrol, and continued to head west. The fuel situation was becoming critical when he spotted North Coates airfield and at 00:50 brought his machine in safely to land.

During 1918, 51 Squadron's personnel strength at Marham was recorded as 14 officers, 15 SNCOs, 14 corporals, 113 other ranks, and three WRAF. By this date the airfield facilities had increased to appoximately 30 buildings, including two main hangars. The overall size of the landing ground was estimated as 740 yd by 530 yd, with 'a good level surface. Its general surroundings being open and flat with large fields.' By the standards of the day it had become a reasonable landing ground. Training sorties continued to occupy most of the

The Marham churchyard contains two First World War airmen's graves, including that of 2nd Lt A.R. Hodges.

squadron's time throughout 1918, and, with little chance of seeing any real action, many pilots became somewhat bored. September brought the Avro 504s and dual-control D.H.9s of 55 Training Depot Squadron to Marham.

Armistice Day, 11 November, was celebrated with an 'attack' on the squadrons at Narborough. The 51 Squadron raiders dropped bags of flour, only to suffer retaliation somewhat later in the form of bags of soot.

The end of the war signalled a rapid reassessment of the Royal Air Force's future, and, in the rush to disarm, the new Service, which had come into being on 1 April 1918, was reduced to almost nothing. Marham was not one of the all-too-few airfields scheduled to survive, and with the departure of 51 Squadron for Hornchurch on 14 May 1919, the airfield was closed down.

CHAPTER 2

BOMBER STATION

After years of neglect caused by Government disinterest and lack of funding for military aviation, the 1930s saw a rapid expansion of the Royal Air Force. In the 1920s analysis of the effect of air power on military operations in the First World War, most 'expert' opinion saw the bomber as the key to future success. With leading theorists such as General Douhet preaching the devastating potential of the bomber, it became air doctrine to favour a strong bomber force that could cripple the military and economic potential of an enemy. When, at long last, the RAF was able to gain enough Government support for even a moderate expansion programme, it was the bomber that became the central element of the strategy.

Any increase in aircraft strength meant that a greater number of airfields would be required, so the airfield construction programme became an integral part of the 1930s' plans. Up to this point most strategic planning had been based upon the perceived need to counter French airpower capability, but now that Germany was regarded as the most likely potential enemy it was essential to establish airfields in East Anglia, Lincolnshire and Yorkshire. Because of the limited range of existing bombers, East Anglia became the initial focus. The search for suitable tracts of land often started with a return to those areas that had been used as landing grounds during the First World War, so both Marham and Narborough were surveyed during the early 1930s. Development potential, land availability (and price), local communications and many other points were taken into consideration.

Work began on the construction of a perma-

A 'sneaky' picture of Marham and its aircraft; this photo later formed part of the Luftwaffe target folder.

38 Squadron was the sole operator of the Fairey Hendon night bomber.

nent station at Marham in 1935. The German announcement that year of the official existence of the Luftwaffe, and the boast that it matched its 'rivals' in size, provided a spur to accelerate the RAF's programme. Work progressed rapidly on the new West Norfolk base, and the distinctive arc of 'C'-type hangars began to dominate the landscape.

On 1 April 1937 RAF Marham was opened as a standard two-squadron Heavy Bomber station forming part of No. 3 Group, RAF Bomber Command. Wing Commander A.P.V. Daly AFC took command the following day, being promoted to Group Captain on 1 July. With an initial strength of two officers and 30 airmen, the unit was in business, although it was to remain some-

Although it looked ungainly in flight with its massive fixed undercarriage, the Hendon had a number of advanced features.

thing of a building site for many months. At 09:30 on 5 May the Handley Page Heyfords of 38 Squadron, under the command of Sqn Ldr W.J.M. Akerman, arrived from Mildenhall, the squadron having formed at that base some two years earlier from a Flight of 99 Squadron.

The squadron hardly had time to settle in before it was split in two, B Flight going to form the second of Marham's bomber units, 115 Squadron, with effect from 28 June. At last, on 9 July, the 14th and last of the new Fairey Hendon bombers was delivered, these aircraft being shared with 115 Squadron until the arrival of the latter's planned complement of Handley Page Harrows. The Harrows arrived throughout the summer, the first, Harrow I K6962, being delivered on 14 June. The Squadron eventually had a mixed complement of Harrow I and II aircraft. In October the squadron deployed to No. 2 Armament Training Camp at Aldergrove, Northern Ireland, for a period of intensive training in bombing and gunnery. The first aircraft loss came during the return flight on 9 November, when K6968 suffered an engine failure on take-off. The Harrow's wing dipped, striking one of the gun butts and causing the aircraft to crash, fortunately without injury to the crew.

As one of the RAF's newest and most advanced stations (the Hendon and Harrow being seen as 'modern' bombers), Marham was subject to numerous visits throughout 1938. The new alliance with France led to many military exchange visits as joint planning became routine. One such visit to Marham was that on 1 June by a French air force mission led by General J. Vuillemin, Chief of the General Staff of the French air force. The team toured all parts of the station, but paid particular attention to the flying squadrons and the various flying demonstrations. From 27 June to 16 July, 38 Squadron had a detachment at No. 7 Armament Training Camp, Acklington, for bombing and gunnery practice. The average bombing error for the 12 crews was 128 yd from 10,000 ft and 36 yd from low level, while the gunners managed to score an average of 37.7 per cent hits. These were very respectable figures on a range in peacetime, but it would be a very different matter under operational conditions. August brought the annual Home Defence Exercise, the Marham squadrons flying a number of sorties on the 5th and 6th of the month and, according to the umpires, performing well against the fighters.

September 1938 brought Britain to the brink of war, with the Munich Crisis. The increasing belligerence of Hitler's Germany led many to believe that it was time to take a stand and support the guarantees given to Czechoslovakia. RAF units were put on standby and aircraft were given new camouflage schemes. The prewar idea of painting the squadron number on the side of aircraft was abandoned in favour of a widespread adoption of two-letter codes. Many of those units already using codes had them changed as part of the new

This 115 Squadron Handley Page Harrow carries its squadron number as a prewar 'code'.

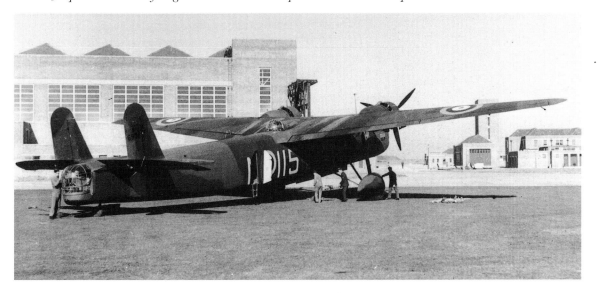

Marham's C-type hangars have seen many occupants since this Harrow.

security awareness. When British Prime Minister Neville Chamberlain's meeting with Hitler resulted in the famous (or infamous) 'Peace in Our Time' document, there was a general feeling of gratitude. On the part of the military this was expressed as a sigh of relief, as it allowed more time in which to continue the expansion and re-equipment programmes that were still very much

Harrow K7019 came to grief at Liverpool on 22 October 1938.

in their early stages. Marham would certainly be a very different place 12 months later; the obsolete Harrow and Hendon bombers would be replaced by the much more viable Vickers Wellington. The first Wellington I, L4230, was delivered to 38 Squadron on 28 September, and over the next few weeks the re-equipment programme went ahead at a steady pace. The last of the Hendons had gone by 12 January 1939.

Meanwhile, 115 Squadron had continued the training routine with their Harrows, including a number of detachments to No. 4 Armament Training Station at West Freugh. Recalled from one such detachment, K7019 was destroyed following a forced landing near Liverpool. Engine trouble was again the root of the problem, engine vibrations persuading the captain to land at Speke. Because the landing looked a little uncertain he ordered the crew of four to bale out, and this was safely accomplished, although two suffered minor injuries. A landing at Speke was now out of the question, so the pilot chose a 'dark patch' that he took to be a field, and put the aircraft down.

Aircraftman E.C. 'Johnnie' Johnson arrived at Marham in early 1939. He recalls:

When we arrived at Marham we found that all personnel had been confined to camp for the past two weeks or so. This of course was an extremely unusual situation, as was the incident

A rare shot of a Hendon having its starboard Rolls-Royce Kestrel engine overhauled.

that had caused it. Apparently, or so we learned later, a few days before Christmas 38 Squadron had been carrying out night flying

A superb line-up of 38 Squadron aircraft.

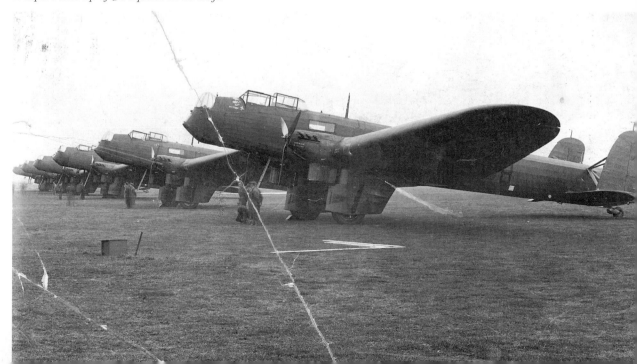

Winching the standard 250 lb bomb into a Harrow.

with their Hendons. During the evening a Hendon had started up, taxied out and received a green lamp for take-off. It was then opened up to full power, rolled across the airfield and became airborne, but almost immediately the engines were throttled back and the aircraft dropped heavily to the ground, smashing its undercarriage and slithering to a stop at the edge of the airfield, extensively damaged. When the fire engine and ambulance arrived at the site, the aircraft and cockpit were found to be empty, with not a soul in sight. It was quickly established that no pilot had been involved in the flight, so the RAF Special Investigation Branch (SIB) were called in. A few days after our arrival two airmen were arrested. It was said at the time that someone fed up with being unable to leave the camp to see his girlfriend had named them to the SIB. It was rumoured that they were going to fly the aircraft to the Civil War in Spain, but how they expected to get there with no navigation aids and probably insufficient fuel no one really knows. They were both uninjured in the crash, jumped out of the cockpit and disappeared into the darkness of the airfield perimeter and walked back to camp. Their Courts Martial took place a few

weeks later and they were sentenced to the military prison at Colchester. One of the first jobs we inexperienced apprentices were given was to cut up the rear fuselage of the crashed Hendon with hacksaws!

Meanwhile, the Wellingtons were kept busy on tours and training exercises, four aircraft going to Acklington in February to be used for training air gunners for No. 3 Group.

Aircraft from Marham ranged far and wide throughout the UK, as well as undertaking a number of exercises to France. Every month the squadrons took part in a station tactical exercise, simulating war conditions with typical targets and, when possible, arranging fighter opposition. On 1 March Harrow K6969 developed engine problems over the North Sea during one such navigation exercise and, with little prospect of curing the problem, the captain ordered the crew to bale out. Three of them safely took to their parachutes, but then the two pilots decided that it was worth trying to make it back to base; and duly arrived back at Marham!

'Johnnie' Johnson recalls the often frightening task of flarepath duty during night flying:

This necessitated the goose-neck flares having

Above *Personnel of 115 Squadron pose with a Wellington IC in 1939: rear; Plt Off Lines, Plt Off Crosby, Fg Off Lambert, Fg Off Gibbes, Sgt Moores, Flt Sgt Powell, Sgt Taylor, Flt Sgt Groves, Sgt Newberry, Sgt Line, Fg Off Gayford: middle; Fg Off Laslett, Fg Off Wood, Fg Off Sheeran, Fg Off Donaldson, Fg Off Clarke, Fg Off Chivers, Plt Off Harris, Plt Off Jaggard, Plt Off Scott, Fg Off Rankin, Fg Off Wardlaw, Plt Off Hughes, Plt Off Craigon: front; Fg Off Gardener, Fg Off Pringle, Flt Lt Vincent, Sqn Ldr Bowles, Wg Cdr Rowe, Sqn Ldr Arglencroft, Flt Lt Guthrie, Fg Off Simpson, Fg Off Newman, Fg Off Wells.*

Below *Wellington X3662 of 115 Squadron.*

to be filled up with paraffin and then laid out in a line into the prevailing wind across the grass airfield, and sometimes a hurried scamper to change the line if the wind changed. After dark the flares were lit and, according to the sergeant who was instructing us, as long as we stayed on the right-hand side of the flarepath when aircraft were taking off or landing, we would be perfectly safe. I must admit it was a bit frightening to be in the middle of the airfield with these huge aircraft hurtling towards you in the pitch dark, and I wish that our sergeant had instructed the one pilot who landed on the so-called 'safe side' of the flarepath, causing me the fright of my life as the wing of this aircraft rushed over my head.

The arrival of the first Wellington for 115 Squadron on 30 March heralded an acceleration of the re-equipment programme, which was now rushed through as quickly as possible. By the middle of May the squadron had a full complement of the new type, and both Marham units now had the RAF's latest bomber. The intensive

An aerial view of Marham, 18 April 1939.

training was to continue throughout the summer; a summer of rising tension on the European political front. However, the country was still at peace as the summer of 1939 opened and, like many RAF stations, Marham held an Empire Air Day on 20 May. With good weather and an active programme of air and ground events the station attracted 12,250 visitors and recorded a profit of £609. Despite such apparently peaceful happenings the military build-up continued. The response of Commonwealth countries to the call for assistance was, as always, excellent, and Marham was chosen as the base for the New Zealand bomber squadron, formed on 1 June under Sqn Ldr M.W. Buckley. The unit was later renumbered following a Bomber Command decision not to create 'national' units, and it was not made into a full New Zealand operational squadron. At this early stage of the war the only 'recognition' of New Zealand was in the title of No. 75 (New Zealand) Squadron. This policy of squadron composition and nomenclature was revised as the war progressed and Bomber Command expanded. The very large percentage of Commonwealth personnel joining the crews made it sensible to create 'national' squadrons within the RAF structure; even then, however, they maintained a mix of nationalities.

April saw a 38 Squadron detachment at Northolt carrying out trials with the Air Fighting Development Establishment (AFDE), night and day phases being flown on fighter affiliation with Hurricanes and Spitfires to examine tactics. The standard formation was a close box of sections of three to concentrate defensive firepower. Evasion was controlled by R/T from the lead aircraft, the formation moving as one with manoeuvres such as rotation, sliding section, acceleration and deceleration, turning and skidding. All of the fighter attacks developed into the stern sector, emphasising the need for strong rear armament.

Wellington L4243 was burnt out after crash-landing in a field; Sgt Summers had to put it down when it caught fire during a training flight, but none of the crew was injured. After the inevitable investigation it was decided to modify the flexible union of the fuel line on all of the Wellingtons.

July brought a much-increased pace of activity with, on the 7th, the first major Bomber Command exercise. This was a large-scale event involving most of the squadrons of the Command, and with fighter Groups, Observer

Corps and ground defences all taking part. Later in the month the Marham squadrons undertook long-range flights to southern France, 115 Squadron sending nine aircraft to Marseilles on 19 July and both units combining to send 12 Wellingtons to Bordeaux a week later. Such exercises were of great value to the crews, as they revealed some of the many problems involved in long-range navigation by day. However, the primary purpose was that of a political show of solidarity between allies. 'Johnnie' Johnson recalls the growing tension:

Indications of the coming war became stronger as the summer wore on. In August, hundreds of reservists were called up and posted to Marham [this was part of a major exercise]. The camp became crowded, tents appeared, the NAAFI canteen bulged at the seams – we'd always been served on tablecloths, cups, saucers and spoons and enjoyed personal service by the staff, but with the sudden influx of people this couldn't continue. Gradually the cloths and saucers disappeared, and even broken glasses couldn't be replaced quickly enough. At times we were reduced to drinking out of jam jars. The exclusive flying club atmosphere was fast disappearing!

The German invasion of Poland on 1 September 1939 brought a British mobilization the following day and, when Hitler refused to abandon the attack, a declaration of war on 3 September. When the mobilization orders arrived at Marham a large number of reservists were already on base, taking part in an exercise, and they were duly called up on the spot. The possibility of a major German pre-emptive air attack on the RAF's bomber airfields was taken very seriously, and dispersion of squadrons was ordered. At first this simply entailed 38 Squadron moving the short distance to the field (almost literally) at Barton Bendish. The initial dispersal of 12 aircraft took place at 10:30 on the 1st, while the squadrons continued their mobilization with the issue of gas clothing, identity discs, small-arms and the like. Barton Bendish 'airfield', often referred to as Eastmoor landing ground, was a 340-acre site that had opened in the latter part of 1939.

However, the declaration of war the following day saw implementation of the full Scatter Scheme. Number 38 Squadron moved to South Cerney, although one aircraft ended up diverting to Little Rissington with engine problems. The order to move came at 12:30; aircraft were to fly below 1,000 ft, carrying a skeleton crew and minimum kit. However, the problems of trying to operate from such dispersed locations caused the Air Officer Commanding No. 3 Group to recall squadrons to their home bases with orders to disperse around the airfield as best as possible. Marham was still very much a large field surrounded by hedges, so it was a fairly simple task to tow the aircraft to the edges of the airfield and shove the back end of the Wellingtons into the luxurious Norfolk hedges and adjacent fields. 'Johnnie' Johnson again:

Aircraft were dispersed in these fields during daylight hours for servicing and refuelling. As winter advanced, my most vivid memory of this period is the cold and the mud. The mud was the worst, the aircraft bogged down, the petrol bowsers bogged down, lorries bogged down – and they all had to be dug out. We were permanently covered in mud – eventually we had to have tractors fitted with tracks to move anything. For night-time dispersal aircraft were towed (or flown) to Barton Bendish – more cold and more mud. Starting the engines at Barton Bendish, after they had stood all night in the middle of winter, was quite an experience and required a special, and very unofficial technique. The Pegasus engine was primed for starting by pumping raw petrol into the top three cylinders, by means of a gas pump fitted to the aircraft. The engine oil was of course now so thick and viscous that the trolley batteries could hardly turn the engine. The trick was to get the engine to backfire into the carburettor, where it would ignite the surplus petrol in the air intake, let it burn for the requisite number of seconds to warm up the carburettor, and then extinguish it by placing your forage cap over the intake. All engine fitters' forage caps had singe marks on them!

In the meantime, Marham had received the first of what were to become frequent air raid warnings. At 02:34 on 4 September the initial warning was given of aircraft approaching Yarmouth. Having been declared RED, the highest state, this was downgraded to Green at 03:27 and, at 03:50, to White, to show that the raiders were no longer a threat. In these early days there would be many 'false alarms', but as the months went by Marham was to be on the receiving end of a number of Luftwaffe attacks. The airfield was provided with an army unit for air defence with additional units

Several of Marham's pillboxes survive. This one, near the main gate, was painted green just before one of the many Royal visits in the early 1990s.

in the local area, such as 407 Battery at Narborough. The defence of the airfield against, for example, a German paratroop assault was left to the base personnel, the airmen having to stand guard duty in addition to their normal duties.

The airfield was given a number of slit trenches for defence duties as well as for air raid protection. It was also provided with a system of pill-boxes. Many of these were of the usual brick-built surface variety, a number of which still survive in the fields around the airfield, but there were also some retractable pill-boxes. These are described in *Air Publication 3236, Works*, as:

> . . . special devices installed at a number of airfields, formed essentially of two large diameter concrete pipes, one sliding within the other, one end of each being closed. These were installed on end in the ground at suitable locations on the landing grounds of airfields. When the pill-box was shut the closed top of the inner pipe lay flush with the surface of the airfield or runway. In an emergency this inner pipe was raised by hydraulic or compressed-air jacks until a field of fire could be obtained from

loop-holes slotted in the wall of the pipe. In the closed position the pill-box was entirely invisible and it therefore provided an element of surprise, particularly in the event of the landing by parachute or airborne troops. The provision and installation of these pill-boxes was given the highest priority, the Prime Minister himself showing an interest in the progress of the work. At a later date, however, provision was discontinued as the structures were not sufficiently large enough to accommodate modern weapons and were insufficiently strong to sustain the weight of heavy aircraft.

On the operational front there was great deal of 'standby' but no action, aircrew and groundcrew becoming frustrated. A typical example was 13 September:

11:45 Ops room state no flying today, stand off (down) until 23:59.
14:40 Station Commander orders 6 aircraft with 6 x 250 lb GP bombs – all 6 already had 8 bombs for the previous op; therefore, drop

Bombing up a 115 Squadron Wellington; note how the aircraft is parked near the hedge, as part of the dispersal plan.

2 and put in extra 100 galls.
15:00   Captains to briefing.
15:20   Aircraft reported ready – engines running, crews standing by.
15:35   Station Commander orders engines shut down to save petrol. Crews to standby in crew-room.
16:35   Station Commander cancels standby, bombs off, stand off.

This was also a time of paranoia regarding spies, and it was feared that German agents were roaming the countryside. This, of course, may have been true in the case of Marham; an over-the-hedge shot of the Hendons later formed part of the Luftwaffe target folder. One such spy scare was raised on 22 September, when all guard posts were told to be on the lookout for 'Flt Lt Weston in RAF van MF203', who had visited anti-aircraft posts in the Duxford area asking questions. Orders were to arrest the man on sight. He never turned up.

Throughout this period there was continued emphasis on training and, as and when standby requirements allowed, using the ranges at Berners Heath, including stick bombing and trials with the new Leica bombing assessment cameras. Occasional detachments went to Carew Sheriton range in South Wales for air firing. The air gunners were making almost daily use of the butts at Marham. New bomb distributers were fitted early in the month, and some aircraft were returned to Vickers for the fitting of armour plate around their petrol tanks.

On 14 September 115 Squadron heard that it was to receive the Wellington 1A, equipped with the new Frazer-Nash turret, and the first aircraft, N2875 to N2878, duly arrived at 18:00 that day. They were put into the A Flight hangar so that they could be fitted with equipment stripped from the Mark I aircraft. The rest of September was devoted to training and familiarization with the new aircraft, including a small amount of night flying.

Warning for operations would come from HQ No. 3 Group on a standard form. The following one for 5 October 1939 was typical of this early period:

A.   Form B.44
B.   5th October 1939.
C.   To destroy enemy warships.

D. Daylight hours 6th October.

E. 6 aircraft of No. 115 Squadron. 6 aircraft of No. 149 Squadron.

F. To attack enemy warships and submarines reported by reconnaissance aircraft.

G. Nil.

H. To be notified later.

J. Any surface warships and submarines recognised as enemy. Order of priority:- Battleships, Cruisers, submarines. Should warships be escorting merchant vessels, warships are to be attacked if there is no risk of hitting merchant vessels.

K. Neutral territorial waters to be avoided.

L. Direct subject to neutral requirements and avoidance of neutral territory.

M. Nil.

N1. Squadrons notified in E. above to stand by at one hour's notice from 1030 hours 6th October.

N2. Attack to be at high altitude using 500 lb SAP bombs.

O1. No action to be taken on this order until further receipt of executive message from this HQ quoting Form B.44.

O2. No G.R observers will be provided.

O3. Except as stated in para O3A below, no RN or neutral surface warships will be in the area nought two degrees three nought minutes East to nought eight degrees three nought minutes East, South of five nine degrees nought minutes North, to North of five three degrees nought nought minutes North.

O3A. Submarines are not repeat not to be attacked in the area five degrees four six minutes North, nought five degrees thirty minutes to five eight degrees nought nought minutes North, nought seven degrees nought nought minutes East, to five seven degrees four six minutes North nought six degrees nought nought minutes East to five eight degrees three four minutes North, nought four degrees four two minutes East.

O4. Signals instructions in accordance with 3 Group Operation Instructions No. 14 dated 1st September. Text of any message transmitted by 6BT will be preceded by code word HOG repeat HOG.

The document continues in the same vein with additional details of the operation, although at this stage of the war crews were given a great deal of flexibility as to route flown, attack profile and so on. Later, when they formed part of the huge bomber stream employed each night by Bomber Command, this would no longer be the case. Co-ordinates were given in words in order to avoid the possibility of corruption if numbers alone were transmitted. The reference to GR (General Reconnaissance) observers is quite relevant, as these were frequently attached to squadrons for anti-shipping sorties; the Marham record books contain frequent references to the presence of such personnel.

The general preparations continued as the so-called Phoney War dragged on. Aircraft flew to the Maintenance Unit at Altrincham to collect 250 lb AS bombs to help build up a stock at Marham.

At 14:20 on 8 October, crews of 115 Squadron were brought to one hour's notice for operations. At 15:00 they were ordered airborne to join up with a 99 Squadron formation for an attack on the German fleet off Norway. The 99 Squadron aircraft appeared overhead Marham at 15:40, and six Wellingtons took off to join them. This was Marham's first operational outing, and the crews comprised:

L4317 Sqn Ldr Bowles, Fg Off Sheeran, Sgt Kirkham
L4324 Fg Off Pringle, Sgt Moores, Sgt McKenzie
L4325 Flt Sgt Boore, Sgt Martin, Sgt Roberts
L4305 Flt Lt Guthrie, Fg Off Simpson, Sgt Tyrell
L4333 Fg Off Newman, Plt Off Gayford, Sgt Lambert
L4299 Flt Sgt Groves, Sgt Newberry, Sgt Juby

'Each aircraft to carry four 500 lb SAP bombs. Form B.44 to be carried out in collaboration with 99 Squadron who are to lead. If junction with 99 Squadron not effected or if it is not possible to stick with them, operation not to be carried out.'

The crew lists are strange; either they flew without any air gunners, which seems most unlikely, or the Operations Record Book (ORB) does not bother to list anyone below the rank of sergeant. At this time most air gunners were airmen.

The aircraft flew the planned route, but it was a fruitless search and no ships were found. The Marham formation returned to base between 19:15 and 19:55. Although this was not a great success, it nevertheless created quite a stir after the weeks of nothing happening. Unfortunately more of the waiting game followed, but with an increased emphasis on fighter affiliation, aircraft co-operating with fighters from Wittering. The Wellingtons would land at Wittering after the 'combat' to debrief.

Tragedy was never far away. Sergeant E.T. 'Slim' Summers was tasked to move Wellington L4239 to Barton Bendish, a short hop at low level. With him in the aircraft went six groundcrew. *En route* it crashed into a tree at Marks Farm, Boughton, with the loss of all seven on board. The official report into the accident reads:

Wellington aircraft 4239 of No. 38 Squadron, piloted by Sgt Summers, left Marham for the satellite aerodrome at approximately 1525 hours and crashed approximately 6 miles away, or two miles south of the satellite aerodrome at about 1530 hours on 5/11/39.

Six of the crew must have died immediately either from multiple injuries or as a result of the fire, with the exception of AC Watson, who was found in the broken off portion of the tail. He was badly injured and died as a result of serious lacerations of the head and shock about two hours after the crash. Two pilots from this squadron saw from the satellite aerodrome this aircraft turning steeply low down and on pulling up sharply on the last occasion it appeared to turn on its back straight into the ground, immediately catching fire.

There were two civilian witnesses to the accident, both of whom made statements. One was Leslie Howlett, a tractor driver at Field Barn, Boughton, who testified:

I was looking out of my sitting room window, which faces Boughton, and was watching an aeroplane flying very low. It came from the direction of Eastmoor and took a left turn over Boughton at a very sharp angle. Before he got out of the turn the left wing struck the top of an oak tree and brought the plane completely over. The plane then crashed in a field about 400 yards from the oak and immediately burst into flames.

This tragic accident, with the death of so many groundcrew, affected the whole squadron for some considerable time.

Social life on the base was kept as active as possible, with numerous concerts and cinema evenings. Leave was still very restricted, the standing rule being that only one crew could be away in any 48 hr period, although up to two crews could be on short leave in the local area.

Excursions into King's Lynn, Swaffham, and Downham Market were quite common, but in these early days of the war most preferred to be on hand to see what happened. As the war lengthened into years, the problem of social life became more acute. Entertainment was often 'home-grown', and a station amateur dramatic society was formed on 23 November. A few days later Marham was delighted to host an ENSA concert by Maurice Dallimore's Bluebird Concert Party. This was voted the best entertainment yet seen, although a number of previous ENSA visits had also proved popular. Such ENSA visits tended to take place every two months or so.

On the same day, the 27th, Gp Capt C.H. Keith took command of the station. He took over at a period of increased tension. Only a few days before, the AOC had sent a signal to all of his stations: 'Bomber Command thought it quite likely that the Germans would celebrate Armistice Day with a mass attack and the C in C was most anxious that aircraft be kept in their dispersal pans when standing to, irrespective of what has been done in the past, and that massing of aircraft should be strictly avoided'.

Activity at Marham was not confined to the home-based units, and there were numerous visitors. Typical of these were a number of Blenheims from 18 Squadron, returning from a photographic sortie over the Siegfried Line. In line with the general war directive that bombers should only attack targets at sea (at this stage there was to be no bombing of land targets, as it would risk causing civilian casualties), the Wellington units had been on standby as Coastal Duty Squadron since the outbreak of the war, each squadron taking it in turns to hold the duty.

In the middle of the month, on 17 November, it was 38 Squadron's turn to go hunting ships, A Flight sending N2908/H (Flt Lt Macfadden), N2907/B (Fg Off Hopkins), and N2910/M (Sgt Sayers), and B Flight contributing N2879/Z (Sqn Ldr Selby), N2878/Y (Sgt Plumb), and N2880/W (Sgt McGregor). The report says:

Aircraft were to leave the ground by 1300 hours. Crews were recalled from early lunch and a slight delay in taking off was caused by last minute amendments to the area free of our warships. Six aircraft each carrying three 500 lb SAP bombs took off at 1306 to proceed to Lowestoft via Honington. Course was set for position 5400N 0600E and hence to position

Wellingtons at the marshalling point ready for take-off.

5450N 0600E and hence to base. Height at first was 7,500 ft over 1–3/10 cumulus cloud at 6,000 ft. Cloud increased to 5/10 and became 10/10 to NW of Borkum when our height was 10,000 ft. The formation arrived at Marham at 1720 hours. Except for the fishing fleet off the East coast and one grey MV seen on the return journey, no ships or aircraft were seen.

Two days later, 115 Squadron's Miles Magister crashed at Newmarket owing to the gusty wind conditions. Having walked away from the wreckage, the pilot had to wait for a vehicle to come and collect him.

At a conference at No. 3 Group HQ a few days later, the C-in-C, Sir Edgar Ludlow-Hewitt, stated:

War Cabinet is anxious to inflict loss or damage to the capital ships of the German fleet. It has been decided to send aircraft in strength to German naval bases to bomb any warships that might be seen. In view of this an exercise was to be carried out against ships in Belfast Lough. All aircraft were to concentrate against a single warship until that was destroyed.

This trial exercise, involving all four squadrons of No. 3 Group, took place on the 28th. For a variety of reasons, including poor weather, it was a total failure; no attacks were made and only one ship was seen. The major problems were poor co-ordination and even poorer R/T. It did not bode well for any major operation.

Nevertheless, the general routine remained one of sitting and waiting, with a great deal of stand-by but little operational employment. The number of available crews was drastically reduced at the end of November, following an outbreak of food poisoning caused by 'dodgy' oysters served at a party in the Sergeants' Mess.

December was to be a far busier month, with operations taking place on five days. Three aircraft flew an abortive sweep on the 1st: 'Three aircraft sweep over the North Sea – small flotilla of destroyers and minesweepers seen and dived on with bomb doors open when British deck markings were observed. Ships opened fire but no damage sustained.' Two days later a 12-aircraft mission, with a further 12 from 149 Squadron, went to attack German warships at Heligoland.

A painting showing 115 Squadron Vickers Wellingtons under attack by three Bf 110s. (Eric Scott)

This was to be the first real test of daylight bombing against a defended target. Nine aircraft of 115 Squadron and three from 38 Squadron reached the target at 11:45 and made their attacks from 10,000 ft, claiming at least two hits on ships at anchor.

The Luftwaffe made an appearance, but failed to make an impression on the bomber formation. However, one of the Marham air gunners, LAC A. Copley, was hit during such an attack. Luckily the bullet struck his parachute buckle and he was uninjured; he managed to find the spent bullet, which he kept as a good luck charm. As the enemy fighter passed his Wellington, N2880, Copley fired and scored a number of hits. The crew made a claim that the enemy aircraft had gone down in flames, thus chalking up Marham's first victory. The Wellington had 29 holes in its fabric and the port tyre was shredded, the latter damage causing the aircraft to swerve on landing. In recognition of his part in the battle, Copley was awarded the Distinguished Flying Medal (DFM).

Three further sweeps were flown that month,

on the 18th (three aircraft), 21st (18 aircraft), and 24th (17 aircraft), all with no result. The last of these called for aircraft to sweep the Danish and Norwegian coastal areas. The six involved in the Danish operation returned with no problems, but those sent to Norway had not returned by the time fog had started to form at Marham. One eventually reached home using direction finding (DF), but, of the other two, Sqn Ldr Glencross landed at Mildenhall and Fg Off Newman crash-landed at Martlesham Heath. The latter aircraft had an hydraulic problem, probably caused by battle damage, and the captain ordered his crew to bale out before he attempted the crash-landing.

As winter took its grip on East Anglia there arose a serious problem of ice build-up on dispersed aircraft, and a number of solutions were tried: 'Aircraft were wiped with oily rags to counteract ice formation. This made a filthy mess and it was found to be completely ineffective. It was decided to de-bomb aircraft and bring them to the hangars overnight; moving them out first thing in the morning.'

Throughout January, anti-shipping duties

A Wellington of 115 Squadron in the winter of 1941, with fabric covering to protect the wings from the inclement weather.

remained the priority, although not many sorties were actually flown, partly because of poor weather but also owing to continued political constraint on the employment of the bomber force. Sweeps were flown on the 2nd, 3rd, 5th, 9th, 20th and 23rd of the month, usually by either three or six aircraft. The most significant operation in many ways was that of 13 January, when a single Wellington from each squadron undertook a leaflet-dropping mission. Flight Lieutenant Newman had earlier visited Mildenhall to discuss techniques and problems with the experienced crews of No. 4 Group.

Flight Sergeant Powell and crew from 115 Squadron took off at 00:18 in Wellington N2950/G (landing at 07:15), while Flt Lt Nolan and crew were airborne slightly earlier (00:02) in N2963/Q. With the injunction not to drop bombs on land targets, these leaflet raids, code-name 'Nickel', were to prove invaluable in providing crews with experience in the problems of finding land targets at night. Peacetime training in night navigation had been quite poor, as the English countryside had been well lit, in contrast to the pitch black conditions over wartime Europe. Crews had to rely on moonlight on water features; the 'coasting-in' fix was very important.

In general, however, it was the more vulner-able Whitley squadrons of No. 4 Group that specialized in this role in the early part of the war, while the Wellingtons of No. 3 Group and the Handley Page Hampdens of No. 5 Group took on the offensive task. While the German air defence system was, at this period, incapable of causing much damage to the night raiders, the winter European weather was a most dangerous foe. There are many recorded instances of the problems of severe icing, crews reporting the horrendous sound of large chunks of ice being thrown off the props and against the fuselage. At other times aircraft were forced down to lower altitudes in search of warmer air to disperse the huge weight of ice that threatened to send the aircraft out of control. It is not known how many were lost owing to such problems; a simple FTR (Failed to Return) is often all that the ORBs provide.

It was not only in the air that the weather caused problems. Throughout the winter period the airfields of East Anglia suffered from snow and fog. The Marham ORB records that on 29 January the snow was one foot deep over the airfield and that operations were restricted to heavy aircraft, while at Barton Bendish the six-inch covering made the field all but unusable. A few days earlier: 'Oil tanks in the majority of aircraft have buckled owing to the intense cold, a lot of snow

Nickel 263, as dropped by Marham aircraft.

had fallen. No flying was carried out and after lectures, crews indulged in snow-balling and "terraplaning" on boards towed by cars.' The oil tank problems continued: 'Owing to the very cold weather, aircraft were difficult to start. An oil tank was split and another overheated through waiting for the others to start. Thus only two aircraft finally took off for the op.'

It was not unusual for aircraft to be diverted upon their return to Marham because the weather had deteriorated during the time they were airborne. Such was the case on 21 February, when crews were returning from an attack on shipping at Heligoland. Aircraft tried to approach Marham from 06:30 onwards, only to find that conditions ruled out a landing. In the event, four Wellingtons went to North Coates, two to Digby and one to Radcliffe. Flight Lieutenant Nolan in P2526/W

made five attempts to get in at Marham and a further three at Digby. With fuel running low he then climbed away from the airfield and ordered the crew to bale-out. All made safe landings except for Sgt Cousins, who injured his left foot. However, the saddest event of the night was the loss of Fg Off Hawxby and crew in N2951/D of 38 Squadron, Marham's first operational loss. It is worth quoting the operational report:

NIGHT 20/21st FEBRUARY 1940

Narrative

6 aircraft from No. 38 Squadron and 3 aircraft from No. 115 Squadron took part in the above operation.

The object of this operation was to destroy enemy warships situated in the HELIGOLAND BIGHT and for this purpose each aircraft carried three 500 lb SAP bombs, except 2876 (Sqn Ldr Glencross) who carried 4 of these bombs. The first aircraft left the ground at 2305 hours 20/2/40 and the last at 0025 hours 21/2/40.

The weather proved treacherous and mitigated [sic] against the successful carrying out of the Operation; furthermore, the rapid thaw had apparently released the warships stated to be frozen up NW of the main island and in fact only one aircraft saw naval craft, viz 2 destroyers about half way up the east side of the main island.

The night proved to be misty and hazy with a series of layers of cloud, the first 600 feet to ground and sea level, the second varied from 1,000 feet to 2,000 feet, and finally a light layer of cloud at about 25,000 feet. The wind too proved to be stronger than anticipated. The visibility on the German coast, subject to haze and mist, was a great deal better than that experienced on the British coast and the conditions from Heligoland to the British coast worsened rapidly.

Course in every case was set direct for Heligoland and to pass south of a point 06° 00′ east, 54° 10′ north, as stated in the Operation Order, and aircraft on leaving the ground flying to the maximum of 10,000 feet. However, as the wind proved stronger than anticipated, and forecast, on losing height and coming down through the clouds, aircraft in every instance found themselves some 10 minutes early and beyond the objective, the landfalls being made from Sylt as far as Borkum, some aircraft even penetrated Germany. This was due to the difficulty experienced in distinguishing the sea from the land on account of the freezing up of the sea, which appeared to extend from Sylt to Borkum, and for some 20 to 40 miles offshore. Pilots and navigators quickly appreciated what had happened, obtaining 'fixes' and thereafter proceeded to Heligoland after a reconnaissance of the German coastline.

This deviation caused aircraft to be late at Heligoland and some therefore passed over Heligoland at heights of 5,000 to 10,000 feet, to avoid aircraft of other stations, with the exception of Sqn Ldr Glencross, who approached the target from the south at a height of 2,500 feet. On the return journey, conditions had adversely affected aerodromes in the 3 Group area, so that aircraft were instructed to proceed and land at Digby. Flt Sgt Roberston and Fg Off McFadden effected safe landings at Digby at 0655 and 0650 hours respectively. Plt Off Hopkins, Fg Off Wells, Plt Off Scott and Sgt Odoire proceeded to Digby, found fog and thence proceeded to Grimsby with similar result, so went on to North Coates, where each effected a safe landing between 0630 and 0720 hours.

Sqn Ldr Glencross arrived over England in a small patch of good weather, remained in this patch, having found a landing ground, landed at Ratcliffe, near Leicester, at 0730 hours.

Flt Lt Nolan made 5 attempts to land at Marham, and 3 attempts at Digby, and then with 10 minutes petrol left he gave orders to abandon aircraft, and he and his crew landed uninjured with the exception of Sgt Cousins, his navigator, who injured his left foot fending himself off a tree. It is regretted that nothing has been heard of Fg Off Hawxby and his crew since 03:30 when he was heard trying to obtain a fix from Heston. His position then was unknown and he has been reported missing with his crew.

Enemy aircraft

One was seen at a distance over Cuxhaven, flying with navigation lights on, by Flt Lt Nolan. Four were seen at Heligoland by Sqn Ldr Glencross, he proceeded between the island along the east side of the main island, went around the North and proceeded down the west side, about one quarter of the way down an enemy aircraft showing a white light came up astern, whereupon it was engaged by the rear gunner with a short burst (30 rounds). It then passed underneath to the green beam and came level. Sqn Ldr Glencross took station astern and at 400 yd his front gunner fired

several bursts (totalling 200 rounds) and the light in the enemy aircraft went out and it disappeared. It is thought that the enemy aircraft was hit. Proceeding down the western side, the Southern Mole was reached and another run to the East side was made. Again an enemy aircraft came up astern and in passing flashed a white light, to which Wg Cdr Mills, who was in the astrodome, replied flashing the letter 'F' with a pencil torch he had with him. Thereupon the enemy aircraft fired a green Very light, passed ahead and the searchlight then operating dowsed its light. A second circle of the main island having been completed, a third was commenced with the object of bombing two destroyers, seen in the second circling, which were about half way up on the east side of the island. A run-up was made but unfortunately the bombs failed to release. Shortly after, two more enemy aircraft were seen. As they did not appear to have sighted our aircraft a quick get-away into the clouds was made.

Flak fire

This was never intense. Such as was experienced appears to have been sighting or signal bursts. Red tracer, red 'Onions' and red balls of fire, giving off 12 small balls or variegated colours of blue, green, red, and yellow, were seen 5 miles south-east of Cuxhaven. Generally the fire was below and astern.

Additional paragraphs dealt with other aspects such as searchlights, blackout details, and other comments.

Only a few days later, on the 24th, the station lost another aircraft when Fg Off Scott crashed N2948 on take-off. Fortunately, the crew suffered only minor injuries. Eric Scott recalls the incident:

One night we were detailed for a night exercise to include identification of a target followed by the dropping of practice bombs on a range to the south of Marham. One of my particular friends at the time was the station dentist. He was aching for a flight, and to his delight the Squadron Commander agreed that he could come with me. I tell this story against myself to emphasize the danger of overconfidence, especially when flying at night. Our concentrated training had brought me to the position where night flying was second nature. That night was a little different, however. The wind direction had changed and we were instructed to take off across the grass airfield up the hill to the north-

Wellington N2948 KO-A burnt out after an accident on 14 February 1940. Plt Off 'Stella' Wickencamp emerged from the wreck with nothing more than a broken nose.

west. On take-off at night, the initial manoeuvres on the ground are visual, but immediately after leaving it instrument flying is essential, as one enters a blind zone on leaving the end of the runway, unless the night is moonlit. On this occasion my overconfidence allowed me to leave the runway without going on to instruments – as I thought I knew the aircraft's attitude by its feel. I was wrong. A moment later I perceived some black shadows ahead approaching me fast – the trees to the northwest of base. I pulled the nose of the aircraft up sharply, but I was too late and we brushed some trees on the brow of the hill in the next field. My controls had been damaged and I was unable to keep the aircraft climbing. We hit the ground with a terrible roar, the engines being at full throttle. The aircraft broke into two and burst into flames. My dentist friend and I were thrown forward into the nose of the aircraft and there, by the grace of God, was a hole where the Perspex turret had split open. We both had been strapped in, but the force of our sudden stop had torn our thick cord straps from their mountings. Flames were all around us and we both scrambled through the hole. We were in a ploughed field. The aircraft was like a huge bonfire. Ammunition from the guns was exploding, Very light cartridges were shooting into the air. One of the six high-octane petrol tanks was split – the others would go off at any moment. The tail section had come away from the fuselage and left a gaping hole through which the other three crew members escaped without a scratch. Fortunately we had no real bombs aboard, but at any moment the other petrol tanks could explode. "For God's sake, RUN!", I shouted, not knowing whether anyone was seriously hurt. We all ran then stood and watched what could have been our coffin. "Are you all right, skipper?", said the dentist, "You've blood all over your face." It was only then that I realized that my nose was pushed in. Soon we heard the sound of a car and saw dimmed lights approaching the edge of the field. We were in a ploughed field and the ambulance could not get to us. We shouted that we were all right and started trudging towards them. I had lost a boot and found it hard to walk across a recently-ploughed field with one foot unprotected! We were soon tucked up in bed in the Sick Bay.

The month had been quiet on the operational front, with missions on the 1st, 11th, 20th, 21st, and 29th, the latter seeing four aircraft drop leaflets on Bremen, Hamburg, Cuxhaven, Brunsbuttel, Wilhelmshaven, Lubeck, and Kiel; places to which they would return in subsequent months with a much more deadly purpose.

As this 'Nickelling' (leaflet dropping) was a standard role for Marham crews, it is worth quoting extracts from the report of a typical mission, that flown on the night of 29 February by an aircraft of 115 Squadron:

Raid KCD.140 (Sqn Ldr Hawkins) left Marham at 01:29 (March 1st) and proceeded via corridor 'C', climbing steadily. On crossing the coastline clouds were 10/10ths below, and after 30 minutes the weather improved steadily until about 0245 hours, when the night developed into a perfect one, except for a slight haze. A 'fix' was obtained at 0324 hours, but this seemed so far out at 54° 35′ north, 03° 50′ east, that another 'fix' was asked for, but as the operator had some trouble, as someone else was being worked, the aircraft proceeded.

At 0215 hours trouble was experienced with both engines in oil and cylinder temperatures, and to keep the engines cool the cooling gills had to be opened, which slowed down the speed considerably. A further 2,000 ft was climbed very slowly to 12,000 ft, which appeared to be the ceiling of the aircraft. The flight was carried on for a further threequarters of an hour, but as the temperatures rose beyond the 'maker's limits', it was decided it was too risky to proceed. Accordingly at 0350 hours a turn was made for home, and as the prospects of the 'Nickels' reaching Wilhemshaven appeared good, they were unloaded at 54° 50′ north, 05° 30′ east.

Six crew were carried, and only the rear gunner complained of cold. The turret was continuously exercised and presented no difficulties, both front and rear guns were regularly fired and no trouble was experienced with either. Oxygen was used by one crew member at 10,000 ft and the rest at 12,000 ft, only 2 bottles were used.

Wireless was on the whole satisfactory, though in the last hour the generator became troublesome and seemed likely to pack up at any minute. Trouble was experienced in getting 'fixes' due to congestion. The first 'fix' took nine minutes, but later 'fixes' took up to nearly an hour. 'Nickels' were stacked, some on the bed and some on the floor, and no difficulty was experienced in getting rid of them by the usual drill by two men.

Petrol consumption was 371 gal for 775 miles = 2.08 m.p.g.

The only casualties for February were the crew of one of the target-towing Fairey Battles, which crashed at Spalding, killing both crewmen.

March opened with the loss in accidents of two more aircraft. Wellington N2907 forced-landed at Christchurch, Wisbech, on the 1st, and N2947 caught fire, the Very pistol having been set off when the aircraft landed, and was badly damaged. In both cases the crews escaped without injury. Eight missions were flown during the month, on the 9th, 15th, 16th, 20th, 21st, 23rd, 27th, and 28th, the major effort going into leaflet dropping. The only loss was N2950, flown by Flt Sgt Powell, which crashed on take-off for the leaflet operation on March 23. A cylinder blew in the starboard engine: '. . . crew escaped with minor injuries due to the coolness of the captain and 2nd pilot in carrying out previously rehearsed force-landing drill. The aircraft was completely destroyed by fire.' There was, however, one casualty in the month, when N2987/O crashed at St Ives, three crew members being killed and the others receiving serious injuries.

Defence of the airfield continued to receive a high priority, and Army units were attached to help, an example being the arrival of 63 men of the 8th (Home Defence) Battalion, Royal Norfolk Regiment, on 4 April to replace a detachment of the 1st Cambridgeshire Regiment. Such units also helped with another of the home-spun entertainments, the RAF v Army sporting events. While April was fairly quiet for the aircrew, with operations being conducted on the 12th, 16th, 21st, and 30th, the month was significant in that it saw the first bombing attacks on a land target. A message from 3 Group HQ on 9 April announced that the Germans had invaded Norway, and that No. 38 squadron was to be at one-hour standby for operations in the Norway area with effect from 06:00 the following day. The operations would probably involve deployment to a northern base, such as Lossiemouth.

In the event it was 115 Squadron that, on 1 April, sent a detachment to Kinloss to co-operate with the 9 Squadron detachment at Lossiemouth on operations over Norway. The first operation was flown on the 7th. Twelve aircraft took off to rendezvous with the other Wellingtons for a shipping attack. The target was not located, but the formation was intercepted by a force of Bf 110s, and two of 115's aircraft were shot down: P2524/F, Plt Off Wickenkamp, and N2949/G, Plt Off Gayford. Three others were damaged and two crewmen injured. The following day crews attacked a cruiser in Bergen harbour, claiming one hit.

Meanwhile, at Marham on 12 April 38 Squadron sent six aircraft on a sweep. Squadron Leader Nolan and crew in P9269 failed to return from this mission, probably having fallen to a fighter, and all of the remaining five aircraft were hit and suffered varying degrees of damage. Two days later another crew went missing. Pilot Officer Crosby in L4339, operating out of Wick, was believed to have ditched near Whitby.

The final series of operations, directed against the airfield at Stavanger, opened on 11 April with the first intentional bombing of a land target on the European mainland by Bomber Command. This first mission comprised six Wellingtons of 115 Squadron, operating out of Kinloss. The Germans had already strengthened the airfield's defences, and the bombers encountered heavy flak, Plt Off Barber (P9284/J) being shot down and at least one other aircraft suffering serious damaged. The hydraulics of P9271/O, flown by Flt Sgt Powell, were damaged, and he had to belly-land back at Kinloss. A week later, news was received that this pilot had been awarded the DFM for this operation. Three aircraft attacked the same target again on the 14th, and that same afternoon the detachment returned to Marham. Number 38 Squadron had also been tasked against Stavanger, flying the first of its three missions on 16 April.

In the early hours of 1 June, Fg Off Gibbes in R3154 crashed on the Lastingham Hills, Yorkshire, and two of the crew were killed. The others were fortunate to escape with shock and minor injuries.

May was a hectic month, the latter part bringing operations almost every night. The Marham units flew operations on the 2nd (Rye), 7th (Stavanger), 9th (security patrol), 11th (Waalhaven), 15th (oil targets in Germany), 17th, 18th, 20th, 21st, 22nd, 23rd, 26th, 27th, 28th, and 30th. A total of 173 aircraft flew missions during the month against a variety of targets, with the loss of five aircraft and crews. The German ultimatum to Holland on 9 May led to renewed fears of air attack, and the dispersal plan was enforced more rigorously. In addition, six aircraft, three from each squadron, took off between 19:33 and 23:21 on 'security patrols'. With the launch of the German offensive in the west on 10 May the real battle had begun, and, in response to the Luftwaffe bombing of Dutch cities, Winston Churchill withdrew certain of the constraints and authorized Bomber Command to attack strategic targets in Germany. This was the true beginning of the Strategic Bombing Offensive. The bomber weapon was being given the opportunity to show what it could do, and the prewar strategic plans for attacks on German industry could be instigated.

All leave was cancelled, and personnel on leave were recalled to base. The 'real war' was about to start.

The initial report on the 11 May operation to Waalhaven stated:

Twelve aircraft (6 from 38 Squadron and 6 from 115 Squadron), TCD 219 to TCD 230 – took off at Marham between the hours of 00:02 and 01:36 for the purpose of attacking WAALHAVEN aerodrome. All attacks were carried out in dives

The award of a DFM to Flt Sgt (Plt Off by time of presentation) L. Boore for a mission on 7 April 1940.

from 4,000–6,000 down to 1,200 to 1,500 ft. With the exception of TCD 227 (Flt Sgt Boore) all aircraft located the target, though many found observation partly obscured by smoke from fires in the town. TCD 227 (Flt Sgt Boore) flew over the town at 7,000 ft and found himself in a thick pall of smoke under the cloud base that obscured all visibility.

He was unable to locate the target and returned without releasing his bombs. Several aircraft were fired at by Dutch AA guns and were engaged by Dutch searchlights, but in all cases where the letter of the day was signalled interference ceased immediately.

In spite of widespread fog in East Anglia, all aircraft except one were able to land at Marham without difficulty. The firing of a succession of mortar shells proved of the greatest assistance in bringing pilots home and preventing congestion of the H.F. D/F station. The lights also enabled four aircraft from other stations to make a safe landing.

Flight Sergeant Boore was one of the 115 squadron crews on the mission. The squadron ORB states:

Six aircraft from this squadron with aircraft from all other squadrons in the Group, a total of 36, attacked WAALHAVEN aerodrome, previously captured by the Germans with the aid of parachute troops. There was little opposition. The later aircraft saw many fires on the aerodrome, caused by previous aircraft. Also fires from Rotterdam from military activity after the invasion. Hits were obtained all over the aerodrome and on the buildings, and aircraft on the aerodrome destroyed and damaged. Flt Sgt Boore failed to locate the target and returned with his bombs. Two of Sqn Ldr DuBoulay's bombs hung up.

A reduced petrol load was carried, allowing 12 250 lb bombs to be carried.

Crews for the operation were:

Wellington 1A P9230/R
Sqn Ldr DuBoulay, Plt Off Sheeran, Sgt Kirkham, AC McNevin, LAC Miller.

Wellington 1A P9227/S
Fg Off Wood, Plt Off Fraser, Sgt Jakeman, AC Chatterton, AC Stow.

Wellington 1C P9285/T
Flt Sgt Boore, Sgt Williams, Sgt Roberts, LAC Smith, AC Jones.

Wellington 1C R3151/D
Flt Lt Newman, Plt Off Hunkin, Sgt Boteler, Plt Off Sydney-Smith, AC Grundy.

Wellington 1C P9235/G
Fg Off Scott, Plt Off Moore, Sgt Hardy, AC Crocker, AC Orford.

Wellington 1C P9297/F
Fg Off Laslett, Plt Off Dodshun, Sgt Flower, AC Ludlan, Plt Off Whitton.

The other 3 Group stations taking part were Mildenhall, Feltwell and Honington. One final drama remained for Marham that evening: 'No. 5 Nissen hut was burnt out while aircraft were taking off, owing to a paraffin lamp, left alight for personnel coming off duty late, falling and bursting.'

The evening of 15 May saw Marham launch 18 Wellingtons to attack oil targets at Homberg, Duisburg, and Gelsenkirchen, with the implementation of 3 Group Operational Instruction No. 34. The first away was Flt Lt McFadden in P9294. Once again the weather caused problems and a number of aircraft had to land elsewhere, including two in France. Flight Lieutenant Pringle had originally taken off at 20:55 in P9299, but the aircraft developed engine trouble. Landing back at Marham, the crew raced to P9229 and, minus AC Butler, who had gone sick, were soon airborne again. On the return trip the aircraft had navigational problems, not helped by the poor weather forecast given at briefing. The aircraft crashed at Bernay, near Rouen, with the loss of all on board.

Other losses that month were R3152/J, Plt Off Morris, on the 20th; P9298/H, Flt Sgt Moores, (20th); P9297/F, Fg Off Lazlett, (21st); and R3162, Fg Off Rosewarne, (30th). Of these, the last was seen to crash in flames some 6 miles south-west of Ostend. The cause of the loss usually remained a mystery unless it was witnessed by another crew or a crew member reappeared some time later to tell the tale. Throughout the war the Germans passed information via the International Red Cross (IRC) regarding the fate of Allied aircrew. Doubtless the tragic loss of life invariably included an heroic struggle, yet the details are seldom known. Postwar studies of German records have allowed some detail to be filled in, but much still remains a mystery.

The collapse of the Allied defences in France

under the weight of the German *Blitzkrieg* led to an all-out employment of air power in an effort to stem the advance of the Panzers. Included in this offensive were the squadrons of Bomber Command, and although No. 2 Group's Bristol Blenheims were to bear the brunt of this, and the associated high loss rate, the other Groups were also involved, attacking lines of communication and troop concentrations. Typical of these was the task issued on 17 May 1940:

To:- Mildenhall, Feltwell, Marham.

A. Form B.139.
B. 17 May.
C. The enemy are making a determined assault against the French position in the vicinity of Sedan and the junction of French, Belgian and British forces covering Brussels.
D. To delay the enemy advance by attacking points on his channels of communication, by sustained attack.
E. Night 17/18 May.
F. Eighteen sorties Mildenhall, twelve sorties Feltwell, eighteen sorties Marham
G. Nine sorties – Mildenhall – AR.1.
   Nine sorties – Mildenhall – AR.2.
   Twelve sorties – Feltwell – AR.20.
   Three sorties – Marham – AR.20.
   Fifteen sorties – Marham – AL.19.
   Targets are roads and river crossings, general dislocation of eastern approaches to towns in this order of priority. One unbroken river bridge at R.20 is of the highest priority.
H. Alternative targets given in 3 Group Operations signal Ops. 4. 14 May.
J. Movement of enemy land forces, trains, vehicles and any large concentrations of troops.
K. Direct via corridor 'G'.
L. Direct via corridor 'G'.
M. The first sortie is not to cross the Dutch coast before 2130 hr, and the last sortie is to have crossed the Dutch coast on the homeward journey by 0315 hr. Attacks are to be spread at intervals between these times.
N1. Each aircraft is to carry twelve 250 lb bombs. A minimum of 25 per cent, and if possible up to 50 per cent of these bombs are to be fused 8 hr and 12 hr delay in equal proportions. The remainder are to be fused DA or NDT.
N2. Attention is drawn to the latest BOMLIN signal.
N3. It is most important that any large movements observed on roads and railways shall be reported as soon as possible by W/T on 4160 K/Cs in accordance with 3 Group Signals Instruction No. 3.
N4. A camera is to be carried by one aircraft from Marham and a photograph obtained of target AR.20. A camera is to be carried by one aircraft from Mildenhall and a photograph obtained of target AR.1.

Such lines-of-communication targets dominated the second half of May, intensive raids of up to 20 aircraft a time being launched against road and rail bridges. Rail facilities such as marshalling yards were the favoured options. Attacking bridges was not easy, as they were very difficult to hit from medium level (success against such targets has only really come in recent years, with the use of Precision Guided Munitions). Even later in the war, with the adoption of dive bombing, it took a great deal of effort to hit a single bridge. Certainly, during this particular phase of the German advance, the bombing of such targets had little effect.

At this stage of the war there were very few Leica bombing-assessment cameras, so this essential aid to post-raid analysis was frequently not available. All bombers were fitted with cameras as the war progressed, and the vital importance of obtaining an aiming point photograph was stressed.

The unleashing of the bomber force to attack industrial targets led to a massive increase in the operational task for every station within Bomber Command, and especially for those of No. 3 Group. Marham squadrons operated on 15 nights in June, attacking a wide range of targets in Germany and France. The overall effort was split fifty-fifty between communications, such as the Somme bridges and French rail facilities, and the growing commitment to the strategic bombing campaign against Germany itself, typical targets being oil installations and industrial plants. With the declaration of war with Italy on 10 June it was inevitable that the bomber squadrons would soon face the long trek across France and the Alps to attack the industrial centres of northern Italy. At this stage the Marham units were too heavily engaged against targets in the Ruhr and France, and it was left to others to take on the new task, although 115 Squadron was put on standby to deploy to the south of France for such operations. In due course both Marham units would make the journey to targets in Italy.

This 115 Squadron Wellington, R1379, was shot down by Lt von Bonin of NJG 1 on 10 May 1941. The aircraft had been on a sortie to Hamburg.

There was still some free time for entertainment: 'much use has been made lately of Narborough lake, by kind permission of Admiral and Mrs Fontain, for swimming by aircrew and maintenance sections'. With the increased emphasis on night operations it was also decided that the aircrew working day should start at 13:45. The other notable event in June was the announcement on the 2nd that all air gunners were immediately promoted to sergeant, the decision at last having been taken that all aircrew should be sergeant or above. This caused a mass influx into the Sergeants' Mess and a few grumbles from some long-serving NCOs.

Despite the increased flying effort, there was only one operational loss; Sgt Morris and crew of 38 squadron in N2953/R failed to return from the attack on Baden-Baden on the 14/15th. Most crews that had been operating this night against targets in the Black Forest reported heavy and accurate flak. This comment is increasingly true of most combat reports from this period onwards, as the strength of German defences increased in response to the obvious threat posed by the RAF's bombers.

Nevertheless, weather and aircraft faults remained the major problems. During his take-off on 8 June, Flt Lt Hopkins in P9920 encountered problems with engine overheating. While sorting out the problem, and with the undercarriage still down, he struck a fence on the edge of the airfield. Keeping control of the damaged aircraft, he flew towards Hunstanton to jettison his bombs in the Wash before returning to base. The bad luck for 38 Squadron continued on 16 June when, on a transit sortie, Plt Off Plumb's Wellington, P9249/HD-T, suffered an engine failure during the final stages of the approach. The aircraft crashed at Marham Fen, the pilot being killed and two airmen, both aircraft fitters, being injured. Fg Off Stuart of 38 squadron and his crew had a hair-raising experience in L7809. Airborne on 24 June to attack Dusseldorf, they had reached the Dutch coast when the accumulation of an increasing amount of ice overcame the aerodynamics of the Wellington and the aircraft went into an uncontrolled dive. The pilots wrestled with the controls and eventually pulled the aircraft back on to an even keel at 7,000 ft.

These were still the very early days of night operations, and most crews had to 'learn the ropes' as they went along. Training covered all too few of the operational problems that crews faced when they reached their squadrons. If you survived long enough you discovered the problems, overcame them and, hopefully, passed on the word to the less experienced. New crews arrived at the rate of one or two a week, the policy being to post in replacements as soon as possible, rather than have 'empty seats' in the crew rooms.

It was not all a one-way trade during June, and on a number of nights the air raid warnings sounded as Luftwaffe aircraft attacked targets in East Anglia, on occasion flying over Marham and dropping bombs in the vicinity. The first 'major' attack on the airfield itself came on 10 July 10th: 'At 06:00 an enemy aircraft dropped 18 light bombs on both sides of the main road leading to the station. A simultaneous attack was made on the dummy site and left 18 small craters.' The main decoy site for Marham was at South Pickenham, this site being classified as both a 'K' (day) and 'Q' (night) decoy. It was provided with 12 dummy Wellingtons that were moved around daily by a tractor to 'convince' any air or ground reconnaissance that they were real aircraft. Various dummy buildings and installations were provided and, for added realism, the airfield was defended by three Lewis guns. The dummy flarepath was operated from an underground bunker. Although the site was marked on some Luftwaffe maps as a decoy, it still attracted a fair number of attacks, some 200 bombs being dropped on the site during the war; more than at

Marham. At one period in May 1941 South Pickenham was given a temporary detachment of 12 Bofors guns and three searchlights. These managed to claim a low-flying Junkers Ju 88, which crashed at Scoulton. The site was so realistic that a damaged Wellington elected to land on the 'airfield', and was subsequently repaired and flown out.

The other means of deterring an attack on the main airfield was camouflage, and throughout the early part of the war a great deal of time and attention was spent on this, the 'boffins' coming up with some amazing concepts. For creating decoys of equipment, especially aircraft, the Ministry turned to the experts, the film industry. Impressive decoys were built to fill any requirement, from a simple two-dimensional aircraft that worked well enough to fool a passing aircraft, to far more complex structures.

Airfields were toned down both through the painting of buildings and the creation of false agricultural land to disguise airfield operating surfaces. This is well shown in a number of aerial photographs of Marham. The official RAF account of such matters (AP3236) says: 'It became obvious by

The AOC 3 Group presents medals, 30 June 1940.

1941 that the camouflage of landing grounds by painting of hedge lines and the break up of field areas by coloured ochres, painting and treatments such as sulphuric acid spraying was entailing not only considerable expense in both labour and materials but owing to the extremely short life of such treatments, repeated renewals were resulting in airfield work on camouflage being almost continuous. Increased operational use of the airfields made it necessary to achieve some more lasting method of aerodrome "break up". It was in this way that a longer term scheme of agricultural treatment was introduced. Field effects were obtained by differential mowing of grass in adjacent areas, by seeding down areas of different grass mixtures, and by chemical fertilizing of selected field areas. Hedge lines were retained in some cases but the costly and slow process of hand spraying was replaced by a rougher method of drag net pulled behind a wheeled tractor. The bitumen emulsion paint was gravity sprayed from a simple tank immediately in front of the net. By 1942 building camouflage had become restricted to simplified painting of greens, browns or blacks.'

July was not as hectic on the operational front, with only 11 active nights, although one of these, 27 July, saw the largest effort so far by Marham, with 24 aircraft, 12 from each squadron, being despatched to attack Hamm, Cologne, Hamburg and Soest. Crew reports continued to emphasize the improving German defences. The flak over Hamburg on the night of 6 July was described by one crew as 'the heaviest in ten months of flying'. The other growing threat was that of the night-fighter. Up to now these had posed little problem, but from this point on the situation would be very different. No fewer than six twin-engined night-fighters had taken it in turns to attack Wellington R3213 of 38 Squadron, but Sgt Giles and his crew were able to fend of all attacks. After the raid of 20 July, Wellington P9287 returned to base with the rear gunner, Plt Off Leach, severely wounded following an attack by a nightfighter. Despite the best efforts of the doctors in the station sick quarters, he died the following morning.

In common with many Heavy Bomber stations, Marham had its own Target Towing Flight, equipped with a mix of aircraft. Unfortunately, details of this unit are very sketchy, and it tends to appear in the record only when something goes wrong, such as the loss of an aircraft. Although the operational squadrons were mounting raids as and when required, there was still a great need for routine training, and the majority of aircraft movements in any day would be connected with this. Among the non-operational flying that the squadrons carried out was the occasional special task, such as examining the effectiveness of the smokescreens provided for certain British cities.

August opened with another crew loss. Following the raid on Hamburg and Hamm on the night of 2/3 August, Plt Off Gerry's aircraft, R3202, sent a distress call at 02:11. The aircraft was expected to ditch in the North Sea some way short of Wells, so two aircraft were sent to search for the dinghy. Meanwhile, the rescue launch from Wells also set out for the approximate area. In the event, none of this assistance proved effective and nothing more was seen of the crew. It is worth stressing the lengths to which the RAF went to rescue its crews, sending out aircraft sorties from the home base or other units as well as the increasingly efficient coast-based rescue craft. Of course, a wide range of naval and commercial shipping was also available.

A few days later, following a raid on Hamburg, Sgt Lupton had to force-land R3293/Y in a field near Driffield, having run out of petrol. On most sorties the fuel load was only just sufficient, the ratio of fuel and bomb load having been calculated at the planning stage. Slightly adverse winds, a poorly performing aircraft, or a host of other reasons could leave the Wellington on the wrong side of the fuel equation during the return sortie. On most occasions crews were able to reach another airfield, but sometimes, as has already been seen, it was a question of bale out or force-land.

The remainder of August was average, operations taking place on the 5th, 8th, 10th, 12th, 14th, 16th, 22nd, 26th, 28th and 31st. All of the targets were in Germany, Hamburg being attacked three times and Hamm six. However, the most significant event was the mission on the night of 28 August, when the first Marham sorties to Berlin were flown (the first raid on Berlin, which had been authorized by the War Cabinet a few days earlier, took place on the night of 25/26 August). Attacking 'the Big City' was a great political event, 'striking at the heart of the Nazi regime', and was always considered something special by the crews. It also made a change from attacking targets in the Ruhr, this increasingly hostile area becoming known as 'Happy Valley' in true air-crew humour.

George Bury was navigator in a 115 Squadron Wellington that night. He recalls:

The target was Klingenberg Electric. Having been warned that the area was very heavily defended, we decided to fly at 15,000 ft, that was 5,000 ft higher than our normal height. At this height it was essential to use oxygen all the time, but after a few hours the masks became wet and uncomfortable to use, but, if taken off, frequent movement was very tiring. As it turned out the flight as far as we were concerned turned out to be fairly uneventful, searchlights were very active and although one did pick us up, he failed to keep us within his beam long enough for the others in the group to join in – when just ahead we saw a Wellington caught by two at the same time, and quick as a flash many others concentrated on the same target and he was caught in a cone of at least ten searchlights. The whole area around the aircraft was as bright as day and no matter which way he turned and twisted, they easily held on to him. The last we saw of him he was in a steep dive with shells bursting all around. This was our eighth flight and the first time that we had seen another aircraft; we were beginning to think that we were fighting the whole war on our own.

That night, Bomber Command's total effort had been 79 Blenheims, Hampdens, Wellingtons and Whitleys to bomb targets in Germany and airfields in France. Losses were one Blenheim and one Hampden. At Marham the following day there was a certain amount of 'banter' between George Bury's pilot, Plt Off Barr, and another young Pilot Officer, the latter scoffing at the 15,000 ft bombing height and claiming to have 'approached at low level and taxied almost the full length of the Unter den Linden Strasse, knocking on front doors to show his contempt for the Germans'. This idle boast earned him a roasting from his Flight Commander and a lecture on the dangers of flying low over German cities.

Four other aircraft suffered problems during the month, three making forced landings in England. Sergeant Upton in R3293/Y landed in a field near Filey, Yorkshire; Plt Off Boggis came to rest in P9294/E near Brundle, Norfolk; and Sgt Cook in R3276 forced-landed at Wood Dalling. With the exception of the last incident, in which the front gunner, Sgt Watts, was killed and the others received serious injuries, all crewmen suffered no

more than minor injuries. However, Wellington '7485', returning from Lunen in the early hours of 15 August, crashed at Brancaster with the loss of Sgt Gregory and crew.

The increase in operations brought an ever-increasing number of gallantry awards to members of both squadrons, and medal presentation ceremonies became regular features of the record. Typical is that of 9 September, when the AOC, Air Vice Marshal Baldwin, presented a DFM to Flt Sgt Boore, although by this time he was Plt Off Boore. Operations took place on 11 nights in September, the 3rd, 6th, 9th, 11th, 14th, 17th, 20th, 23rd, 24th, 27th, and 30th. There were two new trends during the month. On at least two operations crews were sent to attack targets in forest areas using a new type of weapon. 'Razzles' and 'Deckers' were designed as fire-raising munitions for the destruction of forests and crops. They consisted of small phosphorous pellets in celluloid strips ('Decker' at 4 in x 4 in being the larger of the two) that had to be kept in tins of alcohol and water until dropped, the idea being that they would ignite when they dried out. The idea was simply to pour them down the flare chute – and hope that they did not stick to the aircraft, dry out and catch fire!

More important, however, was the employment of the bomber force on anti-invasion work, with attacks on the Channel ports where Hitler was building up his forces. The attack on the concentrations of invasion barges is one of many missions undertaken by Bomber Command during the Second World War that has not received due credit or recognition. Invasion Alert No. 1 had been issued on the 8th, all aircraft being put on standby to support defensive operations countering any attempted German air or sea landing. This continued throughout the next day, and then, at 16:30 on the 10th, there was some relaxation of the rules: 'Squadron (38) allowed to go to King's Lynn to see pictures. News reel taken at Marham of flying crews, provided that they attend the first house and come away directly after the film. The Squadron bus took 32 to the show.'

Ostend was attacked on the night of 11 September, followed later in the month by raids on Antwerp, Ijmuiden, Calais, Boulogne, and Le Havre. A large number of the 248 sorties flown out of Marham still went to targets in Germany, occasionally with spectacular results. Attacking the blast furnace at Cattenoun on the night of 3 September, Sgt Clegg (P9293/S) reported that his bombs caused a brilliant white explosion followed by extensive fires. That same night one aircraft failed to get airborne: 'Plt Off Sargent did not take-off owing to an argument with a fence when taxying to the T/O point'. It is good to see that a sense of humour survived.

The same pilot appears in the record later in the month, on the 24th, when he brought his aircraft back with an 18 in hole in the port engine cowling, having struck a balloon cable. The only other significant damage was to 7854/R a few days earlier, when Plt Off Lane had to belly-land after the hydraulics had been damaged by flak, one crewman being wounded. There was one lost crew; Fg Off Allen in L3237/R on the night of 11/12 September.

Twice during the month German aircraft had tried to attack Marham, but on both occasions they had been fooled by the nearby 'K' site and had delivered their bombs into a vacant field.

On 24 September Gp Capt V.E. Groom OBE DFC arrived to take command of the station. There was also a continual influx of new personnel, especially conscripts who had now completed their training and were arriving in increasing numbers at the operational units. Charles Waring had, on conscription, expressed a preference for an equipment trade in the RAF. Having passed out of the Equipment School at Cranwell, he arrived at Marham in the autumn of 1940:

This was a good posting for me, as my home was in Norwich. On arrival at Marham I was escorted to Block B, a two-storey building, and was allocated a bed on the ground floor, this held about 30 beds – 15 on each side. Whoever was in the room as it became dark had to ensure that all black-out screens were put up at the windows before switching on any of the lights. Each bed had a metal locker by its side and articles therein had to be neatly stored. Periodically a duty officer would make an inspection of the interior of these lockers. Our work day was from 8 a.m. to 6 p.m. with a short break for lunch – seven days a week. The only time that you didn't work on Sunday was when you were detailed for church parade, held in the church at Marham village. When you finished your work you went straight to the mess for tea, which was the last meal you had for the day. If you wanted any supper you had to buy it at the NAAFI. They sold very good rock cakes – cakes with plenty of currants in them. They certainly filled any gaps in the stomach!

Even in wartime, the need to keep the paperwork 'just right' tended to dominate much of what went on, although the reasons behind it were sometimes not as simple as they first appeared. Charles Waring cites an example:

It wasn't long after I had arrived at Marham that I had to be the Duty Store Basher, and I soon had a rude awakening regarding what the Cranwell Equipment School had taught me and what was happening in practice. The bell rang – "I want aviation fuel, I'll be at the pumps". The equipment manual says that first you dip the tank you are going to use and then you dip the bowser; thirdly, after issuing the fuel, dip the tank and bowser again. There is also a large sign on the pumps, saying "Engines must be switched off before delivery of fuel".

It's a cold frosty night as I arrive at the pumps; the engine of the tractor pulling the bowser was still running. "You will have to switch that off," I said. "I'm not doing that; I'll never get it started again," came the reply.

"Right, now I must go down and dip the tank and then I'll dip your bowser."

"You don't need to do that," he says. "I have 40 gallons in my bowser and I want 460. I'll get on top and tell you when I'm full. As soon as I feel the spray on my face then I'll be full."

He signs for 460 gallons and is happy that he can get on refuelling the aircraft. I'm satisfied because I have his signature for 460 gallons but he's probably only had 420 gallons. The Equipment Assistant in charge of fuel is happy because his tallycard shows that he has less fuel than he actually has in the tanks. This surplus was the basis of my next experience of such things.

Before going off duty the Equipment Assistant tells me that three Scammels will be arriving during the night. He wants one emptied in tank No. 1, one in tank No. 2, but the third one he wants diverted to the MT fuel dump, where he wants 500 gallons put in and then the Scammel to come to the aero dump and off-load his remaining 4,500 gallons into No. 3 tank. This was the only way he could balance his tallycards. He always had a surplus on aircraft fuel but a deficiency on MT fuel, and that way he could keep everything correct on paper.

October was a frustrating month, extensive cloud cover over Germany preventing crews from locating their primary targets. Crews were usually given a primary and an alternate target for the night, with the added authorization to bomb suitable targets of opportunity, but only if neither of the others could be located. Furthermore, these were still early days for the bomber force, and in a typical night a 24-aircraft attack force would be tasked against up to three targets, an example being the 15th/16th of the month, when Kiel, Hamburg, and Gelsenk were on the list. In this instance, 20 were tasked against the primary target of major warships at Kiel, with Hamburg as the declared alternate, and a further three were sent to Gelsenk. Aircraft took off over quite an extended period and were given a large degree of flexibility concerning such things as routeing and attack direction. It was not until 1942 that the Bomber Command large-scale Main Force concept was introduced, with its much more rigid requirements.

The list of targets remained extensive, embracing Germany, including Berlin, as well as invasion ports and airfields in Holland. Operations took place on the nights of the 1st (early morning), 7th, 8th (day and night), 11th, 13th, 15th, 20th, 24th, 27th, and 30th. The first raids of the month ended with a double loss, recorded in the ORB:

Of the 10 aircraft detailed to attack the German Air Ministry in Berlin, 7 aircraft attacked the target, 1 aircraft returned with engine trouble, and 2 aircraft bombed other targets. These aircraft experienced intense heavy accurate flak. The flashes of the heavy flak were reported as being very bright with the apparent intention of blinding the pilots. Of the 3 aircraft detailed to attack the marshalling yards at Ehrang, 2 attacked the target and one aircraft attacked Ostende aerodrome.

Of the 8 aircraft detailed to attack Merseburg, 2 located their target, 2 attacked other targets, 1 brought his bombs back, 1 returned with intercom trouble and 1 failed to return. The crew was Plt Off McLean, Sgt Williams, Sgt Tipping, Sgt Gammon, Sgt Hamilton, Plt Off Mathieson.

Of the 3 aircraft detailed to attack Osnabruck, 1 aircraft bombed the marshalling yards to the NW of the town and the other two failed to return. The crews were Plt Off Steel, Sgt Goldie, Sgt Mogg, Sgt Dowsett, Sgt Walter, Sgt

Westwood for sortie CD 334 and Sgt Wessels, Sgt Thompson, Sgt Pennington, Sgt Pritchard, Sgt McNair, Sgt Cameron for sortie CD 340.

The latter crew were flying R3292, and may have been lost to a nightfighter. Sergeant Goldie was flying T2549, and two of this crew, Plt Off Steel and Sergeant Mogg, baled out and were taken prisoner. Both crews were from 115 Squadron.

Squadron Leader Taylor and crew failed to return from the attack on Berlin on 7/8 October, and L7809 with Flt Lt Chivers and crew was lost on the 24th/25th while attacking the Blohm & Voss shipyards in Hamburg. Returning from the attack on oil refineries at Gelsenkirchen, Plt Off Rodgers crashed at Booten, near Reatham, in the early hours of 28 October, two of the crew receiving injuries.

Orders were received from 3 Group to have six aircraft and crews on standby from the 29th to deploy to Malta. Long-range fuel tanks were fitted in the bomb bays, and the selected crews were given briefings on routeing procedures. At 00:11 on 30 October the first aircraft, 115 Squadron Wellington '3278', flown by Sqn Ldr Foss, took off from Marham. By 00:31 the last of the six, three from each squadron, was airborne and *en route*. Tragedy soon struck, however, when '2613' crashed into the London balloon barrage with the loss of Plt Off Pate and crew. Another 115 Squadron aircraft, piloted by Sgt Forrester, had problems with the fuel feed from the long-range tank and returned to base. The remaining Wellingtons arrived safely at Malta between 07:30 and 07:45.

At 09:00 on 4 November, 38 Squadron was ordered to 'prepare for proceeding overseas to a base as yet unknown. All personnel to be recalled from leave.' This was followed 24 hr later by the order 'all squadron ground equipment to be stacked in B Flt hangar ready for transportation to Birkenhead'. Number 115 Squadron was ordered to give every assistance with swapping equipment, aircraft, and personnel, the latter to replace those of 38 Squadron found unfit for service overseas. At the very last minute they took another crew from 115 Squadron to give a full establishment. Nine aircraft that were approaching the 240 hr inspection were also given up, as was 'K', the dual-control Wellington.

A few weeks later, in the early hours of 23 November, a further eight aircraft of 38 Squadron, led by Wg Cdr Thomson, left Marham *en route* for

Malta. Most of the groundcrew had already left Norfolk in the middle of the month for the journey to Luqa, Malta. The remaining eight aircraft departed the following day. Marham was soon back up to strength, however, as the advance elements of 218 Squadron, also equipped with the Wellington 1C, arrived from Oakington on the 25th. The event was recorded by that squadron's diarist: "Squadron a bit depressed at having to move again, having just begun to enjoy the comforts of Oakington. A good deal of cleaning up of hangars and barrack rooms and general sorting out to be done." The arrival at the new base was marred by the death a few days later of one of 218's original air gunners; Sgt King was killed when he walked into a revolving propeller.

With these various changes taking place, November proved to be a light month for operations. Missions were flown on the 5th (Flushing and Bremerhaven), 7th (Essen), 11th (Gelsenkirchen), 14th (Berlin), 16th (Hamburg), 22nd (Bordeaux and Lorient), and 27th (Cologne and Boulogne). On the non-operational side, a sherry party was held on the 8th to bid farewell to 38 Squadron, and on the 16th the aircrew took up residence at Marham Hall, the officers moving to Marham House. Lastly, His Majesty the King paid a visit to the station on the 27th to tour the squadrons and watch the briefings for that night's operations. On the down side, Fg Off Proctor damaged T2511 when, on leaving dispersal, he taxied into a Battle of the target-towing flight.

Neither was it a month free of tragedy. At 18:40 on the evening of 14 November the first of 11 Wellingtons of 115 Squadron were airborne to attack Berlin. Among those getting airborne that night was George Bury, navigator in T2509. He recounts the dramatic events of that night in his book *Wellingtons of 115 Squadron over Europe* (Newton, Swindon, 1994):

We took off from Marham in our aircraft T2509 at 1900 hours, arriving at our target area very quickly as there had been a strong tail wind. The flight was no more difficult than previously, there was a certain amount of opposition from the ground *en route*, but over Berlin it was comparatively quiet, in fact we found that it was less well defended than targets in the Ruhr. After bombs away and confirmation that they had landed we set course for home. It was a very cold night and the captain, who had been flying for over 3 hours, handed over the

controls to the second pilot and came back to the navigation/wireless compartment and squatted on the floor to warm up a bit. Hot air from the engines was ducted to the cockpit but it had very little effect, whereas the nav compartment having a door between it and the main fuselage was almost warm. The second pilot had been given the course to steer with the added instructions to avoid flying through any searchlights if possible. The course was checked from time to time but due to low and medium cloud it was not possible to confirm our position, but we had been adopting our normal practice of flying 270 magnetic after bombing targets in the north of Germany and relying on being able to pinpoint our position upon crossing the Dutch coast. Then came a call from the cockpit.

"Skipper, there are searchlights ahead."

"Well fly around them."

"I can't, every time I turn more pop up and now there is almost a solid wall of them ahead."

By this time the captain was once more in control of the aircraft and we had resumed our correct course. I was then told that there appeared to be a large river on our starboard side, well if that was so then we must be well off our intended track. Had the pilot averaged out his course by flying to the right and then left around the searchlights, or did he turn to the right each time? The answer was, as I feared, always to the right. Maybe the compass was out. I knew that this was not the reason as we had arrived at the target without difficulty, even so I decided to carry out a rough check. I went to the astrodome intending to look for the pole star but the clouds together with the searchlights made it impossible.

I did get a quick glance of the river the captain had mentioned and was making my way forward to the bombing position in order to get a better view when all hell was let loose, they threw everything including the kitchen sink, no nice coloured lights this time, just flashes which burst all around us and were very accurate as to height, also quite close judging by the noise. The Captain took avoiding action but this was very much like avoiding raindrops, if you fly on a steady course they may miss you and if you take avoiding action you might just fly into the path of one which would have missed you – but as you always feel better doing something, violent avoiding action was taken and at last we were clear of it and just about to congratulate ourselves on our escape when it was noticed that the oil pressure of the starboard engine was starting to fall. There is a reserve tank under the stretcher bed on the port side, the transfer of oil is carried out by operating the handle of a small pump, this is no doubt most efficient on the ground or in the tropics, but at 10,000 ft with the temperature well below freezing, the oil was so viscous that I could hardly move the handle. The wireless operator arrived to lend a hand but the extra effort only resulted in the handle of the pump being broken off, it was only made of Dural and not up to the task.

The starboard engine caught fire and was quickly brought under control by the built-in fire extinguisher. We now took stock of the situation. I had only had a very quick glance of the ground and it looked like the river Elbe at Hamburg, but it could have been Bremen. I could not fathom how we could have been so far north of our intended track to be over Hamburg. Now we were over the sea but had not even seen the coast and I could not complete my plotting accurately because during the confusion with the oil pump and fire, I had failed to make a note of important times and courses. The Wireless Operator broke radio silence and sent an SOS on the captain's instructions, not much use as we were somewhere over the German Bight, but at least it would let them know back in the UK of our predicament. I explained to the captain that we were now flying into a 30 knot headwind at this height which would drastically reduce our groundspeed but if we went lower the wind would be less and our groundspeed so much greater. Try explaining that to a pilot who is trying to keep an aircraft airborne on one engine and still has some 450 miles of sea to cross. He is unlikely to relish the thought of deliberately losing height. To help reduce the weight we set about throwing everything we could overboard. The only items of any weight were the oxygen bottles, these went first, through the large hatch in the floor of the aircraft. It was now a very clear night and we could follow the path of each bottle all the way down until it hit the sea.

We were nowhere near the coast of England when the port engine started to falter due to lack of fuel, the second pilot changed over the fuel cocks so that the remaining petrol in the starboard wing could be used. Now we really had a problem, just how far could we go on that remaining petrol. How accurate were the gauges? It was unlikely that we would encounter fog over East Anglia because of the strength of the wind – but there could be low cloud. Could we risk flying the 18 miles from the coast to Marham? Should we land on the beach? But were not all beaches protected by anti-invasion obstruction? Landing close to the shore in the sea might be safer, but it would be a pity after all our efforts to strike a mine and be blown to bits. These were problems for the captain to mull over whilst trying to keep the aircraft in the air. Just what course of action he decided upon we do not know, maybe he just intended to keep on flying on and see what turned up or maybe he just prayed, if so it had very little effect. There was a sudden silence from the port engine, broken only by the eerie whistle of the wind as we headed down towards the sea. There was no requirement now for the intercom, the captain's voice could be clearly heard throughout the aircraft as he called: "This is it, take up your crash positions". We at once went to our previously selected places but just before doing so, the Wireless Operator clamped his key down in the hope that the ground station might at least obtain a fix on our position, and I threw large heaps of paper down the chute. During the last stages of flight we had torn up every scrap of paper we could find, retaining only my chart, log and one local map. The idea was, knowing how difficult it was to spot an aircraft in the sea from the air, it might become more obvious if the whole area was covered by scraps of paper. This was another brilliant idea that came to nothing as the pilot stretched his glide as far as he could, making the point of touchdown miles from where the paper would have landed. The wait for touchdown was painfully drawn out, but at last came the call, "This is it!". The aircraft gently touched the crest of the first wave as the pilot held off, the second wave with a lot more force and the third like running into a brick wall. The time was 04:00.

From my position near the astrodome I pulled the dinghy release lever and shouted that it was released and inflating, I clambered out quickly followed by other members of the crew. I had never been instructed in dinghy drill, all I had ever been told was that in the event of an impending crash always take up a position near the main spar or other structure and that the dinghy would be tied to the aircraft by a line and this should be cut using the dinghy flotation knife, after which we should get away from the aircraft as quickly as possible as it could sink within two minutes and might turn over in doing so. One of the air gunners was fishing about in the dark trying to locate the non-existent mooring line whilst the other fumbled about in the bottom of the dinghy trying to locate the knife. At this stage a wave broke over the wing, snatching the dinghy from our grasp, before it could drift away we all flung ourselves into it, and before we could untangle ourselves we had drifted under the rising and falling tailplane. We had just pushed ourselves clear of this danger when there was a shout of "Help, my arm!". It was only then that we realized that there were only five of us in the dinghy and that the call was from the second pilot (Sergeant Dean), who was only now emerging from the escape hatch over the cockpit. We paddled like mad but could not make any progress as we did not have any proper paddles, and helplessly watched as Dean missed his landing on the wing and fell between the fuselage and the engine – he was not seen again. Naturally we were desolate, we had survived the attack and the subsequent fire, and had made a perfect landing in the sea and whilst we had not yet been saved there was no reason to doubt that this would soon take place – and now we had lost one of our team.

Slowly we drifted away from the aircraft and hours afterwards we could just distinguish her outline on the horizon, there was no sign of her sinking. If only we had known we could now all be sitting on the fuselage, or even inside, warm and safe instead of being cold wet and cramped inside the dinghy. We were told later that the Navy had sunk her by gun fire after 3 days as she was a danger to shipping, a very sad end to T2509 which had served us well.

The survivors were picked up just before dusk by HMT *Pelton*, wrapped in warm blankets and given cups of hot tea. The night was spent in the Naval Sick Quarters at Great Yarmouth before return to Marham for debriefing. For the pilot, Sgt

Morson, it had been his 13th operation. Most of the crew thought he deserved a medal for his handling of the aircraft. The authorities agreed, and both Morson and the wireless Operator, Sgt Cleverly, were awarded immediate DFMs, the latter for his actions in sending distress messages and clamping the key, thus giving the rescue authorities the maximum amount of information with which to effect a rescue. George's tale was worth recounting at some length, as it encapsulates many aspects of Wellington operations during this period; the vagaries of navigation, problems of cold, enemy defences, the 'feel' of what it was like to be in a bomber crew on a dark, lonely night over Germany, and the hazards of a night ditching in the North Sea. This crew were lucky; for many others the cold sea becoming their last resting place.

The operation to Hamburg on the night of the 16th was a disaster. The 11 Wellingtons of 115 Squadron took off from 17:20 onwards. The weather was bad, and only four found the primary target, the others bombing various alternates. The German defences were very much on the alert, flak and fighters proving extremely active. Flight Lieutenant Van, piloting R1034, landed back at Marham with his aircraft badly shot up; two others were damaged and had to make forced landings at other airfields. Pilot Officer Tindall in T2606 was attacked by four Bf 110s in the target area, the Wellington being sprayed with shells and the front gunner, Sgt F. Jarvis, being badly wounded. The pilot managed to make it back to England but had to force-land at Bircham Newton. Jarvis later died of his injuries. Pilot Officer Roy in P9299 crashed at Wittering, but with no injuries to the crew. One other Wellington, P9286/K flown by Sgt D. Larkman, was shot down by nightfighter pilot Oberleutnant Egmont and fell at Winkel, Holland, with the loss of all of its crew. A further aircraft from the squadron, R3213/S, carrying Sgt English and crew, failed to return.

There were also a restricted number of operations in December, although in this case operations were scheduled for most days but were cancelled owing to bad weather in the target areas. For most of the month there was still only one operational squadron, as 218 was still undergoing training and work-up, with an average of nine such sorties a day. It did not fly its first mission from its new base until the early hours of 20 December, sending two aircraft, R1009/L (Sqn Ldr

Richmond) and R1210/O (Fg Off Anstey) to Ostend.

Wellingtons of 115 Squadron were active on eight nights against a wide range of targets, although the Turin raid planned for the 4th was changed into an attack on Dusseldorf. The squadron lost three aircraft during the month. On the 8/9th Plt Off Tindall and crew in T2520/A flew into the hills near Tredegar when returning from the Bordeaux raid; on 11/12th Sgt Hartland and crew failed to return from an attack on Mannheim in T2466/C; and on 29/30th T2465/O, flown by Plt Off Salmon, failed to return.

The night of December 16/17 saw the largest Bomber Command effort to date with Operation Abigail Rachel, an attack ordered by the War Cabinet against the centre of a German city in retaliation for the bombing of British cities. The chosen target was Mannheim, but in the event the raid was largely ineffective, with scattered bombing.

Christmas 1940 came: 'The Airmen's Christmas dinner was held at 12:30 and was a happy affair, everybody seemed in the right spirits, the band played during dinner which seemed to give the right atmosphere. The Officers' dinner was held in the evening.'

January's weather was even worse than that of the previous month, especially from the 16th onwards, and frequent heavy snowfalls made the airfield unusable. Only six operations were flown, on the 1st, 4th, 8th, 9th, 12th, and 15th, the maximum number of sorties on any one night being 12, although this was partly due to the slow work-up of 218 Squadron. No aircraft were lost this month, although Sqn Ldr Lasbrey crashed 115 Squadron Wellington R1179/W on landing back at base; no injuries were suffered by the crew. The

Flt Sgt Stanley Pook with his 115 Squadron crew in 1941: left to right; Sgt Leslie, Sgt Nuttall, Sgt Duff, Plt Off Foster, Sgt Pook, Sgt Scriven.

danger of lurking enemy nightfighters was again underlined when Sqn Ldr Richmond, having returned early because of intercom failure, was attacked at 1,000 ft whilst in the Marham circuit. Dousing his lights, he evaded the fighter and left the area, returning some time later. There were still training losses, Fg Off Maclaren of 218 Squadron crashing on his first solo.

The Luftwaffe's bomber-intruders found Marham at last, and between 04:30 and 04:35 on 16 January ten small bombs were dropped on the airfield. One fell near the station workshops, blowing out all the windows on one side. Three others fell about 300 yd south-east of Ladywood, and a further six in the field next to barrack block 103. There was very little damage and no casualties were suffered.

Charles Waring recalls one of the Luftwaffe's bombing raids:

We had a few air raids whilst I was at Marham. The first one I vividly remember. I had just been to Norwich for the day and I returned with the *Eastern Daily Press* van which left at midnight, dropping papers *en route* to King's Lynn. I was dropped off at the Narborough crossroads and then had to walk from there to the station. Whilst I was walking I was met by a Squadron Leader on a bicycle who informed that there was a raid on. It seems that a German aircraft had followed ours in and bombed the station. The Squadron Leader told me to get into a shelter as soon as I got back. He had no sooner spoken than we heard the German plane. It was flying low and we both dived into the roadside ditch. Fortunately it was a dry one and so we didn't get too mucky! I later learned that one bomb had dropped close to the Sergeants' Mess but there was not a lot of damage.

The major effort during February was against invasion ports, Le Havre, Boulogne, Rotterdam, and Brest being targeted on seven nights. The Boulogne raid of the 7/8th was typical of the operations at this period, ten aircraft of 115 Squadron leaving the ground from 20:16 onwards:

Aircraft bombed quays and docks with some success, all bombs falling across the docks, from 7,000–12,000 ft. Visibility good, with high cloud. Big fires and explosions seen, also fires breaking out on the quays.

During the first 10 days of the month the squadrons of 3 Group were heavily tasked, Marham contributing 46 sorties, and this was reflected in a message from the AOC:

Congratulations to all units on the successful conclusion of last night's operations. These were by far the most ambitious as yet undertaken by this Group. 104 aircraft were briefed and 101 carried out the operation, of which only one is at present outstanding. A fine achievement reflecting the greatest credit on all members of units comprising the Group.

Marham's contribution had been 10 aircraft from 218 Squadron and 11 from 115 squadron, with Hannover and Rotterdam as the targets. Crews returning from a mission tended to relax as they crossed the English coast, thoughts turning to the hot chocolate and breakfast that would follow the intelligence debrief. However, the skies over England were by no means safe. The German nightfighter force had extended the intruder programme aimed at destroying aircraft as they returned to their bases. On this night Sgt Rodgers of 115 Squadron, flying Wellington R1084, was attacked over the Swaffham beacon. Having just missed a mid-air collision with other Wellingtons, the crew decided to switch on their navigation lights. Almost immediately they saw an enemy fighter to starboard; moments later they had been hit and the port engine was damaged. Trying to avoid the fighter by going low, Rodgers was left with little option but to make a forced landing, his aircraft having been hit at least twice. The Wellington came to rest on the railway tracks near Swaffham and quickly burned out. Fortunately the crew were able to scramble to safety, only the rear gunner, Sgt Hill, being wounded in the engagement.

The danger was brought home two weeks later, on the night of 25 February, when '1009' of 218 Squadron, piloted by Sgt Hoos, was shot down some 4 miles from Marham. In the ensuing crash the front gunner, Sgt Stanley, was trapped in the wreckage and suffered severe burns. Once rescued he was rushed to King's Lynn hospital, where his leg had to be amputated. These two incidents in one month showed that vigilance was essential at all times.

The only other nightfighter combat had taken place on the Brest raid of the 22nd, when a 115 Squadron Wellington had a brief tussle with a Bf 110.

Fog was still causing problems – and losses. The records describe a return from the Hannover–Bremen–Magdeburg raids on the night of 11 February:

The Station Commander had been informed by HQ No. 3 Group that most of the aerodromes would have bad visibility. Instructions were afterwards received to divert, if petrol would allow, to Lossiemouth and Kinloss. This was not possible. A general broadcast was made to all our aircraft to hasten home, but only a small number acknowledged this signal. Our visibility at Marham was then down to 500 yards, the sky being completely obscured. All aircraft were told to home on Wyton. This aerodrome became unserviceable about 0055 hr. Every available flare etc was prepared at Marham for the reception of aircraft, but the visibility at this time was down to nil. Eventually none of our aircraft was able to land at the parent station.

Wellington 3238 Wg Cdr Evans-Evans, 115 Squadron 'baled out' and the aircraft crashed at Wicken Bonhunt. The crew landed safely with the exception of the Wing Commander, who sustained injuries to his leg. He was admitted to Saffron Walden hospital. A/C 1210 Fg Off Anstey abandoned his aircraft and 'baled out' in the Cambridge area. All crew safe, but unfortunately his aircraft crashed on a house and killed three civilians. 1326 Sqn Ldr Ault, 1063 Flt Lt Giles, 1221 Plt Off Curry landed at Wyton; 1034 Sqn Ldr Lasbrey, 7854 Plt Off Loder landed at Alconbury; 1025 Flt Lt Shaw landed at Driffield; 2887 Plt Off Bois landed at Newmarket; 1135 Fg Off Agar landed at Bassingham; 2885 Sgt Adams force-landed at Frampton on Severn. His aircraft was stuck in the mud and owing to the tide being at its height at 0900 hr it was impossible to salvage same. 9290 Fg Off Kirk landed at Gravesend; 1238 Sgt Whittaker force-landed at Finningley without injuries to his crew; 7895 Flt Lt Clyde-Smith landed at Tangmere; 2801 Fg Off Smith landed at Withernsea; 2958 Flt Lt Mitchell landed at Lindholme.

An incredible saga! Without any interference from the Germans, the Marham bomber force was spread across England; aircraft had been lost and crews injured. As stated previously, the weather was an enemy almost as dangerous at times as the human one. It also restricted operations: 'Owing to the lack of crews who were scattered about the country after last night's ops, no flying took place today, 13th.'

February had not yet finished with 115 Squadron. The early hours of the 23rd brought another round of casualties. The target was a Hipper-class cruiser reported at Brest, and the squadron launched nine aircraft from 02:38 onwards. Plt Off Clarke, in T2511/P, returned early with an aircraft problem, but on landing swung to starboard to avoid some buildings, ending up in the trees to the west of the airfield. None of the crew was injured and the aircraft was repairable. Returning from the mission, Sgt Milton in R1221/F called for a bearing at 08:25; this was acknowledged and orders given to divert to Feltwell. Nothing more was heard, and a few minutes later the aircraft crashed at East Winch, hitting some trees and catching fire with the loss of all six crewmen. Some revenge was claimed by R1469/Q, flown by Sgt Bright:

When about 8 miles N of Morlaix (French coast) his rear gunner, Plt Off Milles, observed Me 110 flying about 500 ft below the red quarter and astern. The rear gunner opened fire with about 300 rounds from each gun into the 110's cockpit. The E/A was seen to shudder and dip its port wing as it turned to port. Plt Off Mills asked the captain to turn quickly to the green side and a stall turn and dive brought his guns to bear again on the enemy's tail unit, which, after about 200 rounds from each gun, was seen to lose the port fin tail and rudder. the enemy's nose came up and stalled into a spin disappearing through the clouds at about 4,000 ft.

Later that same day a single aircraft, L7810/R, was sent to attack Boulogne. The aircraft was airborne at 19:43, and some two hours later was heard calling for a fix from Hull. Nothing else was heard, and Sgt Lloyd and his crew were listed as missing.

In the early hours of 3 March 1941 a message was received from the Observer Corps that a Wellington had been seen to dive into the sea near Teignmouth. The staff at 3 Group assessed that it was a Marham aircraft and notified the station, which confirmed that '3279' had yet to return. In the meantime rescue craft had gone to the area, where they recovered two parachutes and the body of Sgt Fanwick. The W/T operator was the only member of the crew to be found, the rest of Sgt Elliott's crew having vanished. A second aircraft was lost on the 12th. Flying Officer Crosse and crew from 218 Squadron in

'1326' failing to return from operations. The following night the squadrons visited Hamburg and Rotterdam, crews noting severe flak. Sergeant Donald's Wellington, '1183', was badly hit and the W/T operator, Sgt Huffingley, was killed. The pilot brought the damaged aircraft back to base but crashed on landing.

With continuing winter weather problems, operations had only been flown on the 2nd, 12th, 13th, 15th, 18th, 21st, 27th, and 30th. The mission on the 30th was to be the first of many to Brest to attack the German warships *Gneisenau* and *Scharnhorst*, both of which were in dock undergoing refit. The Admiralty had expressed, in very strong terms, that the RAF should attempt the destruction of these ships before they cut loose on Allied shipping. For the night's efforts, 21 aircraft went to Brest and the other one to Calais, and all crews claimed to have straddled the dock area with their bombs. RAF crews were to attack these targets numerous times over the next few months; throughout Bomber Command the ships became known as 'Salmon' and 'Gluckstein'.

This same target was visited five times during April, a total of 87 sorties being flown on the 3rd, 10th, 12th, 14th, and 22nd. The squadrons lost six aircraft in the process, three failing to return and the other three crashing in England. Sergeant Thompson and crew in R1470/H were attacked by an enemy aircraft, probably a Ju 88 of 1/NJG2, when returning from the first raid of the month, and the Wellington crashed into the mud banks off King's Lynn. All were killed in the impact except the rear gunner, Sgt Russell, but he subsequently died from exposure. Sergeant Brown and crew in '1442' were lost on the 10th of the month, and Sgt Swain and crew, in '7798', on the 22nd. Sergeant F. Shaw, second pilot in T2560/E, was killed when the aircraft crashed on diversion to Wroughton after the 22/23 April operation to Brest.

The station ORB for May 1941 contains an unusual section headed 'Notable War Service':

The Commander in Chief desires to bring to the notice of all ranks in the Command the coolness and devotion to duty shown by No. 938896 Sgt Burke H. a Wireless Operator/Air Gunner in No. 218 Squadron. On the night of 8/9th April, 1941, this NCO was member of a crew of a Wellington aircraft detailed to attack Kiel. In the course of this operation the aircraft was very badly hit and was eventually flown back to England across the North Sea on one engine after all moveable equipment and maps had been jettisoned from the aircraft. Great dependence, therefore, had to be placed upon the assistance which could be obtained by wireless in order to bring the bomber back to England. The fixed aerial, however, had been damaged by enemy action, and before any wireless could be obtained, Sgt Burke with more than half his body outside the astro hatch repaired the damage.

The aircraft returned to England on a course guessed by the Navigator, who had no means of sextant and by wireless bearings which were obtained by Sgt Burke once he had repaired his wireless. Throughout the whole trip Sgt Burke's coolness and efficiency resulted in the aircraft being brought back safely to an aerodrome in England. He had to change frequencies and wavebands at the pilot's request with great rapidity and finally home the aircraft successfully at Horsham St Faith. It is considered that this NCO's coolness and skill resulted in the safe return of this aircraft.

Although Brest was on the list twice during May (3/4th and 7/8th), most attention was paid to targets in Germany, with visits to Mannheim (5/6th), Hamburg (8/9th, 10/11th, and 11/12th), and Cologne (16/17th). During the second Hamburg raid a 115 Squadron aircraft flown by Plt Off Saunderson dropped a 4,000 lb 'cookie'. From now on these blockbuster weapons were to become a regular part of the bomb load, the experts having decided that the blast effect of this bomb would prove highly effective. The only casualty during May was a 115 Squadron Wellington, R1280, piloted by Sgt Sayers, which lost a propeller and, unable to maintain height, had to force-land half a mile short of Oakington.

In addition to operational flying from Marham, there were numerous other aircraft movements in a day. Each of the flying squadrons mounted two or three training sorties, the total depending on the operational task scheduled for the next 24 hr and the amount of conversion or continuation flying that needed to be done. Other sorties were flown by station flight aircraft, and there were quite a regular number of visitors in and out. There was also a routine requirement for post-rectification air tests and night-flying tests. Consequently, in common with most grass airfields, the surface at Marham began to suffer from

The Secretary of State for War visits Marham on 14 July 1941 and inspects the airfield defences.

wear and tear. This was never much of a problem in the summer, although it could be somewhat rough on undercarriages, but it was a potential disaster for winter operations. As already stated, Barton Bendish was often unusable for long periods.

As the summer wore on, the take-off times became later and later, the June period having first take-offs at around 23:30. Operations were flown on 11 nights during June, the majority being in the first half of the month.

Kiel and Cologne were the most frequently visited targets this month, although various 'fresher' crews went to the usual locations such as Boulogne and Dunkirk. The policy of sending 'freshmen' to what were considered 'easy' targets on the coast of France had been employed for some time, and most considered it a good idea. That is not to say, however, that such sorties were free from hazard, and losses were suffered.

The first casualties in June occurred on the night of the 12th. Sergeant Robson was one of 12 115 Squadron captains destined for Hamm, but shortly after take-off R1805/T developed engine

trouble and he was forced to jettison its bombs over the Wash and return to Marham. The aircraft was proving difficult to control, and as it crossed the airfield boundary the second engine failed. In the ensuing crash it hit a tree. Two of the crew were seriously injured, Sgt Aikenhead later dying from his injuries, but the others escaped with hardly a scratch.

Routine flying continued to claim casualties. On the 17th R1517 crashed at Palgrove Farm, near Sporle, during an air test. Only one man survived. A few days later, on the night of the 23/24th, Plt Off Sharpe forced-landed T2963/A at Moat House Farm, Martlesham, while returning from bombing Kiel–Cologne; Sgt Tingley died of wounds. The following day another Wellington, R1501, crashed on take-off, Sgt Skillen and his crew escaping unhurt as the aircraft burned out. The squadrons then had a few days without operations, but on the night of the 29th 115 Squadron suffered a double loss. Flight Lieutenant Bailey in W5459 was shot down by Hauptmann Ehle of II/NJG1, the Wellington crashing at Altenwerder with the loss of all of its crew. Then, whilst running in to

An effigy of Hitler hangs in a tree in front of the Officers' Mess, summer 1941.

the target at Bremen, Plt Off McSweyn's aircraft, R1509, was hit and damaged by flak. It was then attacked in quick succession by a Bf 109 and a Bf 110, although the rear gunner laid claim to the former. The rear gunner and second pilot had been injured, and the aircraft was in a bad way. McSweyn ordered the crew to bale out, and all did so. Unfortunately, rear gunner Sgt Gill landed

Groundcrew at work on the port engine of a Wellington.

in a tree and broke his back in the subsequent fall to the ground, later dying of his injuries. After numerous attempts to escape back to England, including the attempted 'borrowing' of a Bf 110, McSweyn made his way to England via Spain. In recognition of his determination he was awarded the Military Cross. A third aircraft had problems during the raid, Sgt Payne crash-landing at Manston in R1805.

July was a busy month operationally, and also one in which an increasing number of nightfighter combats were reported by crews.

The first operation of the month was flown by 115 Squadron, who sent three aircraft on a sea search for a dinghy on the morning of 1 July. Sergeant Smith in R1063 was jumped by three Bf 110s, but although the aircraft was hit three times it escaped serious damage. None of the aircraft sighted the dinghy. Messerschmitt Bf 110s were in evidence again on the following night, when at least one crew reported combats; X9663 came back with a liberal peppering of cannon holes. It was the same story again on the night of the 4th, although this time Sgt Parsons, the rear gunner of Wellington X9671, claimed to have downed the enemy. Two nights later the same pilot, Sgt Wallace, was found by Bf 110s again. In the ensuing eight-minute combat the crew co-operated superbly and only very minor damage was suffered. Wellington X9672 was not so lucky; Sgt Berney could not shake off the fighter and had to jettison his bombs. During this combat the rear gunner, Sgt Kerruish, was killed. German nightfighter pilots appreciated the threat posed by the Wellington's four-gun rear turret, and their usual tactic was to silence these guns; hence the high loss rate amongst rear gunners. With the guns silenced the fighter could then finish off the bomber. Yet another aircraft of 115 Squadron failed to return, R1063/D, piloted by Sgt Matthews, having been damaged by a fighter and forced to ditch in the North Sea. Although an SOS was sent, the subsequent air and sea search failed to locate the crew.

Aircraft were lost on all but two of the remaining operations flown by 115 Squadron during July. The squadron sent four to attack Osnabruck on the night of 9/10th, and all went well until the return leg. Squadron Leader Sindall had a double engine failure in X9673, and with the aircraft showing no inclination to recover, he ordered the crew to bale out. Almost as soon as they had done so, and just before he himself was preparing to leave, the engine picked up again and Sindall landed the Wellington at Brackley.

During the Bremen raid on the night of 13/14th, R1502 was shot down by a fighter, the crew baling out and becoming POWs, with the exception of Sgt Tipper, whose body was found in the wreckage. Two nights later R1798/B (or R1222?) failed to return from Brest, and the aircraft was subsequently found to have crashed near Nederweert, Holland. The Mannheim raid of 21st/22nd cost the lives of Sgt Payne and his crew when Z8788/H failed to return.

On rare occasions the night bomber force was called upon to make daylight raids, and such was the case on 24 July 1941. The Marham units sent a number of aircraft on the major attack to bomb the *Gneisenau* and *Prinz Eugen* at Brest. The overall raid plan was complex, involving strict timing to make best use of the escort by long-range Spitfires. However, all three Wellingtons of 115 Squadron were engaged by Bf 109s. During the combats the bombers were not hit, but their gunners laid claim to no fewer than three of the fighters. Two of the bombers were damaged by flak, but all claimed to have hit the target, Sgt Prior claiming two Direct Hits (DHs) on *Gneisenau*. Ten out of the total force of 79 Wellingtons were lost on this mission.

Intensive operations continued into early August, seven missions being flown in the first 12 days. This included a double operation on the 12th. Taking off at 00:15, 115 Squadron sent ten aircraft to Munich, and all had returned safely by 05:50; then, at 21:25, nine (including five crews who had flown on the earlier operation) were airborne for Essen–Hanover. A significant aspect of the earlier raid was the squadron's first operational use of the new Gee navigation aid. Selected crews had undergone a training course in the new system, and a number of aircraft with the appropriate installations had been received. Gee was to prove a great boon to the bomber crews, not only for navigating to the targets and bombing them (until jammed by the Germans somewhat later), but also for helping aircraft find their home bases. The second mission was not without loss. Wellington Z8835, piloted by Sgt Wallace, was shot down by an aircraft of 6/NJG1, crashing at Grafel with the loss of all on board. Returning to base and aware of the risk of collision in the congested skies around the East Anglian air bases, Plt Off Wood in T2563/D switched on his navigation lights. Almost immediately he was pounced on by a Ju 88 intruder, and in the sub-sequent attacks the Wellington caught fire and was forced-landed at Smith's Farm, near Scottow. All escaped from the destroyed bomber except Sgt B. Evans.

The second half of the month saw only four operations; Emden–Osnabruck–Hanover on the 14/15th, Duisberg on the 18/19th, and Mannheim on the 27/28th and again on the 29/30th. Nevertheless, 115 Squadron alone lost five more aircraft, three in the early hours of the 28th, two crews baling out over Norfolk and the other crash-landing at West Raynham.

The high loss rate continued through September as German defensive capability improved and the Wellington found it increasingly harder to survive. Number 115 Squadron flew 81 sorties over nine missions, for the loss of six aircraft. The worst night was that of the 29/30th over Stettin, when two fell to nightfighters, X9673/B, Sgt Ellis, and X9910/Y, Sgt Hulls, only the rear gunner of the latter aircraft surviving to be taken prisoner.

The large number of operations meant that Marham personnel were frequently in the news regarding gallantry awards, and the tally of Distinguished Flying Cross (DFC) and DFM recipients rose rapidly, although the MC to Plt Off McSweyn was certainly unusual. Awards were, in essence, of two types; those granted for a single operation, and those in recognition of a period of notable service. It is not possible to list all of the honours and awards received by Marham personnel during 1939–45, but a short reference and a few examples are certainly justified.

On the night of 16/17 October 1941, Sgt Allan George, a New Zealander with 115 Squadron, took off from Marham at 00:50 in Wellington 1C Z8399/Z. The citation regarding his award of a DFM is contained within RAF Awards List No. 291:

One night in October 1941 this airman was the pilot of an aircraft detailed to attack Duisburg. On the outward journey, shortly after passing the Zuider Zee, both engines of his aircraft commenced to lose power and the aircraft would not maintain height. In spite of this, Sergeant George resolutely continued his flight to the target area, where, although subjected to most accurate and intense anti-aircraft fire and unable to take complete evading action, he released a very heavy bomb. Although his aircraft was gradually losing height, and in spite of

being further handicapped by an unserviceable radio transmitter, Sergeant George skilfully flew back to this country and made a safe landing.

Throughout, this pilot displayed outstanding coolness, courage and determination. On a previous occasion, Sergeant George carried his mission through to a successful conclusion in conditions of great difficulty.

The crew of Z8399 had been one of 11 sent out that night by 115 Squadron. All reached the target and dropped their bombs, although with a height over target of only 9,500 ft, Allan George's aircraft was certainly the lowest. The squadron records mention that one aircraft was carrying a 4,000 lb bomb, although they do not state which aircraft was so burdened; however, bearing in mind the comment on the citation, it seems likely that it was this Wellington. Surprisingly, there is no mention in the squadron ORB of the problems faced by this crew.

Compared with recent months, October was a good one, with operations on nine nights for the loss of two 115 Squadron aircraft (Z8844/S on the Nurnberg raid of the 14/15th, and X9873/P on the Bremen raid on the 31st). With deteriorating weather, November and December were much quieter, with a total of 11 operational nights against targets in Germany and French ports. The loss rate also fell, 115 Squadron losing three aircraft, but with all the crews safe. There were, however, still stupid losses. On the 24th March Sgt Bruce was flying with his crew and three passengers on a local sortie when the aircraft hit a railway truck near March and crashed among the coal wagons, starting a major fire. All on board the Wellington were killed.

One happy note at the end of the year was the announcement of the award of the Distinguished Service Order (DSO) to the CO of 115 Squadron, Wg Cdr Trevor Freeman. The citation read:

This officer has been engaged on active operations over a long period. Wing Commander Freeman has carried out sorties, involving attacks on Kiel, Berlin and other important targets in Germany, a daylight raid on Brest and an attack on Turin in Italy.

As commanding officer of the squadron he has set a splendid example by his leadership, enthusiasm and courage. In September 1941, he led the squadron in an attack on Cologne and, in spite of fierce opposition, descended to low level, flying over the area for over an hour

Wellington IC R1448 HA-L survived its time with 218 Squadron and moved to 20 OTU.

searching for his objective which he eventually bombed.

Later he led the squadron in a raid on Turin. In the face of heavy opposition, he made a successful attack from low level. Wing Commander Freeman has spent many hours flying with young crews on operational sorties and his personal example in the face of the enemy has proved a source of inspiration. While employed as a navigation officer at station headquarters he continually carried out operations with the various units of the Group, thus taking the opportunity to demonstrate, in a practical manner, the theory he was endeavouring to teach.

The squadron also received two DFCs (Sqn Ldr Foster and Plt Off Miller) and two DFMs (Sgt Berney and Sgt Gilpin) during December.

Marham had been very busy during 1941, and losses had steadily risen. Many new faces appeared each week, most new crews at this period coming from 15 Operational Training Unit (OTU). It was among some of the ground staff that the losses seemed to have the worst impact, and the WAAFs in particular. There was little doubt that the Wellington was reaching the end of its front-line life.

1942 – The Decisive Year for Bomber Command

As the war dragged on into 1942 and Bomber Command became an increasingly effective offensive force, the pace of operations increased and station personnel were hard-pressed to keep up with the work. Social life was virtually limited to that to be found at Marham, and, if it was possible to get away, a visit to one of the pubs in Marham village. The need to allow personnel some free time was, however, recognized by the station executives, and it was possible to get the odd day away from the station. Charles Waring remembers such occasions:

On Friday evening a truck would take to King's Lynn any who had a pass out. You had to give notice to the MT section if you wanted to go. At a given time the truck would return to the station – and you had to make sure that you were at the return point or it would go without you. On a day off you could catch the King's Lynn to Norwich bus at Narborough crossroads. There was one in the morning, and this returned at 8 p.m. from Norwich. So it was possible to have a day out in Norwich if you could afford it (LAC pay – one shilling and sixpence a day). I did this journey one Saturday with AC Smith. We went to a dance and missed the bus back. Smith was confident that we would get a lift back. We managed to get a local bus to Costessy, but from then on it was a case of walking. Not a single vehicle passed us all night and we had to walk all the way to

A Gold Coast town name being painted on a Wellington of 218 (Gold Coast) Squadron.

Marham – result, a whopping great callous on one foot!

January and February were reasonably quiet, as the Norfolk weather caused problems at Marham and the forecast over the target areas made operations difficult. Nonetheless, operations were flown on 11 nights in January, with no loss, and on a further five in February, again without loss. However, 115 Squadron had another training loss on 15 January, Z1563 crashing near the airfield while on an air test, killing all six crew. A number of aircraft suffered flak damage during the month. Wellington X9755 had to land at Exeter after being hit by flak while attacking Brest on the 11th: 'This aircraft was shot up rather badly while over the target, causing damage to the starboard wheel and bomb doors. WOP Sgt Allen was injured in the eye by shrapnel, also the Front Gunner, Sgt Morrison, was hit in the jaw by shrapnel.'

On the night of the 28th, five aircraft, three of 115 Squadron and two of 218 Squadron, were tasked to attack Munster, but only three found the target area. Sergeant Smithson in 'B' had flown

through thick cloud, and layers of ice were building up on the airframe. The instruments were showing strange readings and the aircraft suddenly went into a spin at 19,500 ft. As the aircraft reached 2,500 ft the pilot called to the crew to bale out, but before any could respond it was discovered that the front gunner was jammed in his turret. The entire crew elected to stay with the aeroplane while the pilot fought with the controls. The warmer air at the lower altitude and the sheer determination of the pilot brought the aircraft out of the spin and, shaken but relieved, he flew the Wellington back to Marham.

The other reason for the lighter operational workload for the Wellingtons was the continued re-equipment with the Mk III version and working-up with the Gee system. As part of the latter requirement, squadron crews took part in Exercise *Crackers* on 13 and 19 February. The most significant operation during the month was *Fuller,* which took place in the daylight hours of 12 February. This was an attempt to intercept the warships that Bomber Command had spent so much time trying to destroy at Brest. The 'Channel dash' by *Scharnhorst* and *Gneisenau* caught the RAF on the hop, and by the time bombing sorties were mounted it was too late. Marham sent nine Wellingtons, two operating out of Lakenheath, where they had been on standby. Although four of the aircraft found their targets near the Dutch coast, no hits were scored. In the event, the two major vessels struck mines that had been laid by Bomber Command and were damaged; the so-called 'dash to freedom' did no more than bottle up the ships in a German rather than a French port.

Meanwhile, the task of crew conversion to the Short Stirling had been taken over by 218 Conversion Flight. Formed on 28 February, this unit carried out most of its training flying from Barton Bendish. It was to be a fairly short-lived organization, leaving Marham in October to join 1657 Conversion Unit at Stradishall.

The snow having cleared at last, March brought the seasonal fog. Nevertheless, the pace of operations increased and the bombers were airborne on 11 nights from the 3rd onwards. Essen was the main target, being visited no fewer than six times,

27 bombers from Marham, including 17 Stirlings, attacking on the night of 25/26th. These formed part of Bomber Command's largest effort to a single target, 254 bombers taking part for the loss of nine of their number. Unfortunately it was not a good attack, many of the bombs falling on the decoy site at Rheinberg.

Four aircraft were lost during March, including two over Essen on the night of 26/27th. The only other casualties had occurred after the first operation of the month, when 'Y' blew up on landing, killing two of the crew and seriously wounding the flight engineer. The subsequent investigation attributed the cause to the explosion of two 1,000 lb bombs that had been 'hung up' in the bomb bay.

A further mission, a daylight cloud-cover attack on targets in the Ruhr, was scheduled for the 18th. Few of the crews had any desire to visit 'Happy Valley' by day, and fortunately a recall was sent when it became obvious that cloud cover was inadequate. The air gunners continued to notch up claims, two being made by the

Sir Alan Burns, Governor-General Designate of the Gold Coast, visits 218 (Gold Coast) Squadron in 1942.

Stirlings of 218 Squadron over Lubeck on the night of the 28th.

April was the busiest month since the previous July. The Wellingtons flew 189 sorties over 16 nights, most consisting of 12 to 20 bombers. This was an excellent effort and a credit to both groundcrew and aircrew. The majority of these operations were to targets in Germany, no particular city receiving attention. In view of the overall effort, losses were remarkably low. Wellington X3596/B, piloted by Sgt Holder, was shot down by a nightfighter over Holland on an Essen raid on the night of 12th/13th; X3633/Y, flown by Sgt Fone, was another nightfighter casualty, crashing near Toftlund, Denmark in the early hours of 26 April; X3639/K, with Sgt Harris in command, was lost on the attack on Cologne on the 27th/28th; and, finally, Sgt Reynolds, flying X3593/C, was shot down near Paris on the 29/30th. Although the Stirlings of 218 Squadron contributed 191 sorties, only one aircraft failed to return, Plt Off Millichamp and crew in W7506/Y being lost on the 25/26 April Pilsen raid. However, an earlier trip to Rostock, on the 23/24th, had cost the lives of Sgt Davidge and crew in Stirling 'F', which crashed near King's Lynn.

The most unusual operation of the month was that flown by six Stirlings to the Skoda armaments factory at Pilsen, Czechoslovakia. This long-range sortie was a difficult task fraught with many prob-

lems. Having reached the area, the crews were frustrated by almost total cloud cover, but five aircraft made attacks, losing one as detailed above.

At the beginning of April 1942, station strength had stood at:

No. 115 Squadron	aircrew	–	136
	others	–	362
No. 218 Squadron	aircrew	–	164
	others	–	439
Stirling Conversion Flight	aircrew	–	38
	others	–	97
SHQ Squadron		–	285
AA Flight		–	86
WAAF		–	235
Army:			
70th Btn Beds and Herts Regt		–	130
282 LAA		–	121
317 Searchlight Regt		–	41

This gave a total station strength of almost 2,800 personnel.

The above statistics come from a routine medical report issued by the Station Sick Quarters (SSQ). These reports are full of information that does not appear in the standard ORB entry. For obvious reasons, a typical element of the report is the medical state of the unit. The entry for this particular month gives the following information:

Condition of aircrew – some healthy tiredness

Wellington X3662 of 115 Squadron, April 1942.

A trio of 218 Squadron Short Stirlings.

and morale very good. Recently there has been an abnormal amount of airsickness, mainly in observers – undue concentration on TR1335 [Gee] with resultant strain upon the eyes for those training in the apparatus appears to be a contributory factor.

It would be interesting to know what the MO considered to be 'healthy tiredness'! He was obviously having a busy period, as in the middle of May: 'the gunners of 218 Squadron have been medically examined. Their physical efficiency has almost invariably deteriorated since their original examination as air gunners. More PT recommended.'

The early part of May saw a continuation of the intensive operational period, but this had slowed down by the latter part of the month in preparation for Bomber Command's major new tactical gambit, Operation *Millenium*.

Missions were flown on the 2/3rd (minelaying); the 3rd (St Nazaire); the 4/5th (Stuttgart, Pilsen – with the loss of another Stirling, Nantes, and Lyons – the sole Stirling from this 'Nickel' operation crash-landing at Tangmere); the 6/7th (Stuttgart, Nantes – with the loss of X3591/K and X3466/N, seven crewmen surviving from the two aircraft to be taken prisoner); the 8/9th

(Warnemunde); the 17/18th (one to Boulogne and 12 minelaying, with the loss of X3644/A); the 19/20th (Mannheim – with the loss of one aircraft, and St Nazaire); and the 29/30th (Cherbourg and Gennevilliers).

Regarding minelaying operations, an entry in the Marham Line Book comments: 'We go in so low that we don't have to worry about the flak ships. It's depth charges that we worry about.' An entry a few days later contains a reference to flak:

Bill Blessing describing a 'do' to an amazed bunch of listeners casually remarked, "Of course we weren't hit at all by the flak-wallahs but unluckily stopped a 5 inch shell from somewhere or other!" Noting the gasps of disbelief among his audience he added, "I know it's hard to credit, but I measured the diameter of the hole in my flap and it was exactly 5 inches."

Thousand Bomber Raids

On 30 May 1942 operation orders were issued by all the Groups of Bomber Command, including the two training groups, No. 91 and No. 92, for what was to be by far the biggest effort made by the Command to date. Since his appointment as Commander of Bomber Command in February 1942, Air Marshal Arthur Harris had been determined to prove that his strategic bombing tactics were capable of winning the war. However, in the face of evidence that most bombs were missing their targets, plus rising loss rates and calls from other Commanders to put bomber resources to other uses, his most urgent task was to prove that the bomber had an independent role to play. Harris intended to combine both objectives in a series of major attacks against German industrial cities, called Operation Millenium and otherwise known as the Thousand Bomber Plan.

In common with all Bomber Command stations, Marham saw a relaxing of its commitments in April and May as resources were concentrated on building up the required strength of aircraft and crews for the planned offensive. However, Marham mounted 19 sorties on the night before the all-out effort; eight to attack Cherbourg, eight to Gennevilliers, and the remaining three, comprising Stirlings of 218 Squadron, being tasked to plant *vegetables* at Nectarines II (the Frisian Islands). All returned safely, but the engineers now had to work flat-out to get the maximum number of aircraft ready for the next day.

On 30 May 1942 the following signal arrived at Marham:

From:-   HQ No. 3 Group.
To:-   Feltwell, Honington, Marham,
         Mildenhall, Stradishall, Oakington,
         Tempsford, Waterbeach, Wyton.

A. Form B.826.
B. 30 May for night 30/31 May.

C. Other Groups	Sorties	Target
No. 1	150 Wellington	TROUT, Thousand Plan
No. 4	8 Whitley	
	9 Wellington	
	138 Halifax	
No. 5	33 Hampden	
	45 Manchester	
	79 Lancaster	
No. 91	240 Wellington	
	21 Whitley	
No. 92	48 Wellington	
	46 Hampden	

1. TR Force
Mildenhall	16 Wellington
	6 Stirling
Feltwell	29 Wellington
Honington	15 Wellington
Stradishall	12 Stirling
Marham	17 Wellington
	13 Stirling
Wyton	7 Wellington
	12 Stirling
Oakington	12 Wellington
	16 Stirling

Non TR Force
Mildenhall	3 Wellington
	4 Stirling
Feltwell	14 Wellington
Honington	7 Wellington
Stradishall	8 Wellington
Marham	4 Stirling
Wyton	14 Wellington
Oakington	3 Stirling
	10 Wellington
Waterbeach	8 Stirling
Tempsford	20 Wellington

NOTES
1. Operation to be carried out according to the THOUSAND PLAN.
2. Zero hour – 0055 hours.
3. Aircraft which fail to get off through unserviceability, or aircraft which return early, are if possible, to be de-bombed and made ready for search in the morning if necessary.
4. 'J' beams – Haine 052. Cransford 112. Fulstow 100. TR Co-ordinates 'TROUT' B 7.48.
5. TR aircraft are to approach the target from West along 'B' lattice line 7.48.
6. Bombs are to be released visually on the homing run when target is identified and position confirmed by TR.1335.
7. If the main target is not identified visually, the alternative target 'STOAT' is to be attacked.

The ORB records (a combination of the Marham and individual Squadron ORBs) detail this historic mission:

Form B.826 received from HQ No. 3 Group. The undermentioned aircraft took off for operations.

115 Squadron		**218 Squadron**	
X3750/B	Plt Off Patterson	A	Flt Sgt Johnston
Z1574/C	Plt Off A'Court	B	Sgt Boyd
X3601/V	Sqn Ldr Grant	(other crews not
X3471/G	Sqn Ldr Cousens	listed)
X3721/F	Fg Off Williams	
X3635/J	Plt Off Wood	
X3662/P	Plt Off Slade	
X3445/S	Plt Off Perry	
X3724/T	Flt Sgt Beckett	
X3749/D	Sgt Fry	

Z1614/R Sgt Edwards
X3343/Z Sgt Williams
X3412/L Plt Off Felt
BJ796/H Plt Off Stanford
BJ797/M Plt Off Rohde
X3539/W Flt Sgt Loughead
X3488/X Flt Sgt Hyde
X3540/K Sgt Dunn

115 Squadron – five aircraft carried a 4,000 lb HC, two aircraft carried a single 1,000 lb GP plus five 500 lb GP, and eleven aircraft each carried 9 SBCs. 18 aircraft took off between 2250 and 0021 hours to attack target COLOGNE. Visibility over the target was found to be good. Bombs were dropped from heights ranging from 10,000 to 15,000 feet on the target area. Fires were started which spread until the whole of the town was ablaze. Leaflets were dropped and photographs attempted.

For 115 Squadron, the involvement of 18 aircraft represented their entire strength, a remarkable achievement by the groundcrew, while 218 went one better and sent 19 aircraft, one of which carried the AOC No. 3 Group, A.V.M. Baldwin.

Wellington Z1614, which had taken off at 23:59, was the only one of 115's aircraft not to return. This aircraft, manned by Flt Sgt W. Crampton and crew (Sgt M. Boyle, Sgt E. Edwards, Sgt W. McLeod, Sgt H. Sproston), was shot down by Oberleutnant Barte of 4/NJG1, and crashed near Wijchmal in Holland. Number 218 Squadron lost Stirling 'N'.

In the event, 1,047 bombers took part in this operation, the 602 Wellingtons involved playing the major part. It seems that just under 900 aircraft actually bombed Cologne, releasing a total of 1,455 tons of weapons, about half of which were incendiaries. The raid caused over 2,000 fires and destroyed factories and houses. The RAF lost 41 aircraft, including 29 Wellingtons. At an overall 3.9 per cent loss rate for all types, the raid was considered a success.

There was to be no respite, and a second major attack was mounted the following night, 956 bombers attacking Essen. Marham contributed 32, 18 of which were Wellingtons of 115 Squadron, all crews except two (Flt Sgt Hutchison and Sgt McKee) having flown on the first raid. The weather conditions were poor, and most aircraft had trouble finding the target, releases being by Gee or dead-reckoning navigation. Again 115 squadron lost an aircraft, X3721/F, Fg Off

Williams and crew, as did 218 Squadron, Stirling N3753 failing to return. The problems caused by the haze layer resulted in scattered bombing and a far less effective raid than that of two nights previously. Losses, at 31 aircraft, were slightly less as a percentage of the force involved.

In the period 7–18 June, the Stirlings flew 23 gardening sorties over four nights.

Two nights later, on 3/4 June, 115 Squadron sent 15 aircraft to attack Bremen, losing two of their number; X3724 flown by Flt Sgt Hutchison and X3635/J, Plt Off Wood, with no survivors. A third aircraft, X3749, forced-landed back at base. Seven Stirlings were on the same mission, and one, W7474/K, was lost. Operations continued throughout the month, including a number of 'gardening' sorties as this was now a major role for Bomber Command. Each Wellington carried two 1,500 lb mines, whereas the Stirling could carry four, and these had to be delivered as accurately as possible from low level. The two most frequent targets for June were Emden and Bremen, the latter being on the receiving end of five Marham attacks. Stirling losses continued to be high, a further four aircraft being lost in the space of a week, two each on missions to Emden (W7530 on the 20th/21st and N6078 on the 22nd/23rd) and Bremen (W7503 on the 25/26th and DJ974 on the 27/28th). The high loss rate of the Stirling had been under investigation for some time, the Bomber Command Operational Research Section (ORS) undertaking a number of studies. It was eventually agreed that the problem was one of lack of performance; Stirlings could not get as high as the other 'heavies', and so bore the brunt of the flak.

It was not only the Stirlings that suffered in June. The Wellingtons of 115 Squadron also had problems, X3554 with Sgt Abbott and crew being lost over Bremen on 25/26th. In addition, Fg Off Freegard had to ditch X3555/W some 60 miles north-east of Cromer on the outbound leg of the attack on Emden on the 22/23rd. None of the crew was injured, and all were subsequently rescued.

Harris was determined to use his '1,000-bomber' force again while it was still available, bearing in mind that the OTU Groups could not maintain their operational status on this scale for very long without seriously hindering the training effort. The third and final 1,000-bomber raid took place on the night of 25/26 June, when 960 bombers attacked Bremen in another devastating

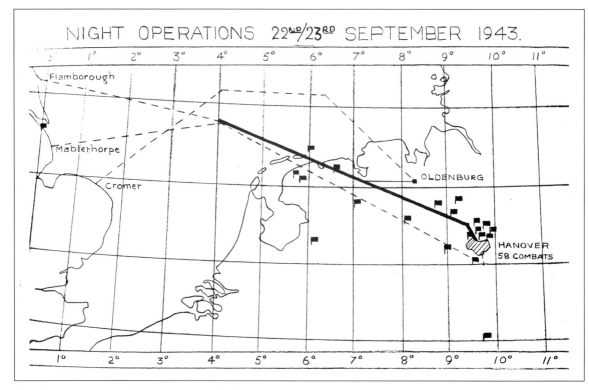

NIGHT OPERATIONS 22ᴺᴰ/23ᴿᴰ SEPTEMBER 1943.

The Hanover attack of 22/23 September 1943.

demonstration of the bomber force's destructive capability. Once again 115 Squadron sent 18 aircraft and, once again, one of their number failed to return; X3554, with Sgt H. Abbott and crew.

Aircraft of 115 Squadron were airborne twice more in June. During the Bremen raid of 27/28th the nightfighters were again very active, and in one engagement Flt Sgt McCann, the rear gunner of BJ589, was killed. Two nights later Plt Off Stanford was outbound for Bremen when BJ796 suffered an engine failure. Even with the bombs jettisoned the aircraft continued to lose height, and Stanford was forced to ditch some 40 miles from Lowestoft. All of the crew except Flt Sgt Linwood made it safely to the dinghy.

July started quietly, but operations were flown almost every night from the end of the first week onwards. Duisberg and Hamburg were the chief targets, receiving four and two visits respectively. It was a month of heavy casualties. While 115 Squadron lost 11 aircraft, and another two crash-landed at other bases in England, 218 Squadron lost one more Stirling, N3718/M, which fell to a Bf 110 nightfighter on its final operation from Marham, to Bremen on the 2/3rd. Another Stirling

had to fight off three other fighters, but returned safely. The station sent two aircraft on an ASR search for the missing bomber, but to no avail. Of these losses, six were on missions to Duisberg.

The Stirlings of 218 Squadron moved to Downham Market on 7 July, and although they were still associated with Marham, and were usually included in the Marham ORB, they now leave this story. New arrivals joined the Marham strength on 13 July in the form of 1483 Target Towing and Gunnery Flight (TT&GF) from Newmarket. Although a training unit, it also appeared in the operational record, sending two aircraft against Hamburg on the 28/29th as part of the Marham effort. Little is heard of this unit. Its Wellingtons can be seen in one or two photographs of the Marham Mosquito period, but details of their activities are lacking.

August started well, 115 Squadron flying 74 sorties without loss. Then, on the 20th/21st, ten aircraft went 'gardening'. Nothing more was heard from Flt Sgt Newman's crew in X3989/V, and Plt Off Grimston in BJ660/H had to crash-land at Exeter. Another loss that month was Fg Off Skelton in BJ710/L on the night of the 27/28th, during a raid against Kassel. The WOP, Flt Sgt Middleton, was the only one to escape from the Wellington. However, it was on the final operation of the month, on August 28/29, that the worst losses occurred. Five aircraft were to attack Saarbrucken, and another ten went to Nuremburg. The Saarbrucken raid had few problems, although one aircraft landed at Manston, short of fuel. Two of the Saarbrucken force returned early with various problems.

Targets in Germany and minelaying kept the Wellingtons busy throughout the first half of the month, operations being flown on 14 nights up to the 21st. During this period the squadron lost a further seven aircraft:

Saarbrucken	1st/2nd	BJ895/C Plt Off Shires
Bremen	4th/5th	BJ771/L Sgt Keith
		BJ663/N Plt Off Davies
Duisberg	7th	BJ724/P Flt Sgt Lanceley
Wilhelmshaven	14th/15th	BJ693/J Sgt Boaden
Minelaying	18th/19th	X3718/Q Plt Off Owen
Minelaying	21st/22nd	BJ962/D Sgt Evans
Lingen	28th	Z1663 Sqn Ldr Parsons.

With the exception of one crewman who survived the crash-landing on the 7th, and three who baled out of Z1663 to become POWs, all of the crew members were killed.

A signal arrived on 19 September that was to herald major changes for Marham, No. 3 Group outlining plans to move the bomber squadrons out of the station in order to transfer the base to No. 2 Group. This was part of a plan to free Attlebridge and Horsham St Faith for use by the Americans, the resident squadrons at the latter station being moved to Marham. This move of the de Havilland Mosquito-equipped 105 and 109 Squadrons, along with 1509 Beam Approach Training Flight (BATF), was to be completed by 1 October. The situation was clarified in a follow-up signal on the 21st:

Following moves proposed to make Marham available for No. 2 Group by 28th September, 115 Squadron to move from Marham to Mildenhall, the advance party to move on 23/9 and the move to be complete by 26/9. No. 218

Conversion Flight to move to Oakington, to be complete by 2nd October. 1427 Flight to return to 41 Group immediately as it is understood that the training commitments are completed. 1483 TT&G Flight to remain at Marham as lodger unit in No. 2 Group. Downham Market to remain in No. 3 Group as a separate entity, but Marham to be responsible for rations, pay and equipment accounts.

The movement orders were duly issued on 22 September 1942, and the Wellingtons ceased operations until the move was complete. Number 218 Squadron flew two more operations, on the 23rd and 24th, before they, too, ceased operations. The move by this unit and 1427 Flight was completed on schedule; but to Stradishall.

After its unbroken spell of three years operating from Marham, during which time it had taken part in the full spectrum of Bomber Command activities, 115 Squadron began its move to Feltwell on 23 September to stay within No. 3 Group. Marham was about to acquire a new role and new aircraft.

Marham – The Premier Mosquito Base

Late 1942, and particularly 1943, marked the heyday of the Mosquito, and Marham established an

Mosquito crews of 105 Squadron.

unsurpassed reputation with this aircraft. Flying Officer Hayes of 105 Squadron expressed it well in May 1943 (over a pint): "Why listen to the news? We made it." The station was transferred to No. 2 Group with effect from 28 September, the day that saw the arrival of advance parties from Horsham. On the following day 105 Squadron declared 14 aircraft and seven crews available for operations. The cadre element of 139 Squadron arrived on the 30th, as did 1655 Conversion Flight, more usually referred to as the Mosquito Training Unit (MTU). With the new units came a new Station Commander, Gp Capt Wallace H. Kyle, DFC.

During the Mosquito period three operational squadrons used the base:

105 Squadron   29 Sep 1942 to 23 Mar 1944
109 Squadron   5 July 1943 to 2 Apr 1944
139 Squadron   29 Sep 1942 to 4 July 1943

Number 105 Squadron was led by the famous Wg Cdr Hughie Idwal Edwards, an experienced medium-bomber pilot who had earned the Victoria Cross for a daring daytime low-level attack on Bremen. Having settled in at Marham, the unit flew its first operations in dusk raids on 1 October 1942. Warrant Officer Nolan and Sgt Urquhart took Mosquito IV DK336 on a low-level attack against an oil refinery at Ghent, and their bombs fell on a group of large buildings just west of the storage tanks. Meanwhile, Fg Offs Bristow and Marshall attacked the chemical works at Sluiskill in DK315, and Plt Offs Bruce and Carreck in DZ312 went to Entvelde. The last of these missions proved abortive, as the bombs failed to release. Such nuisance raids were the *raison d'être* of the Mosquito force at this period, the idea being to keep the German defences on alert (and thus wear them down) and disrupt German, or German-controlled, industry through constant air raid alerts. If the workers were in the air raid shelters, production would at the very least be slowed.

The Mosquito crews ranged over most of Northern Europe, attacking pinpoint targets or flying nuisance raids over cities. Many of the missions were either dawn or dusk attacks, partly to sustain the 24hr nuisance value (Bomber Command at night, USAAF by day), but also because of the tactical advantage of operating at these times of day, although, as shall be seen, this also brought additional hazards. There was no time to settle in to the new base, as 105 Squadron

were active almost every day. Six aircraft undertook a shallow dive attack on the John Cockerill works at Liege as dusk fell on 2 October; this was to be a frequent target over the next few months. It is impossible to list every operational sortie, as on most days the squadrons would be operating against a number of targets. This account will therefore be limited to an overview, with a closer look at typical missions and the handful of exceptional missions for which the base became famous.

Illustrative of the varied nature of operations was that of 6 October 1942, when two aircraft carried out high-level bombing at Essen and Bremen, three were tasked with bombing the diesel engine works at Hengelo and the power station at Twensche, and a fifth undertook reconnaissance in the Münster–Osnabruck region. Flying Officer Bristow in DZ316 was airborne at 17:04, but before he could reach his target area he encountered one of the most dangerous of low-level hazards; a flock of ducks. A number of birds smashed into the canopy, shattering the Perspex and injuring both crewmen. Bristow wisely decided to return to base, landing at 19:10 after jettisoning his bomb load in open country. 'Natural' low-level hazards such as this, and trees and wires, were major factors in the Mosquito operations, most low-level attacks being delivered at 50 ft! Although 139 Squadron was still not declaring any aircraft or crews, the ORB records that one of the crews, Sqn Ldr Knowles and Flt Sgt Gartside, took part in this operation, going to Trier in an aircraft borrowed from 105 Squadron.

The remainder of the month was hectic, with meteorological reconnaissance, high-level bombing, cloud-cover raids, and low-level and shallow dive attacks being carried out on a wide range of targets, including Saarlouis, Gelsenkirchen, Dusseldorf, Hanover, Sluiskil, Den Helder, Hengelo, Osnabruck, Kassel, Midne, Münster, Oldenburg, Emden, Hamburg, Borkum, Leeuwarden, Langaroog, Deelen, Jever, Lingen, Ghent, Antwerp, Ijmuiden, Flensburg, and Genoa. This list gives a good impression of the nature of the missions. As to scale, targets in this period received only four or five 'visitors', and most were only attacked by pairs of aircraft. The attack on Flensburg, which took place on the 27th, was directed against the dock area, three aircraft going in below 50 ft to attack shipping and installations. Mosquito DZ355, piloted by Fg Off Bristow, was hit by flak and subsequently

An atmospheric view of Mosquito dispersal at Marham, complete with groundcrew.

crash-landed at Swanton Morley. The second aircraft was unable to complete its attack because it was thrown off balance by slipstream from the leader.

Heavily defended targets such as these were not places to hang around. German light flak was notoriously effective, and the quadruple cannon that seemed to be almost everywhere were the ideal weapons to tackle low-flying aircraft. The attackers' aim was to sweep in on the target at ultra low level without being picked up, deliver a first-pass attack and then exit as quickly as possible, using natural or man-made features as cover.

By the latter part of the month 139 Squadron was declaring itself operational, although for a few more weeks the operational burden still rested with 105 Squadron. The sortie to Genoa took place on the 24th and was flown out of Tangmere, the intention being to use an F.52 camera to obtain high-quality reconnaissance pictures. Having arrived in the target area, the crew were frustrated to find 10/10ths cloud; no pictures this time. For the last operations of the month, on the 30th, the targets were airfields – Leeuwarden, Deelen, Jever, and Lingen. Five aircraft of 105 Squadron and four of 139 took off late morning. Attacks on German air bases, especially night-

fighter bases, were to be a common feature of the Mosquito period. Airfields were also among the most dangerous of targets, bristling with anti-aircraft weapons. Sergeants Levy and Hogan were both injured when DZ340/X was hit over Leeuwarden. The aircraft subsequently crash-landed in a wood near Cockley Cley, the crew escaping from the aircraft and then being taken to Swaffham hospital. On this mission 105 Squadron lost 'J', crewed by Sgt Simon and Sgt Balmforth.

In this first full month of operations from Marham, losses totalled five aircraft, all from 105 Squadron. November was to be far quieter, partly owing to the usual poor autumn weather, but also because 139 Squadron still do not appear to have been fully operational.

The major attack of the month was on the 6th, when six aircraft were tasked to attack two merchant vessels (MVs) reported by a reconnaissance aircraft. Flight Lieutenant Ralston led the attack in 'E', but was unable to find any shipping at the stated location. Searching around, he spotted two MVs of approximately 2,500 tons in the River Gironde area, and positioned for an attack. The first Mosquito dropped its bombs at 16:11, followed by the rest of the formation, all of whom claimed hits. After DK328/V had been seen to make an attack and leave the target area, no more was seen or heard from the aircraft. Fg Off Bristow and Flt Lt Marshall were listed as missing, and it was later discovered that they were safe as POWs. Flight Lieutenant Ralston landed at Predannack, while the other four landed at St Eval. It was usual for aircraft to deploy to bases nearer the target whenever this made sense.

The bad luck continued on the next operation, when two aircraft were tasked with attacking shipping in Flushing harbour on the 13th. They left Marham at 12:08, but neither returned. Later that afternoon the squadron sent four aircraft on an ASR search along the planned route, but nothing was found. Although no details ever emerged, it is possible that they collided with each other.

There were only three more operational days in November, and two of those saw the Mosquito force tasked against what was to be one of the most frequent target categories; railway installations. The disruption of the German-controlled rail network formed a central part of a strategy designed to bring military and commercial transportation to a halt. At this time the strategy was fairly low-key, but as D-Day approached it would become a leading element of the air power offensive. It had already been realized that the cutting of railway lines was of limited value, repair being a fairly simple matter, and that a better tactic was to destroy rolling stock and, in particular, locomotives. The usual rail targets for the Mosquito units were therefore repair shops, locomotive works, engine sheds and the like. The targets on the 16th were the marshalling yards at Lingen and Emmerich, and the railway shop at Zulich, pairs of aircraft going to each place. It was rail again on the night of the 29/30th, four aircraft getting airborne at midnight to attack railway installations at Mons St Gluslain, Montzen, Monceau, and Luige.

December brought the first of what have been seen as the 'classic' raids – the 6 December attack on the important Philips works at Eindhoven. This mission featured as follows in the ORB:

8 Mosquito aircraft took off at 11:22 for low-level attack on Philips Valve & Radio Works at Eindhoven.

(1) Wg Cdr Edwards and Fg Off Cairns led squadron of 12 Mosquitoes in a combined low-level attack by Bostons, Mosquitoes, Venturas on primary target. Bombed in shallow dive from 1,000 ft. Good weather condi-

A low-level photographic reconnaissance shot of the Philips factory one hour after the attack of 6 December 1942.

tions and attack highly successful.

(2) Sqn Ldr Parry and Fg Off Robson led second section of six Mosquitoes. Successfully bombed primary from 1,000 ft after evading Me 109 on run-up. Photos taken.

(3) Flt Lt Patterson and Fg Off Mills bombed target from 1,000 ft. Cine camera carried and films taken.

(4) Flt Lt Blessing and Sgt Lawson – forced to abandon at TURNHOUT owing to interception by Fw 190. Enemy successfully evaded and bombs brought back.

(5) Fg Off Kimmel and Fg Off Kirkland successfully bombed primary target from 1,000 ft.

(6) Plt Off Bruce and Plt Off Carreck forced to abandon task at TURNHOUT owing to interception by two Fw 190s. Enemy successfully evaded and bombs jettisoned. Aircraft damaged by cannon fire from the Fw 190s.

(7) WO Noseda and Sgt Urquhart bombed primary, intercepted on return in OVERFLAKEE area by two Fw 190s. Enemy successfully evaded but aircraft damaged by cannon fire.

(8) Flt Sgt Monaghan and Flt Sgt Dean bombed primary from 1,000 ft. Photos taken and bombs from other aircraft observed bursting in target area.

The Marham effort was part of a total force of 93 aircraft, the majority being from No. 2 Group. As it was a daylight precision attack, the aircraft would be beyond fighter escort range, so the plan involved a low-level approach and attack. The weather was good throughout, and accurate bombing runs were made by the Mosquitoes, Venturas and Bostons. The raid took place on a Sunday in an attempt to minimize casualties amongst the mainly Dutch civilian workforce. Although this was effective, a number of civilian deaths occurred from bombs that fell in the nearby streets. Losses were also high among the attackers, 14 aircraft failing to return. The Lockheed Venturas suffered the highest casualties, nine out of 47 aircraft failing to return. Subsequent photographic reconnaissance showed that severe damage had been caused, and the factory did not resume full production for many months. This raid even drew the press to interview crews and photograph their aircraft.

Rail targets remained high on the list throughout December, the most unusual being a tunnel on the Paris–Soissen line on the 9th. The idea was to run in along the railway line and 'skip' a 500-pounder with an 11-sec delay fuse into the mouth of the tunnel. The first bomb went well, but the second bounced off the mouth of the tunnel. Two aimed at the other end overshot the target, and then a train appeared and entered the tunnel. The crew circled for 10 minutes to see if it would emerge, but had to leave before it did so. Two other aircraft of 105 Squadron attacked targets in the Criel and Laon area.

A few days later the station suffered a fatal loss when Mosquito 'A' crashed near Kimberely while on a training flight during a low-level 'operational exercise'. The Observer, Plt Off Barnes, was killed, but the pilot survived, albeit with various broken bones. The aircraft appears to have broken up in flight. The pilot remembered hearing a loud crack and then found himself falling away from the remains of the cockpit. A second aircraft also had a problem: 'Pilot of one aircraft struck forcibly by bird through windscreen. Lucky to make a forced landing at Bottesford – severe bruising of forehead.' Birds were such a problem that they often appeared in combat reports as an 'encounter with a *staffel* of ducks'.

The second half of the month saw an intensification of the anti-rail campaign by both squadrons, with a corresponding increase in the recorded incidents of flak damage. The best news of the month came on the 23rd, with the announcement of a DSO for Wg Cdr Edwards, who thus became the first officer to achieve VC*DSO*DFC during the war.

January was to prove equally hectic, with the rail network again receiving the most attention. Operations were flown on the 2nd, 3rd, 9th, 13th, 20th, 21st, 23rd, 26th, 27th, and 30th. A few of these were singleton reconnaissance missions, but the rest, with the important exception of an attack on Berlin on the 30th, were against rail targets. The month also saw the loss of one of 105 Squadron's most experienced crews, WO Noseda and Sgt Urquhart failing to return from a mission against rail sheds at Rouen on 9 January. The Stork Works at Hengelo was visited by eight aircraft of 105 Squadron on the 20th:

The formation took off at 13:54. The first three bombed from 50 ft at 15:15 but no results were observed. The next two hit the boiler shops. The formation lead, Squadron Leader Ralston in DZ353, had been hit by flak over Lemmer and received damage to elevator, rudder trim, pitot head and hydraulics. Nevertheless, he continued to the target. He subsequently belly-landed at base at 16:53. One aircraft hit by flak over Lemmer returned to base, this confused his wing-man but he subsequently went on to attack lock gates on the Dortmund Canal just south of Lingen. Flight Lieutenant Gordon, DK296, was hit by flak at Terschelling on rtb [return to base]. His aircraft was damaged in the starboard engine and hydraulics, and after recovering on one engine he belly-landed at base.

Mosquito DZ311, piloted by Fg Off L. Skinner, was lost in a cloud-cover operation against rail targets on 23 January.

A week later, on 27 January, a combined mission of three aircraft from 109 plus six from 105 Squadron flew to Denmark to attack the Burmesiter & Wain diesel-engine works at Copenhagen. This operation was recorded thus by 105 Squadron:

Six Mosquito aircraft detailed to attack BURME-

Three 139 Squadron aircraft await their crews.

SITER & WAIN DIESEL ENGINE WORKS, COPENHAGEN.
1. Wg Cdr H.I. Edwards and Fg Off H.E.P. Cairns
2. Fg Off A.T. Wicken and Plt Off W.E.D. Makin
3. Sgt J.G. Dawson and Sgt R.H. Cox
4. Flt Lt W. Blessing and Sgt J. Lawson
5. WO H.C. Herbert and Sgt C. Jacques
6. Flt Lt J. Gordon and Fg Off R.G. Hayes

These aircraft took off at approximately 1420 hr and set course in starboard echelon in company with three aircraft of 139 Squadron. The first five stated aircraft reached the primary objective and bombed at 1706 hr from low altitude with various calibre bombs i.e. 11 sec, 30 min and 36 hr delays. Hits were seen in test shops by various aircraft and verification of red sheets of flame by last two aircraft. Light flak was encountered by flak ships on way in, and intense light flak at the target. Aircraft piloted by Flt Lt Gordon turned back after crossing enemy coast. Trailing edge of starboard wing was seen to be enveloped in blue smoke. Thinking he had been hit by flak the pilot carried out evasive action and in so doing caught port wing in telegraph wires, damaging his port aileron. The rest of the formation had gained considerable lead and the pilot decided to abandon the trip. The bombs were jettisoned at 1609 hr and the aircraft returned to base safely. Aircraft piloted by Sgt Dawson successfully bombed primary and was last seen in position 5535N 1132E at 1713 hr to have exploded on ground in sheet of flame. All other aircraft returned to base safely.

Catching a wing in telegraph wires means you are flying VERY low – and manoeuvring!

The Nazi regime was very propaganda orientated, and speeches by the leadership, especially Hitler, Goering, and Goebbels, were important elements in the propaganda war. The Mosquito force was tasked with disrupting such rantings, and took great delight in making unscheduled appearances during major speeches. Such was the case on the morning of 30 January, when three aircraft were sent to disrupt a speech by Goering:

After the opening announcement that Reichsmarschall Göering would speak, a few muffled words followed by confusion of many voices could be heard, then another shout or bang after which the mike was apparently switched off and martial music played. It was then announced that the Reichsmarschall's

DZ.365	W/C.H.I.Edwards VC.DSO.DFC. F/O.H.H.E.P. Cairns DFC.	Low level attack Burmeister & Wain Diesel Wks. Copenhagen.	1426	1935	Test sheds bombed from 50' at 1708 hours with 4 X 500 H.P. L. No results seen. Received two holes in starboard nacelle from light flak.
DZ.415.	F/O. A.T. Wickham. P/O. W.E.D. Makin.	-do-	1426	2010.	Target attacked but bombs believed overshot owing to aircraft getting in slipstream of leading aircraft. Intense accurate light flak encountered.
DZ.413	F/L. W.W. Blessing. Sgt. J. Lawson.	-do-	1426	1940	Target attacked from 100' at 1705 hours. Intense accurate light flak. Bursts seen. Two flak ships – moderate – Fairly accurate in position 55°35'N 11°32'E at 1715 hours. Height 20 terrific sheet of flames seen found to be aircraft on approach. Photos attempted.
DZ.302	W/O. H. Herbert.	-do-	1426	1952	Primary attacked from 50' at 1705 hours. Cloud of dust or smoke seen from N.W. corner of test shops after leading aircraft had attacked. Fairly accurate light flak from dock area. Photos attempted.
DK.338	F/L. J. Gordon. F/O. R.G. Hayes.	-do-	1426	1800	Task abandoned north of GRINSTRUP position 55°33'N 08°40'E at 1605 hours 50' owing to trailing edge of starboard wing being enveloped in blue smoke. Pilot thinking aircraft must have been hit by flak took evasive action and in so doing port wing caught in telegraph wires damaging port aileron. This together with the fact that rest of formation had gained considerable lead caused pilot to decide to abandon. Bombs jettisoned at 1609 hours. Position 55°34'N 08°27'E.
DZ.407	Sgt. J.G. Dawson. Sgt. R.H. Cox.	-do-	1426	–	Successfully bombed primary. Last seen in position 55°35'N 11°32'E at 1713 hours to explode on ground in sheet of flames. Missing.

The Operational Record Book entry for the 105 Squadron raid on the Burmesiter & Wain works at Copenhagen.

speech would be delayed a few moments – but after 3/4 hour martial music was still being played.

February saw 105 Squadron say farewell to its popular CO, Wg Cdr Edwards, who had been posted to HQ Bomber Command. He was replaced by Wg Cdr G. Longfield, although, sadly, this officer was to be killed two weeks later in a mid-air collision. Railway installations remained the principal targets, although other missions were flown against objectives such as the steel and armament works at Liege, and, on the 26th, the naval stores depot at Rennes. It was on the latter mission that 105 Squadron lost their CO. This was one of the largest single operations to date, each squadron contributing ten aircraft. The formation left Marham at 16:45, and the attack, by the 15 aircraft that located the primary, went in between 18:43 and 18:46. The chief danger during this highly compressed attack was that of self-damage from fragmentation (weapons effect and debris from explosions), which presented a serious threat. During the jinking over the target Wg Cdr Longfield manoeuvred sooner than expected, right into the path of the next Mosquito, and a collision was unavoidable. The CO's aircraft was seen to spin down out of control, while the other was reportedly leaking glycol and losing height, apparently under control. Nothing more was heard of either crew.

Another training loss was suffered on the 27th, Plt Off McCormick of 105 Squadron, with Wg Cdr Deacon as passenger, crashed at Brick Kiln Plantation. The aircraft had been on a high-level reconnaissance test.

Led by Wg Cdr Shand, ten aircraft of 139 Squadron attacked the Knaben molybdenum mines in Norway on 3 March. The raid plan was for nine aircraft to bomb the flotation plant whilst the tenth Mosquito attacked the nearby AAA site. The attack was delivered in a six-minute window between 14:28 and 14:33:

. . . bomb bursts accompanied by orange flashes and a red glow were seen on and around the target, which resulted in the plant being enveloped in clouds of white and brown smoke, and debris being blown to a height of 1,000 ft. Photographs subsequently showed a concentration of bombs on or near the ore bins, conveyors, ball mills, and classifiers. Four Fw 190s endeavoured to intercept our aircraft on the return journey. Aircraft M was hit and badly damaged, making a successful crash-landing at Leuchars. Fg Off Bulpitt in aircraft O was last seen being pursued by 2 Fw 190s and since he has failed to return it is feared he might have crashed into the sea.

The following day the squadron received a message from the AOC:

This typically posed public relations photograph provides a good illustration of Mosquito-period flying kit.

Please convey to all concerned my best congratulations on your well planned and splendidly executed attack on the important Molybdenum works at Knaben. Mosquito stings judiciously placed are very painful.

One new aspect to the campaign against the railways was the introduction of the *Rover*, with crews cleared to destroy trains found within specified areas. The first recorded day of such operations is the 24th, when 105 Squadron claimed three trains. The guiding principle behind this 'escalation' of the rail campaign was that only military/industrial services would be operating, so all trains were fair game. It was important to destroy the locomotive, but some crews were reluctant to

The Mosquito's glass nose was great for visibility but, at the low heights favoured by the crews, birdstrikes were a major problem.

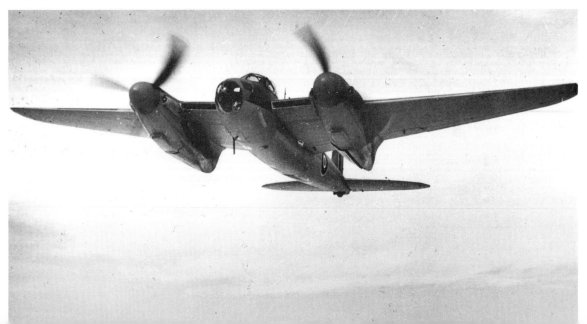

fire on the first pass, preferring to buzz the train to allow the driver, who was probably French or Dutch, to stop the train and get clear. The 20mm Hispano cannon proved very effective against the boilers of the locomotives, and success was evident when a cloud of steam emerged from the stricken engine. Strafing the rest of the train also produced results, but secondary explosions from fuel or ammunition were potential dangers.

Losses increased during March, seven aircraft failing to return and another, 'J', crashing at Martlesham Heath with the loss of both crew members after struggling back to England with severe flak damage sustained over Blankenburg. An increasing number of debriefs mention sightings of, or combats with, Fw 190s, as the Luftwaffe attempted to curb the antics of the RAF Mosquito units. Two aircraft were lost on the 28th after a formation of six *en route* to the marshalling yards at Liege was bounced by four Focke-Wulfs. These fighters were still much in evidence later in the month. On the 28th a six-ship Mosquito formation was bounced by Fw 190s, and two aircraft (DZ416 and DZ522) were last seen being chased. Both failed to return.

After the 9 March operation, Plt Off Thompson was heard to remark: "Yesterday the flak was so thick that I could not see the aircraft in front of me", to which his Observer, Plt Off Horne, added: "We couldn't even see our own wingtips." The standard rule for the daylight harassing raids, known, for obvious reasons, as cloud-cover raids, was to abort if the weather was too clear. There are various comments about this in the Line Book, one of the best being that for 1 September 1944: 'Curtis and his crew pressed on without cloud cover so far that eventually they had to turn back for treatment for sunburn!'

There was also another training loss, a Wellington of 1483 Flight crashing between Barton Bendish and Marham with the loss of the pilot, Flt Lt Greenup, and eight groundcrew. The ORBs are not very revealing as to the activities of the 'non-operational' units at Marham, 1483 Flight and the MTU tending to feature only when they lose an aircraft or if they are engaged on some specific mission. In the case of 1483 Flight, this tended to be their involvement in search and rescue, with frequent references to HQ No. 3 Group requesting aircraft of this unit to help with such duties.

It was important for morale that life continued as normally as possible despite the rising number of losses, although these were, of course, much less in personnel terms than they had been in the days of Wellington and Stirling operations. The social aspects of station life were, therefore, as important as ever:

Another performance by the Station concert party "Out of the Blue", produced by Flt Lt Napier-Pearn, was given. The concert party, who gave their first show on 23 December, have been on tour to the neighbouring RAF stations and from 15 performances have raised £200 for the CO's Benevolent Fund.

Visits to local pubs remained a popular way of releasing tension, each squadron having their own favourite watering hole. The Hare Arms was one of the most popular.

The operation on 1 April was typical of the low-level raids against the railway system, the targets being Trier and Ehrang:

6 Mosquitoes of 105 Squadron, led by Sqn Ldr Ralston, and 4 Mosquitoes of 139 Sqdn led by Sqn Ldr Berggren, bombed railway workshops and power station at Trier and engine sheds at Ehrang respectively at 1555–7 hr from 50–400 ft. Individual results were not observed, but bombs from the first formation were seen to fall in the middle of the railway workshops, throwing up quantities of debris followed by showers of green sparks. Bomb bursts were also observed on the power station followed by a sheet of flame which rose to a height of 100 ft. The attack on the marshalling yards by the second formation resulted in a huge explosion and a red flash from a coal container. A rectangular building in the SE corner of the yards was also hit and coaches of two trains – followed by large explosions. One bomb was seen to bounce off railway tracks into a house which blew to pieces. On leaving target area smoke seen rising to estimated height of 1,500 ft. Aircraft 'W' of 139 Squadron was hit by blast from bomb bursts and also by flak and came back on one engine and with Gyro artificial horizon and turn-and-bank indicator u/s, making a good landing at Manston. Aircraft 'N' of 139 Squadron reached target area, crew thought to have bombed, but subsequently discovered that selector drum was set to 'Container'. Bomb load brought back. Aircraft 'K' of 139 Squadron was hit by flak on crossing enemy coast, causing hydraulics to become u/s

Armourers at bomber stations worked hard to cope with the demand for bombs.

and consequent inability to open bomb doors, so abandoned task.

The same ORB entry records that Flt Lt S. Clayton had been awarded the DSO after completing 100 operations as an Observer, and that he would soon leave the squadron to train as a pilot.

On 7 April two German aircraft landed at Marham; a Junkers Ju 88 and a Heinkel He 111! These were from the Enemy Aircraft Circus (EAC), and provided much interest. This was yet another busy month, with either squadron, or both, operating most days. The rail network remained top of the target list. Combats with Fw 190s continued to increase, a number of sorties being aborted after they were intercepted on the way in. Mosquito DZ472, piloted by Fg Off Polglase, was last seen being chased by Fw 190s on an 11 April operation. Although there were fewer losses this month, the situation with the Luftwaffe certainly did not bode well. Flak, too, remained a problem; Flt Lt Gordon was lucky on the 26th when his petrol tank was hit by a Bofors shell over Eindhoven. The shell failed to explode.

On the night of 20/21 April 1943 the squadrons mounted a raid on Berlin to 'celebrate' Hitler's birthday. This marked the start of the night nuisance operations. Aircraft left Marham at two-minute intervals to arrive over target in the bracket 00:24 to 01:00. It was cloudless with bright moonlight as the Mosquitoes flew over Berlin at 15,000–23,000 ft, unloading their bombs. Flak was moderate and quite accurate, and some shrapnel damage was suffered. Crews also reported seeing a number of nightfighters. Of the nine aircraft from 105 Squadron and two from 139 Squadron that took part, only one of the latter failed to return. The squadron commander, Wg Cdr Peter Shand, and Flt Sgt Handley, in DZ386/H, were shot down by a nightfighter over the Dutch coast. It was a grievous loss to the squadron.

By the end of May Berlin had been attacked five times, and the German leadership was furious that the Mosquito force appeared to be immune to the defences of the Reich capital. Much invective and a great deal of resources were to be expended over the next months trying to counter these raids. During the 21 May raid Flt Sgt Walters in 'L' of 139 Squadron was hit by flak over Berlin just after he had completed his bomb run. Both engines cut out and the aircraft went into a steep dive from which he managed to recover at 11,000 ft. However, only the starboard engine would pick up. Unable to maintain a reasonable height on one engine, the crew elected to drop down to 200 ft and return to base at that height. Sergeant Burke, the Observer, navigated the aircraft to avoid the known flak zones. On the same mission the squadron lost aircraft 'C', Sqn Ldr Harcourt and WO Friendly falling to flak near the coast.

Wing Commander John Wooldridge was one of the great exponents of low-level attacks. In his 1944 account, 'Low Attack', he succinctly described the Mosquito's role:

For those of us who flew the Mosquitoes on these attacks the memory of their versatility and their achievements will always remain. It would be impossible to forget such experiences as the thunderous din of twenty aircraft sweeping across the hangars as low as possible, setting course like bullets in tight formation for the enemy coast. The whole station would be out watching, and each leader would vie for the honour of bringing his formation lower across the aerodrome than anyone else. Nor would it be possible to forget the sensation of looking back over enemy territory and seeing your for-

mation behind you, their racing shadows moving only a few feet below them across the earth's surface; or that feeling of sudden exhilaration when the target was definitely located and the whole pack were following you on to it with their bomb doors open while the people below scattered in every direction and the long streams of flak came swinging up; or the sudden jerk of consternation of the German soldiers lounging on the coast, their moment of indecision, and then their mad scramble for the guns; or the memory of racing across the Hague at midday on a bright spring morning, while the Dutchmen below hurled their hats in the air and beat each other over the back. All these are unforgettable memories. Many of them will be recalled also by the peoples of Europe long after peace has been declared, for to them the Mosquito came to be an ambassador during their darkest hours.

The most significant raid of the month was, without doubt, that to Jena on the 27th, the targets being the Schott glassworks and the Zeiss works. Six aircraft of 139 Squadron, plus eight of 105, took off for this operation. The 105 Squadron report reads as follows:

Standard aircrew relaxation! The local pubs in the Marham area were also frequent haunts for the aircrew.

The Zeiss optical works at Jena were well camouflaged, as evidenced by this reconnaissance shot of 27 May 1943. This target was attacked by 105 Squadron.

8 aircraft of 105 Squadron to attack ZEISS WORKS, JENA. Bomb load: 6 aircraft – 24 x 500 MC 11 sec delay; Aircraft 'O' & 'N' with 6 hr delay.
'O' – Sqn Ldr Blessing and Fg Off Muirhead
'N' – Fg Off Fisher and Flt Sgt Hogan
'C' – Plt Off Herbert and Sgt Jacques
'V' – Sgt McKelvie and Sgt Heggie
'E' – Flt Lt Patterson and Flt Sgt Howard
'P' – Plt Off Massie and Sgt Lister
'R' – Fg Off Rea and Plt Off Bush
'D' – Fg Off Dixon and Fg Off Christensen

Two ('O' and 'C') aircraft attacked the works at 2131/2 hrs from 200–300 ft. Bombs were seen to fall in the glass grinding and polishing shops and a cloud of grey smoke was seen after bombing. Aircraft 'N', prevented from attacking primary by the balloon barrage, bombed the town at 2130 hrs from 200 ft and as long delay bombs were used, no results seen. Aircraft 'D' attempted 3 runs on the primary but was also prevented from bombing by the balloons and intense flak. As an alternative this aircraft bombed goods train at Lastrup,

and although bursts were not seen the tail end of the train was derailed.

Mosquito 'E' having lost the formation in cloud and being unable to find the primary by DR identified and attacked Weimar railway station at 2133 hrs from 300 ft. Bombs which were dropped in a salvo on second run over target fell between platforms near 2 goods trains with steam up. The explosions threw debris 150 ft into the air. A cine camera was carried by this aircraft. Mosquito 'V' having also lost formation in cloud and failing to locate primary bombed a factory at Lobeda. The bombs were seen to explode in the buildings. Mosquito 'R' was seen over the target but crashed on landing at base, killing the crew.

Mosquito 'P' was last seen as formation entered cloud prior to reaching the target, but has failed to return to base.

Weather over target: Cloud 10/10 at 1,000ft, light bad, vis 500–800 yd.

The report of 139 Squadron's part in the operation states:

139 Squadron to SCHOTT OPTICAL
GLASSWORKS, JENA
'B' – Wg Cdr Reynolds and Fg Off Sismore
'D' – Flt Lt Sutherland and Fg Off Dean
'N' – Fg Off Pereira and Fg Off Gilbert
'K' – Fg Off Stovel and Sgt Nutter
'W' – Flt Lt Sutton and Fg Off Morris
'R' – Fg Off Openshaw and Sgt Stonestreet

This factory, closely associated with the Zeiss Works, was the target of 6 of the 14 aircraft led by Wg Cdr Reynolds. 3 Mosquitoes (aircraft 'B', 'D' and 'K') successfully bombed the target between 2131 and 2132 hrs from 200 ft. The 6 hr delay bombs dropped by the first 2 were seen by 'K' to fall into the southern and eastern section of the factory, immediately causing a sheet of flame 100 ft high. The crew of 'K' believe that their bombs fell in the centre of the SW section of the factory. Aircraft 'N' was forced to abandon primary owing to an engine defect and bombed a railway bridge over the river Fulda at 2100 hrs with unobserved results. This aircraft returned to base on one engine.

Aircraft 'W' and 'R' were seen to collide directly after light flak had been fired at approx 20:57 near Helminghausen Dam. Aircraft were seen to disintegrate in the air, explode and then seen to burst into flames on the ground. Intense light flak was encountered over Jena and there was a barrage of 10–20 balloons around the town flying at about 1,000 ft. Wg Cdr Reynolds's aircraft was hit in the port airscrew, part of which came into the cockpit, injuring the pilot in the left hand and knee. The intercom was also rendered useless by flak which narrowly missed hitting the pilot.

Flt Lt Sutherland and Plt Off Dean were seen to bomb the target but crashed near Coltishall on their return journey, both crew being killed.

The following day the BBC turned up at Marham to record the story of the raid.

Throughout June 139 Squadron flew most operations, its sister squadron only being active on four days, flying a total of nine sorties. The primary reason for this was the impending change of role for 105 Squadron, which was to become a Pathfinder unit. Most crew spent periods with the Pathfinder Force (PFF) Navigation Training Unit (NTU), learning the ins and outs of a new piece of equipment – Oboe. The search for an accurate

Groundcrew pause while servicing an aircraft to 'admire' another low pass.

Gp Capt Wallace Kyle, Marham's Station Commander, in another posed shot, listening to a debrief.

blind-bombing aid had been under way since the outbreak of war. Although the Gee system had proved, and was still proving, very useful, it had severe limitations. This new system developed by the Telecommunications Research Establishment (TRE) used two ground stations from which the aircraft received signals. The basic method was to fly an arc on one signal and use the other as a release cue. With the two initial ground stations at Dover and Trimingham, the system gave adequate coverage of the Ruhr and, before it was really ready, was employed by a Mosquito force from 109 Squadron on 20/21 December 1942 to attack Lutterade power station. Only half of the six aircraft had serviceable systems, and the results were hard to determine. Trial raids continued, and Oboe soon proved an excellent precision aid, although it was still very prone to failure.

For 109 Squadron the major effort of the month was, for a change, against cities, including six trips to Berlin. Other targets were Cologne, Duisberg, Dusseldorf, and Hamburg. It was also the first month with no losses to aircraft or crews. Crew reports state that, although the searchlights

and flak still seemed very active, there appeared to be little sign of any nightfighter activity.

July opened with a change of squadrons at Marham, 139 departing for Wyton on the 4th and being replaced by 109 Squadron, equipped with 18 Mosquito IVs and six Mosquito IXs. With the conversion of 105 Squadron to the target-marking role, this meant that Marham was home to the PFF Oboe-equipped Mosquito marking force; a force that was to play a major role in most future Bomber Command Main Force operations.

The principles of target marking were simple. An initial force of aircraft would bomb the target to create a visible signal for the following Main Force to use as an aiming point guide. To provide better illumination than simply bombing, special target indicators (TIs) were developed in a variety of types and colours, red and green being the most usual. This is not the place to discuss the wide range of marking techniques that were developed in the coming months, from basic sky marking and ground marking to route marking and so on, but, needless to say, it became a very specialized role, requiring exceptionally accurate navigation and bombing skills. Oboe certainly helped, but it was not the whole answer.

The new squadron flew its first mission from Marham on the night of 8 July, six aircraft carrying a load of red TIs, green flares, and triple flares. Cologne was the target, and Flt Lt Stevens and Sqn Ldr Gallagher acted as primary marker. Oboe sky-marking was used to mark for a force of 282 Avro Lancasters in what was to prove an accurate attack centred on the western side of the city. Seven Lancasters failed to return.

Air Vice Marshal Don Bennett, as AOC No. 8 Group, took a deep interest in the activities of all of his squadrons. The marker units were among the most important, and he visited Marham almost weekly. The pace of operation had slowed somewhat during July, missions being flown on the 2nd (Cologne and Duisberg), 3rd (Duisberg and Hamburg), 8th (Cologne), 9th (Gelsenkirchen), 13th (Aachen and Cologne), 25th (Gelsenkirchen and Essen), and 30th (Remscheid). The majority of tasking was for the marking role, but the Mosquito was still called upon to undertake a pure bombing role as flown by the units of the Light Night Striking Force (LNSF). The operation to Aachen on July 13 was part of a Main Force raid comprising 374 aircraft, 214 of which were Handley Page Halifaxes. Of the 13 aircraft airborne from Marham, the two from 105 Squadron provided a diversion by dropping green TIs, plus one 500-pounder apiece, on Cologne while the rest went to the real target. The other 11 Mosquitoes comprised eight markers, with red TIs, plus three aircraft carrying a

A Mosquito is bombed up. Although 500 lb and 1,000 lb bombs were the norm, the aircraft could also tote a 4,000 lb 'cookie'.

mixed bomb load of three 500-pounders and one 250-pounder.

As the night battle intensified and the German

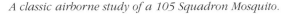

A classic airborne study of a 105 Squadron Mosquito.

night defences became ever more effective, Bomber Command developed a comprehensive system of spoof and deception tactics. Anything that would put even a few of the enemy night-fighters in the wrong place was of great value. The Marham units played a key role in this, in addition to their attacks on nightfighter bases, and must have saved countless 'heavies'.

The third major unit at the base, 1655 Mosquito Training Unit (MTU), usually had between 20 and 30 trainee crews on strength at any one time. Although the unit flew a large number of sorties each day, these are usually not mentioned in the ORB. However, July was an exception, with three references. On 15 July four aircraft flew on ASR for three hours in the afternoon, but with no success; on the 18th a Norwegian crew, Capt Stene and Lt Lochen, were killed when DZ495/N crashed near Cranfield while on a cross-country navigation exercise; and on the 24th another aircraft was written off in a night-landing accident. The only other aircraft casualty in July was 'H' of 105 Squadron, which suffered an engine failure after take-off on the 16th and had to forced-land.

By the start of August both operational squadrons had Mosquito IVs and IXs on strength and had settled into an operational routine that some of the 'older hands' on 105 Squadron found a great deal less exciting than the days of late 1942. It was now very rare for the crews to operate at low level, and the majority of sorties were at night; a very different proposition to racing around the countryside at 50 ft, beating up trains.

Operationally, August was very quiet, a mix of target marking and bombing being required on only four nights, all in the last week of the month. The mission on the night of 23rd/24th was a major effort against Berlin involving 727 aircraft, the predominant type (335) being the Lancaster. Route marking was carried out by the Mosquitoes, which dropped red LBTIs at 5250N 0650E and green TIs at 5235N 0702E, the idea being to keep the bomber stream on track by marking the route, thus avoiding flak hot-spots and achieving the desired concentration over the target. Many questioned the value of such a tactic, arguing that the TIs would simply attract the German fighters to the scene. It was often a question of bluff and counter-bluff, a balance of risk and advantage which is easy to question in a post-event analysis but was, perhaps, the best option available at the time. It actually turned out to be the worst night of the war so far for Bomber Command, with losses of 56 'heavies'. The Stirling force alone lost 16 out of 124 aircraft.

A week later, on the 31st, 47 of a 622-aircraft force were lost on a similar raid, with route marking, to Berlin. Although the 'heavies' were going through a very rough period, the Mosquito units were proving virtually invulnerable, and no operational losses were suffered for months. Many historians have since argued that an all-Mosquito force would have been a far better choice for Bomber Command from 1942 onwards.

There were only two incidents in August. The first was again to an MTU aircraft, 'B' crashing when landing on the 11th and the navigator, Flt Lt MacDonald, dying from his injuries. The second occurred on the 30th, when 'U' of 105 Squadron crashed after take-off, but without injury to the crew.

September opened with a number of 'special operations'. The first two of these, on the nights of 2nd/3rd and 3rd/4th, were unusual in that the PFF Mosquitoes marked ammunition depots for a force of Wellingtons provided by the OTUs. A double operation on the 8th/9th was another special, the Mosquitoes marking a long-range gun battery at Boulogne. The force of 257 aircraft included, for the first time, a small number of Boeing B-17 Flying Fortresses from the USAAF's 8th Air Force. There were then two weeks of little activity before the next operation, when 12 aircraft, six from each squadron, took off on the evening of the 22nd on a diversion mission to attack Emden. The Main Force of 711 aircraft went to Hanover, and a second diversionary raid attacked Oldenburg. Throughout this period the Command experimented with variations on the diversionary tactics; this particular one appeared to be successful, as Main Force losses were lower. The last third of the month was far busier, operations being flown on the 22nd/23rd, 23rd/24th, 26/27th, 27/28th, and 29/30th. Cities were the targets, Emden, Mannheim, Aachen, Bochum, and Gelsenkirchen being visited. Upon returning from the final operation of the month, Mosquito 'E' of 105 Squadron crash-landed at West Raynham with the loss of its crew.

October was far busier, with major involvement on 12 nights during the month, 109 Squadron flying 101 sorties and 105 Squadron flying 76. As usual it was mix of marking, both route and target, and bombing. The station ORB mentions that an aircraft of 105 Squadron failed to return from the attack on the power station at Knapsack on the 22nd/23rd made by 12 of Marham's Oboe-equipped aircraft. The loss is not mentioned in the Squadron Record Book. That same day, however, the MTU also lost an aircraft. Mosquito 'U' was on a night cross-country exercise when it went into a spin. The navigator baled out, but the pilot, Plt Off Jackson, was still in the aircraft when it hit the ground at Chimney Farm, Spalding.

Night intruder work continued to be a major part of station activities in October 1942. Reginald Levy recalls one such operation with 105 Squadron:

[On] 30 October 1942 my flight commander, Bill Blessing, and myself set out to attack the Luftwaffe nightfighter aerodrome at Leeuwarden in Holland. This we did successfully, but I was hit by flak from the ground defences coming across the boundary of the airfield. The port engine was set on fire, the instrument panel and windscreen disappeared with the nose of the aircraft. I was hit in the leg – although I didn't feel it at the time – and my observer, Les Hogan, in the arm.

At 40 ft or so control was tricky, so I called Les to press the extinguisher button on the port engine, which I had feathered. He promptly pushed the starboard one! The good engine was filled with foam, coughed once or twice and then, miraculously, the good old Merlin caught again and we snaked along almost sideways at about 160 mph I had to jam my foot under the rudder bar to keep it straight as the rudder-trim handle had been shot away. We went out over the aptly-named Frisian island of Overflakee straight between two German ships, who opened up on us. Luckily we were so low that they could not get their guns to bear down on us, and the ship on the port side hit the ship on the starboard side, starting a fire in the bows. During the return flight over the sea Les wound down the trailing aerial to try and signal base. The aerial hit the sea and Les yelled that he had been hit again, but it was the handle whizzing round which had banged him in his seat. We managed to get back to Marham, but I couldn't go into cloud as we had no instruments, and we were actually in the circuit when our long-suffering Merlin packed up. We went down into a nearby wood, skating along the tops of the trees, demolishing about 30 (according to the farmer who claimed compensation) before we came to a standstill and promptly blew up.

My feet had gone through the side of the fuselage and I was helpless, but Les Hogan stepped out of the front (there was no nose, it was in Leeuwarden), took my boot off, and we ran like mad despite the wound in my leg, which was now making itself felt. We didn't have a scratch on us from the crash, which had completely demolished the Mosquito. Had the Mosquito been a metal aircraft I am sure that my foot would have been severed, and I am sure that we were saved by the complete break-up of the aeroplane. After three weeks in Ely hospital we were back at Marham and operating again.

The following month was even more hectic, with operations being flown on 20 nights against a wide range of industrial targets in Germany, such as Rheinmetal Borsig at Dusseldorf (a quite frequent target), the August Thyssen foundry at Duisberg, IG Farbenindustrie at Leverkusen, the Goldenbergwerke power station at Knapsack, and, of course, the Krupp works at Essen. On the nights that Main Force was not operating, it was left to the Mosquito force to harrass Germany and keep the defences on alert. On other nights the Marham units would provide aircraft both in support of the main attack and for independent action against industrial targets. The night of 3/4 November was typical, with 12 aircraft (seven from 109 Squadron and five from 105 Squadron) supporting the Main Force attack on Dusseldorf, while a further 13 aircraft (seven and six respectively) attacked the Krupp works at Rheinhausen. The defences appeared to be stronger than ever, and even the Mosquitoes suffered from the attentions of heavy and accurate flak. Having been damaged on the Bochum raid of 5/6 November, DZ587/B crashed with the loss of both crew while trying to land at Hardwick. A few days later, on the 9/10th, 'W' of 109 Squadron, flown by Plt Off Leigh, crash-landed at Wyton after being damaged by flak; Bochum had claimed its second Marham Mosquito. The final operational loss of the month occurred over Dusseldorf on the night of the 15/16th. Ten aircraft of 105 Squadron were sent to attack this target and 'T' failed to return, Flt Lt Hampson and Fg Off Hammond being listed as missing.

The Essen operation on the night of the 7/8th was typical of the non-Main Force nights. The only Bomber Command aircraft airborne were six

The OC 139 Squadron, Wg Cdr Reynolds, with crews in 1943. Note the impressive squadron badge above the door.

Mosquitoes of 105 Squadron *en route* to Essen and 35 aircraft laying mines off the coast of France. The report of the Essen raid records:

Four Mosquitoes attacked the Essen area with

A crew from 139 Squadron studies the met forecast before planning their sortie.

24 x 500 lb MC between 0215 and 0300 hrs, 32,000 to 35,000 ft. Each aircraft bombed on DR run from the last Gee fix. The Special Device [the Oboe equipment, which the records never mention by name] proved a failure because one of the ground stations was not in operation. When this was made known the aircraft were recalled, but only two aircraft received the recall signal. These two jettisoned 2 x 500 lb MC and brought back 4 x 500 lb MC to base. Two of the four aircraft which continued to the target returned home on one engine, and one aircraft landed at Coltishall.

From late November 1943 to March 1944 the major Bomber Command effort was devoted to what has been called the Battle of Berlin. As the Marham units were seldom involved with this, its progress is beyond the scope of this history. The Marham squadrons were certainly kept very busy, but the majority of their operations were concentrated on pinpoint industrial targets, special targets and diversionary raids.

December brought operational flying on 15 nights. The major effort in the latter half of the month was against a new type of Special target that was of crucial importance; the V1 flying-bomb sites. By mid-1943, intelligence assessments had proved the existence of the new German weapon programme, and, given the mass of evidence as to the likely nature and the targets (i.e. London) of these weapons, action had to be taken, at least to delay progress. The initial response was to launch a bombing campaign against the sites, and 'Crossbow' missions to attack 'Noball' sites became regular tasks for strategic and tactical bombers. The Mosquito units were destined to play a full part in this successful venture; the V-1 programme suffered significant delays and the first flying bomb was not launched against England until 13 June 1944.

The first Crossbow attack was flown on the night of 16/17 December, the target being two sites near Abbeville. Twelve Mosquitoes (six from each squadron, three plus three going to each target) marked positions 5003.4N 0205.35E and 5005.15N 0159.1E for a bomber force of 26 Stirlings and nine Lancasters (of 617 Squadron) carrying 12,000 lb bombs. Neither raid was a great success, the markers falling too far from the targets. These sites were to prove very difficult to mark, often being in woodland and covering a fairly small area. That same night, Marham also

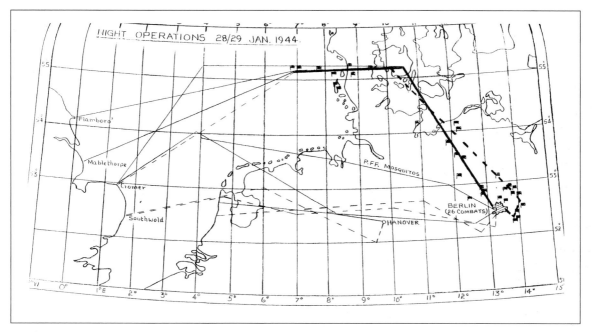

The Berlin attack of 28/29 January 1944, including the diversionary raid on Hanover.

sent six aircraft of 109 Squadron to bomb Duisburg.

Five more attacks on V-bomb construction sites were flown during December, two each on the nights of the 22nd/23rd and 30th/31st, and one on the 29/30th. The only one that appears to have achieved any measure of success was the first, a site at Abbeville being heavily damaged. Two Mosquitoes were lost during the month. Flying Officer Bickley and Fg Off Jackson in 'O' of 109 Squadron failed to return from Bochum on 2/3 December, and Fg Off Reynolds and Fg Off Phillips, in 'D' of 105 Squadron, went missing over Essen on the 12/13th.

Marham also received a great many diverted aircraft, heavy bombers frequently landing at the Norfolk base, often with wounded or dead crewmen on board. There were also losses among these aircraft as pilots struggled to bring badly-damaged bombers in for a landing. Such was the case on the 16th, when Lancaster 'R' of 405 Squadron crashed at Castle Acre with the loss of all but two of its crew.

As part of a reorganization of the squadrons, each unit formed a Servicing Echelon, Nos. 9105 and 9109, from its groundcrew. The change, effective from 14 December, was intended to make the squadrons more mobile.

Another Christmas came and went, and still the war dragged on. In common with most stations, Marhám endeavoured to release its squadrons from operational duties on Christmas Day so that at least some festive spirit was possible. Having landed in the early hours of Christmas Eve, the squadrons were not called upon for operations until the night of the 28/29th, although training flying continued.

January 19 1944 heralded 19 nights of operations, with 20 plus aircraft airborne on some nights. Up to the 14th of the month the squadrons had been active on 11 nights. Tasks were very much as before, area marking and attacks on industrial targets and V-weapon sites, no fewer than 21 of the last being visited. On the night of the 25/26th, 14 aircraft of 105 Squadron visited the Nazi HQ at Aachen. Eleven of the Mosquitoes identified the target and dropped 40 500 lb bombs, scoring a number of hits. That same night 109 Squadron attacked four V-weapon sites, sending three aircraft to each.

The continued and, indeed, growing success of the German nightfighter force against the bomber stream was causing great anxiety among the Bomber Command planners. Deceptions, decoy, spoofing, and *'Serrate'* sorties (British nightfighters operating with the bomber stream) all helped, but it was decided to expand another dimension by increasing the attacks on German nightfighter bases. Typical of this policy was the night of 28/29 January. While 677 aircraft attacked Berlin, almost 100 were engaged on various supporting operations. Among these were 23 Mosquitoes from Marham. Number 109 Squadron sent aircraft to attack Leeuwarden (six) and Deelen (four), and 105 Squadron went to Gilze-Rijen (five), Venlo (six), and Deelen (two). The final attacks of the month, in which 23 Mosquitoes took part, were those against Elberfeld on the 30th/31st.

Although flak was reported as moderate and not very accurate over the target, at least two of 105 Squadron's aircraft were hit near Cologne, WO McPherson's aircraft receiving several hits in the port engine, and Flt Lt Raybould having the nose of his Mosquito shattered.

There had been losses earlier in the month, all to 109 Squadron. One aircraft, returning from the Duisburg attack in the early hours of the 8th, crash-landed at Narborough. The pilot scrambled to safety, but a crane was needed to move wreckage to allow the navigator to be freed. A week later, on the 13/14th, Fg Off Stead and WO Flett went missing in 'F', and 'H' went out of control shortly after take-off for Dusseldorf on the 20/21st, the crew, Sqn Ldr Comar and Fg Off Jenkins, baling out before the aircraft hit the ground near King's Lynn.

The ORB compiler for 105 Squadron recorded a good month's work: '173 sorties for no loss and with only five early returns (2.8 per cent). 89 aircraft (53 per cent) found the primary target(s).' This excellent record was maintained throughout February, although the Squadron did suffer a fatal accident on the 5th, Flt Lt Slater and Fg Off Hedges being killed when DZ548/J crashed during a night-flying test flight. The only other loss to Marham units was an MTU aircraft, 'U', which crashed at Fincham in the early hours of 26 February with the loss of Fg Off Taylor and Plt Off Mander. A number of aircraft were damaged by flak during various operations, and crewmen received injuries, but overall the Mosquito was still proving virtually immune. The major operational emphasis remained on night intruder missions, attacking German nightfighter airfields. The success of this policy was recorded thus: 'News received that only 13 nightfighters seen by PFF on night of 15/16 and only 6 combats. In the area covered by 105 Squadron, only one nightfighter seen, so testifying to the effects of the intruder activity carried out by the squadron.'

The 105 Squadron ORB for the night of 23 March 1944 is typical, although in this instance the operation was not without loss:

Ten aircraft were detailed to bomb nightfighter airfields in Holland as support for an attack by 660 heavies on Frankfurt. 6 x 500 MC were carried by all aircraft with the exception of Sqn Ldr Bird and Flt Lt Clayes, who carried 3 x 500 MC and 1 x TI white.

LEEUWARDEN was successfully attacked by four aircraft with good results. Bombs were seen to burst and the TIs were seen to cascade as markers for Fighter Command intruders. There was 10/10 cloud over the target. Both the aircraft with 6 x 500lb MC had a wing bomb hang up.

Three aircraft attacked VENLO with excellent results through small amounts of cloud, but Flt Lt Ford had a wing bomb hang up.

Sqn Ldr Wills and Flt Lt Castle attacked DEELEN through 5/10 cloud with excellent results. Flt Lt Boxall was also despatched to this target, but 1 x 500 MC which had hung up exploded when the aircraft landed. Flt Lt Boxall was killed and Flt Lt Robinson seriously injured.

This proved to be Marham's last operational Mosquito loss.

The problem of wing bomb hang-ups had been taxing the armourers (and aircrew) for some time,

Berlin on the night of 24/25 March 1944. Cloud, searchlights, TIs and fires confuse this aiming point photograph.

Fg Off Fisher, an American pilot serving with 105 Squadron, admires his appropriate nose art and mission tally.

but a solution was not easy to find. Moreover, the hang-ups seemed to be very spasmodic, a few trouble-free weeks being followed by a spate of failures.

All the usual enemy airfields were visited during this period: Deelen, Venlo, Leeuwarden, Twenthe, Volkel, Gilze-Rijen, St Trond, and Florennes, many of them on two or three nights in succession. While such missions caused very few losses among the German fighters, they certainly caused an enormous amount of disturbance, thereby reducing the overall efficiency and effectiveness of the night defence system. This was subsequently revealed in the reminiscences of a number of German pilots. Kenneth Wolstenholme, a pilot with 105 Squadron (and later a well-known sports reporter), recalled this statement from Emil Nonnenmacher:

Some 20 aircraft were to scramble shortly before midnight. The bombers were approaching abeam Brussels. Four aircraft were already off. I was No. 5 when a Mossie dropped some medium bombs in front of my just rolling aircraft. Post-war investigations revealed that the Mossie concerned was ML938 with pilot Flt Lt Kenneth Wolstenholme and navigator Fg Off Piper. I managed to cut the power and bring

my aircraft to a halt. The bombs had perfectly hit the junction of two crossing runways. In the confusion I took, after a while, the chance via some taxiways to get off a few minutes after midnight, catching up with the bombers in the Nuremberg area and shooting down a Lancaster. All the rest of our Gruppe were delayed up to one hour and they totally missed the bombers. Only the first five aircraft were to see any action, and they shot down eight bombers. I would not hesitate to say that the conditions to bring down a bomber were so excellent as never before or thereafter. Thus at least this one Mossie was to prevent some of your bombers from becoming an equal easy prey.

As usual, operations were not confined to intruder missions, and Mosquito tasking included industrial targets, a favourite this month being the G & J Jaeger ball-bearing works at Elberfeld, plus a number of special targets. It was more of the same into March, with a major effort directed against airfields during the first week, although a few aircraft were tasked to act as formation leaders for Second Tactical Air Force (2nd TAF) attacks on flying-bomb sites. The first such operation was flown on 1 March, the intention being

'No-ball'. The attacks against V-1 sites were very important, the Marham Mosquito units undertook the marking of these pinpoint targets, but with mixed results. This site at Bois de Cassan was attacked on 3 August 1944.

that the Oboe-equipped Mosquito would find the target and drop its bombs to signal a drop by the rest of the formation. During the 18 nights of operations the two squadrons attacked a wide range of targets, and the dropping of a 4,000 lb 'cookie' on Krefeld by Flt Lt Falkinder in 'F' of 109 Squadron marked the first use of this blockbusting weapon by a Marham Mosquito. The crew reported seeing an enormous flash as the bomb exploded.

Bomber Command continued to attack lines of communication, March being the first month when this particular type of target increased in importance. As part of the overall air strategy for Operation *Overlord,* the invasion of Europe, the air planners had decided on a 'Transportation Plan' aimed at isolating the Normandy area. Rail installations, especially the major marshalling yards, were central to this strategy. Amiens was among the targets in this category:

> Amiens marshalling yards was the main target for the squadron tonight [15/16 March]. Two aircraft were detailed to mark with four TI red LB and two with two TI red LB and two 500 MC, but Flt Lt Almond returned early with u/s generator. Technical failures prevented both Flt

Lt Wolstenholme and Fg Off Holland from attacking, but Flt Lt Humphrey was able to make two runs, dropping two TIs each time with excellent results.

There was some cloud and very thick haze over the target, and as only four sets of TIs (2 sets from 109 Squadron) went down at very irregular intervals it is doubtful whether much success was achieved. 132 Halifaxes and Stirlings were despatched and 105 claimed to have attacked with 605 tons of bombs. Little concentration of bombing was reported by our crews, which in view of the poor marking is not surprising, but some of the main force were bombing to the north-east of the target before zero hour. Numerous searchlights were in operation and many fighter flares were seen.

This report highlights the continuing technical problems with the Oboe system and the limitations of poor marking. The marker squadrons also invariably reported that bombing started *before* the first TIs had fallen. However, post-attack photographic reconnaissance often confirmed just how effective attacks had been. By 13 March the reconnaissance feedback was available for the raid against Trappes marshalling yards on 9/10 March:

> This shows that the engine shed has been 75 per cent destroyed and six wrecked locomotives are to be seen lying in the almost demolished building. The water tower has been completely destroyed. Throughout the yards there is a heavy concentration of craters affecting tracks and all the internal lines are blocked. There is also considerable destruction and derailment of tenders and rolling stock. Seventeen direct hits on the main PARIS–CHARTRES lines have put all but one line out of action.

The Marham Mosquito squadrons were now running like well-oiled machines, and the various PFF techniques were starting to bring results for Bomber Command. However, the run-down of the Marham Mosquito force began in March 1944 with the departure, on the 7th, of 1655 MTU to Warboys. Two weeks later 109 Squadron and its associated 9105 Servicing Echelon moved to Bourn, followed in early April by the departure of 109 Squadron (and 9109 Servicing Echelon) to Little Staughton. With the move of 2722 AA Squadron, RAF Regiment, to Horsham on 3 April, Marham passed into the custody of the Clerk of

Works. The airfield was to be closed for major restructuring work, including the laying down of concrete runways.

The decision to turn Marham into a 'Very Heavy Bomber Station' was to virtually shut the airfield for 18 months while the construction teams moved in to create a three-runway pattern, one main runway being 3,000 yd x 100 yd, and the other two being 2,000 yd x 100 yd. The specification was high, calling for a 10–12 in high-grade concrete surface laid on a stabilized and consolidated foundation. It was a huge project, involving the laying of 1,010,000 square yards of concrete for the runways, taxiways and hardstands, plus a further 23,500 square yards of road work. The workforce reached a maximum strength of 1,100, and at the peak of this period they were laying 1,850 cubic metres of concrete a day.

The cost was high. The bill for rebuilding Marham came to £1,740,000, a huge sum at the time. However, when the work was finished the airfield had some of the best facilities in the RAF, and this helped to ensure its survival in the post-war run-down. The station was about to enter a new phase.

Marham's operational life had ended before the momentous events of June 1944 and the invasion of Europe. The Allies faced another 14 months of struggle, as, even in the face of obvious defeat, the German forces withdrew reluctantly and even fought back through the introduction of new weapons. The V-weapon campaign, which had been delayed largely through the efforts of Bomber Command with attacks on research, production, storage, and launch sites, was at last

October 1945, and the major construction work at Marham is almost complete.

begun. The German jet fighters created problems for the Allied bombing offensive. The war in Europe was hard-fought to the bitter end, Victory in Europe (VE) Day on 8 May 1945. Although Marham played little part in the latter stages of the war, its overall contribution to the Allied air effort in Europe had already been significant.

It was now time to look to the future; to formulate a policy for the peacetime RAF and to try and ensure that world peace would be more than just a dream.

CHAPTER 3

CENTRAL BOMBER ESTABLISHMENT

On 1 February 1946 the Development Wing of the Central Bomber Establishment (CBE), one of the most important Bomber Command organizations, arrived from Feltwell to complete the move of this unique body to the West Norfolk base. With the arrival of the rear party on the 28th of the month, Marham was ready to play a crucial role in bomber tactics and development in the postwar era.

It is almost impossible to compile a list of aircraft types operated by the CBE, as there were constant arrivals and departures, some aircraft staying no more than a few days. The principal types, however, were the Lancaster, Lincoln and Mosquito, although the unit also did some work with Halifaxes and used Spitfires for a variety of tasks. A list of other aeroplanes is much harder to assemble, as most types of training and light communications aircraft were to be seen at Marham. In common with most units there were various Avro Ansons, Airspeed Oxfords, and de Havilland Tiger Moths, but the Station Record Books rarely record any details. Typical of the entries for this period, when the RAF was reorganizing, are comments such as that for 14 March: 'The Warwick was disposed of to Lossiemouth as being of no further use'. Unfortunately the Warwick is not identified.

The station was still very much under reorganization postwar, as was the rest of the country, and rationing was still in force. To help overcome this problem, the station ploughed a 12-acre area for a potato crop (9 acres) and a tomato crop. The plan was to use German POWs as labourers, rather than take up the time of the all-too-few RAF personnel. At the end of March, station strength stood at 136 officers (plus 4 WAAF), 86 Warrant Officers/SNCOs (8 WAAF), 631 airmen and 153 airwomen. The large number of air-women caused several problems, and steps were taken to reduce this number as soon as possible. Within a month, 100 German POWs were housed at Marham to help with a variety of manual tasks. Their numbers were increased in October as the shortage of RAF personnel grew even more acute; there was a natural desire among the 'duration only' men to return to civvy street. The main problem now was one of accommodation, and part of a barrack block was converted and given extra security.

Lancasters and Mosquitoes undertook most of the development work, typical trials covering aspects such as improved H_2S radar, the Lancaster Automatic Gun Laying Turret (AGLT – a radar-directed gun), and the SHORAN navigation system.

In this first month at its Norfolk base, the Development Wing flew just over 182 hr. It is impossible to overstate the importance of the CBE within the organization of Bomber Command. It was a vital element of the Command, acting as a centre of excellence, and this can be partly seen in the large numbers of visits both to the unit and by the unit. Most Bomber Command units received visits from time to time, but it was mostly at Command and Staff level that this took place, including very close liaison with the United States Army Air Force (USAAF, which became the USAF in 1947). The CBE was often tasked to take part in the Command's major 'Bullseye' exercises in order to observe the accuracy of the target marking and to comment on the overall bombing techniques being employed. Typical of this was the exercise on 4 April, in which three Lancasters and three Mosquitoes participated.

While the unit was settling in operationally, the extensive rebuilding work continued, Marham acquiring a second Officers' Mess and a station

A very rare shot of Lancaster LL780, with its two remote-control turrets, at the CBE for trials.

cinema, the latter's opening being delayed because the projection equipment had not been collected from RAF Kinington. The cinema eventually opened its doors in August. The importance of local entertainment has already been mentioned, and the station authorities devoted much attention to this aspect. Most personnel of this period remember with particular affection the weekly dances held in the gym at Marham village. Sport was also considered an essential part of RAF life, and Marham teams were soon competing in both RAF and local leagues, the cricket team getting off to a particularly good start with a string of victories.

The impending closure of the satellite airfield at Downham Market meant that a large number of aircrew had to be relocated. So, on 15 May 1946, Development Wing formed a C Flight under Sqn Ldr C.B. Owen. A week later the station celebrated St Dunstan's week with a variety of events in the local area, including, on the 25th, an open day from 14:00 to 23:00, culminating with a dance in No. 2 Hangar. A number of aircraft were on show, and many sections opened their doors to let the public get a close look at Marham's activi-

ties. At the end of the day the station had raised the respectable sum of £1,131 10s to donate to RAF charities. Even more people attended the station's Battle of Britain 'At Home' day on 15 September.

Most of the trials were long-term investigations requiring extensive ground and air appraisals, and each one was given a project leader with wide-ranging responsibilities. Each trial's progress was summarized in the monthly CBE report, and a final report was eventually published as a comprehensive document. The remote-controlled gun turret trial was one of the most important undertaken during this period. The concept was one that the USAAF favoured and had used on its Boeing B-29s. The aircraft used for this trial were Lancasters, such as LL780, and Lincolns; most flight trials involved the use of cine gun film to allow detailed interpretation of the operation of the turret.

In July 1947 the Project Ruby team returned to the USA, the two air forces having acquired a mass of information on the best way to destroy massive concrete structures. Since September 1946 this special force of American B-17s and B-

29s plus modified Lancasters from 15 Squadron had been conducting bombing trials against some of the old German fortifications in mainland Europe.

As one of the major East Anglian stations, and with the general postwar run-down of the RAF, Marham acquired parenting responsibilities for a number of other units. For example, Methwold was held under Care and Maintenance for its stock of bulk petrol for the Fog Intensive Dispersal Operation (FIDO) system and its substantial bomb dump. Such parenting responsibilities have existed throughout the history of the station, but it is not possible to refer to all of them in this history.

Another aspect of the CBE's work, and one that was always popular with aircrew, was the routine of overseas tours. These usually had the dual function of allowing the crew to give lectures to host air forces and, if appropriate, conduct trials on new equipment or techniques. Lincoln RF486 *Excalibur* returned from a very successful Far Eastern tour in mid-October. There were other special flights, such as Operation *Frontline* in December, when CBE aircraft joined a number of Lancasters from No. 3 Group on a route that overflew towns in the British-occupied zone of Germany. However, the most interesting long-range tours seem to have been undertaken by *Crusader*, Lincoln RF498. This aircraft left Marham on 6 January 1947 for a major tour of the Middle

East and South Africa. The tour was headed by the Commandant, Air Cdre G.R.C. Spencer, CBE, and had as its primary aim an in-depth lecture tour and exchange of ideas on bomber operations, plus a study of the problems of long-range reinforcement using the Lincoln. The data acquired was to prove very useful in the near future, when Lincoln squadrons deployed to Malaya and Kenya on active anti-terrorist operations. *Crusader* eventually returned to Marham in February.

The continuing restructuring of the CBE meant that by January 1947 it comprised four main Wings; Development, Tactics, Technical, and Executive. The first two were the 'operational' elements, undertaking the trials, while the latter two were the support elements. It should be borne in mind, of course, that the CBE WAS Marham, and *vice versa*. Among the final reports issued during 1947 was that on Trial 101, concerning the remote-controlled barbettes for Lancasters. Issued on 13 June, the report explained in detail the nature of the trial and the conclusions reached. Lancaster LL780, the primary trials aircraft, had been fitted with upper and lower rear fuselage turrets, each mounting a pair of 20 mm cannon, plus a rear sighting station. The aircraft itself, like a number of other such trials aircraft, belonged to the Royal Aircraft Establishment (RAE) at Farnborough, the tactical trials performed by the CBE being only one ele-

A CBE Lincoln on one of the many overseas tours.

Crusader *and crew before departing on the South African tour.*

ment of a whole series of flight trials. Flight trials were undertaken with a variety of single-engined 'enemy' fighters carrying out a series of 'canned' (i.e. pre-planned) attack profiles. After a number of sorties the basic conclusions were not favourable, the recommendations being for a power seat for the air gunner, improved visibility, and a much improved AGLT scanner.

The station still operated a few Spitfires, but these went through a bad patch with a number of incidents; an accidental jettisoning of a canopy in March, followed by a wheels-up landing in June. Generally, serviceability of the major types was very good, with Technical Wing producing the right aircraft at the right time; not always an easy task when trials requirements were frequently subject to amendment at short notice. The major factors affecting the progress of the trials in the winter of 1947 were the weather and a fuel shortage. The Norfolk weather was dreadful in February 1947, and for most of the month the station achieved nothing. March brought a series of gales, that on the 17th being particularly fierce, the 90 mph winds damaging three Lincolns.

Every Saturday morning there was a colour hoisting parade at 08:30, followed by an hour of drill and PT, after which one third of the assembled 'crowd' had to reappear in best blues for an inspection while the remainder were involved in various domestic tasks around the station. From midday onwards the rest of the weekend was 'free', subject to various constraints, passes, and so on. Once a month this parade was a full Commandant's parade.

The close links with the USAF were once more stressed with the arrival, on 9 September 1947, of the B-29s of the 340th Squadron, part of what was to become a regular coming and going of Strategic Air Command (SAC) aircraft over the next 40 years.

Typical of aircraft movements were those listed for July to September 1947:

July	Mosquito XVII HK327 to 47 MU, Sealand
	Mosquito XVI PF407 from 51 MU
	Lincoln II RE378 from modification at TRE Defford
August	Anson VP513 from A.V. Roe, Woodford

Spitfire PK658 from 833 MU
September Lincoln I RE251 to 10 MU
Lincoln I RE252 to 10 MU
Lancaster I LL780 to 10 MU

It would not, of course, be worthwhile to list every aircraft movement in this short history, but this at least highlights the scene – and these were fairly quiet months. Meanwhile, the routine of trials and tours continued apace. Lincolns RA686 and 722 spent a few weeks in the Sudan during the summer, undertaking hot-weather trials on the H_2S Mk IVA, the airfield at Khartoum being the RAF's tropical test site. Eventually, three Lincolns became involved with these trials. The major tour of this period was, however, a Far East and Australasia extravaganza by *Crusader*. A major expedition such as this took a fair amount of planning and organization, not least of which was preparation of the nominated personnel. The ORB reports: 'Preparations went on for the Far East flight. Half the station has a sore arm from inoculations these days. Cholera is the latest to be added to the list.' The detachment, commanded by Air Cdre Bufton, an established Second World War bomber expert, left Marham, the first major stop being Singapore and the Far East Air Force (FEAF). After a profitable few days with FEAF, the Lincoln left on 6 November for Darwin, Australia. The route then led to New Zealand via Sydney, *Crusader* arriving at Auckland on the 9th. Wellington and Christchurch were visited over the next 10 days, as the Royal New Zealand Air Force was given an opportunity not only to assess the Lincoln (both Australia and New Zealand being potential customers for the aircraft), but also to hear the CBE lecture programme. *Crusader* returned to Marham on 17 December, via Brisbane, Darwin, Tengah, Negombo, Karachi, Habbaniyah, Castel Benito, and Manston, having covered 25,709 miles in a flying time of 144 hr 44 min. The only aircraft problem had been an engine change at Negombo, Ceylon, which caused a five-day delay early in the tour.

Meanwhile, at Marham the so-called 'de-Waafing' process had been completed and the station was now devoid of uniformed females; a major change from the position just a year earlier. Problems arose almost immediately, as there was now no female attendant to help with families!

1948 opened with another major tour, again by *Crusader*, comprising a trip around the Middle

East, Rhodesia, and South Africa. As with most expeditions of this type, the crew list included a Flying Medical Officer (FMO), in this case Sqn Ldr Dhenin, to investigate the aviation medicine aspects of such flights and of operations in the different locations. The year also saw other major trips to the Sudan (H_2S trials again), South Africa, and Nairobi (for 'hot and high' trials). It is worth quoting extracts from the official report on the first of these flights:

The purpose of the flight was:

a) To discuss bomber tactics and developments with the RAF in the Middle East, and the Rhodesian and South African Air Forces.
b) To investigate problems peculiar to the operation of bomber forces in the areas visited.
c) To give lectures, if required, on bomber tactics and development.
d) To practise the technique of long-range reinforcement flights by standard heavy bomber aircraft.

The flight was made in Lincoln II aircraft 'Crusader'. This is a standard Lincoln bomber except for the following:

a) The removal of the B-17 mid-upper turret.
b) The fitting of three bunks and a divan seat in the centre portion of the fuselage, and four small observation panels along the starboard side of the fuselage.
c) The fitting of one 400 gallon tank in the forward end bomb bay, and spares back-up and spare undercarriage wheel in the remainder of the bomb bay.

The mission left Marham on 17 February, and returned on schedule on 21 March. Total flying time, including demonstrations, was 68 hr 52 min, 12,913 track miles were covered at an average groundspeed of 202 knots. During the course of this liaison flight 37 lectures were delivered.

The remainder of the document gives details of each stage of the tour, the entry for Langebaan Weg being typical:

On Monday 15 March, the party left in 'Crusader' for Langebaan Weg, where it was met by Colonel B. Viljoen. Langebaan Weg was constructed during the war and is built upon the most modern lines. It is ideally suited to its role as an Air Navigation, Bombing and Gunnery School. At present, owing to an acute shortage of technical personnel, no aircraft are based on the station. Long range navigation and bombing is carried out in Sunderland aircraft, and for this purpose a detachment of No. 35 Squadron is based at Langebaan. As previously stated, gunnery and bombing are carried out in Ventura aircraft of No. 17 Squadron, which are flown up daily from Brooklyn. The day of arrival at Langebaan was devoted to meeting individual officers and generally becoming acquainted with the lay-out of the station. Needless to say, the very excellent swimming pool was very popular with crew members. The morning of Tuesday 16 March was devoted to lecturing and the standard four-lecture programme was delivered. In the afternoon, Gp Capt Bufton, Sqn Ldr Runciman and Sqn Ldr Austin paid a visit to the flying boat base to see the 35 Squadron detachment.

A new shape and sound arrived at Marham on 9 April, when Meteor III EE340 came on strength from 32 MU. This was the CBE's first jet, and as soon as the staff were converted to the aircraft it undertook tours of bomber bases, the first three being Stradishall, Upwood, and Coningsby, to give crews jet familiarity. Meanwhile, the ongoing gun turret trials continued, Lincoln RF339 going to St Athan on 28 April to have a different turret fitted. As one would expect, bombing was a major part of the unit's task, and a great many practice bombs were dropped on a variety of ranges in the UK. The CBE's 'experts' could only comment on front-line squadron techniques and problems if they themselves were 'up to speed'; in addition, of course, there were the bombing requirement of various trials.

The standard practice bomb was the 25-pounder, and many hundreds of these were dropped in a year, usually without any problems. One of the few incidents to occur was that in June 1948, when armourers opened the doors of Lincoln RE378 to remove the remaining three bombs after a sortie. Something went wrong, the bombs fell to the floor and one exploded, injuring Aircraftman Chaney. The worst incident of 1948 occurred on 14 September, when the starboard engine of Mosquito B.35 TK649, piloted by Flt Lt Sailes, caught fire when the aircraft was at 37,000 ft. Try as he might, the pilot could not get the extinguisher to work, and the propeller would not feather. Keeping control as best he could, Sailes headed back towards Marham. In the event he had to put the aircraft down in a field adjacent

to the airfield, but it was a good forced landing and both crewmen walked away uninjured.

The Americans arrived in some force in mid-July, with two squadrons of the 307th Bombardment Group (BG), the 370th and 371st under Col C.J. Heflin, plus the HQ of 3rd Air Division under Col S. Wray, taking up residence. Other squadrons of this B-29 Division went to Waddington and Scampton. This move was announced by the American authorities as follows:

Two B-29 Superfortress medium bomber Groups have left their base in the United States *en route* to bases in England for a short period of temporary duty. The move of the planes is part of the normal long-range flight training programme which was instigated more than a year ago by SAC. The 28th Group from Rapid City, South Dakota, will fly to Scampton. The 307th Group from MacDill AFB, Florida, will fly to Marham and Waddington. Each Group will consist of three squadrons of ten aircraft each.

On arrival at Marham the Americans were met by the No. 3 Group Senior Air Staff Officer (SASO), Air Vice Marshal S.C. Strafford. It was a time of increasing tension on the world political scene, and many thought that the increased belligerence of the Soviet Union, exemplified by the Berlin blockade, would lead to a major conflict. Large-scale American reinforcements moved into a number of air bases in Britain and on the Continent.

To keep the aircrew on their toes it was decided to introduce a regular escape and evasion exercise. The first of these took place at the beginning of the month, and crews were dropped 20 miles away and told to make their way back to 'safety' at Marham, avoiding all contact with the 'hostile' local population.

In October the Commandant, Air Cdre Staton, issued the following message:

CBE is now approaching its third birthday, and few could have foreseen, three years ago, that we would at this time again be sharing our facilities with our American allies. They have visited us before, but never on a scale that has virtually made them part of the establishment. They have, in somewhat overcrowded conditions, settled down very happily and have knitted into the organization extremely well. The congestion caused by the virtual doubling of personnel at Marham is such that could not be sustained were it not for the co-operation and unobtrusive spirit shown by them on all occasions.

The presence of the Americans meant that Marham received even more visits. The records for most months list at least 30 major visits, a large proportion of which were considered to be VIPs, so the level of 'bull' tended to be quite high!

As part of the American rotation, the 307th BG were replaced by the 97th BG in November. The training routine for these units remained the same, and very similar to that of the home-based squadrons, the emphasis being on long-range navigation exercises to 'attack' a variety of strategic targets in Western Europe. Fighter affiliation was still an important aspect of training, and the B-29 crews were confident of their ability to survive and reach their targets.

As the year came to a close the Establishment was busier than ever, as evidenced by the list of summaries included in the monthly progress report, which included:

1. Attack on ships under way by Heavy Bomber aircraft.
2. Tactics of future jet bomber force in relation to potential enemy defences, including subsonic fighters and guided missiles.
3. Bomber operations over Arctic conditions.
4. Minelaying in sea area by jet-engined bomber aircraft.
5. Minelaying in inland waterways by jet-engined bomber aircraft.

To make best use of the wealth of expertise at the CBE, the Tactical Wing, now renamed the Tactical Training Wing, began a regular course for 12 or so officers a time to look at bomber theory, tactics, and future developments. Meanwhile, Development Wing was ploughing through the trials programme and reacting to urgent special tasking. An example of the latter came in December 1948, with an investigation into:

. . . the overshoot capabilities of the Lincoln aircraft where centre of gravity position is near the aft limit. This arose from a recent incident at Shallufa to an aircraft from Wyton as a result of which HQ 3 Group consulted this establishment. It is clear that, when landing with c of g more than 61 inches aft, overshoot will be difficult; moreover if the undercarriage is raised before half flap is taken off, as was the case in the accident, the aircraft will become uncontrollable.

It is somewhat strange that the CBE became involved in such trials, as they would usually be the province of the RAF's Handling Squadron.

Among the forest of paperwork produced by the unit each month was a comprehensive sports bulletin, the first page of which included the statement: 'it should be the ambition of every officer and airman to represent the station in some form of team competition'. The unit was certainly doing very well in most of its wide range of sporting ventures.

It had been decided that Marham would return to operational status as a front-line bomber station,

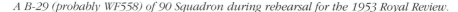

A B-29 (probably WF558) of 90 Squadron during rehearsal for the 1953 Royal Review.

for the introduction of the RAF's Boeing B-29 fleet, so the CBE moved to Lindholme in Yorkshire, the move being completed by April 1949.

The overall political situation of the late 1940s caused a reappraisal of RAF strength and equipment. The Berlin crisis and the Korean War, plus the various anti-terrorist operations, proved that the Second World War had not brought world peace in its wake. 'Cold War' was the phrase in currency, and the old allies endeavoured to strengthen the defences of western Europe. The RAF's re-equipment plan was under way, with Canberra and V-bomber types under development but not ready for squadron service. The English Electric Canberra entered service, with 101 Squadron, in 1951, but the first of the new jet 'heavies', the Vickers Valiant, would not see squadron service (with 138 Squadron) until February 1955. This left the Lincoln as Bomber Command's main offensive bomber.

The decision was therefore taken to acquire the B-29, to be named Washington in RAF service, as a stop-gap measure under the Mutual Defense Assistance Program (MDAP). Although B-29 production had ceased in 1946, the USAF still had a number of squadrons and there was also a large number of airframes in storage. It was from these that the first RAF aircraft were to come, after a series of modifications. The initial RAF requirement was for 70 aircraft, although this was later increased to 88.

At a press conference on 20 March, Sir Oliver Franks, Britain's Ambassador to the United States, said:

These planes are evidence that we are fire-proofing all the houses in our street . . . a preventative medicine in the cause of peace. This ceremony today shows that the words 'Collective Security' are not just a clause in a treaty. These B-29s are a visible and effective warning against aggression and proof of American confidence in the determination of Britain to ensure the general stability and security of the democratic world.

Behind him at Andrews Field, Washington, stood four B-29s freshly painted in RAF markings.

The first four aircraft, led by WF437 (ex-44-69680), arrived at Marham 22 March 1950. The other three first arrivals were WF434 (44-61599), WF435 (44-61787), and WF436 (44-61792). In fact, WF437 was first to land only because it was flying on three engines, the starboard inner having been feathered owing to an oil leak.

With its 141 ft wingspan (the Lincoln spanned 120 ft) and loaded weight of 120,000 lb (Lincoln 82,000 lb), the B-29 (Superfortress in American service) presented a number of problems. The most pressing concerned the airfield surfaces. As a Class A airfield Marham had an adequate runway and taxiway system, but it lacked suitable hardstandings. A rebuilding programme was initiated, including the provision of 12 concentric hardstandings to suit the new aircraft, the first pair being due for completion in February 1951 and the whole programme to be completed within a year. It also required the extension of the apron in front of the hangars to a width of 70 ft,

Washington WF445/F; note the squadron commander's pennant near the cockpit.

The official B-29 handover parade, March 1950. The parade was led by Flt Lt V. Taylor and Lt W. Wasner.

giving Marham one of its distinctive features, known ever after as the 'waterfront'. There was an associated major rebuilding programme for squadron accommodation, technical support, and even new Seco huts for the expected increase in numbers of airmen. There were even plans to build a railway branch line to Marham from Downham Market, but these came to naught.

The Washington was very different from any RAF bomber, and made the Lincoln look antiquated. Powered by four 2,200 h.p. Wright R-3350 Cyclone engines, the B-29 had an impressive performance; a maximum speed of 350 mph, a service ceiling of 35,000 ft, and a range of just under 3,000 miles (over 4,000 miles maximum). Its bomb load, however, was only 6,000 lb, a common feature of American bombers being heavy defensive armament but low bomb loading. The B-29 was defended by five pairs of 0.5 in guns, all in remote-controlled barbettes. The crew of ten were accommodated in luxurious conditions, by RAF standards, within a pressurized crew compartment.

Marham was now commanded by Gp Capt P.W. Stansfeld, DFC, and the station's strength stood at 157 officers and 1,497 airmen. The official description of the unit's role was that of a 'Heavy Bomber base, part of Bomber Command Main Force'.

As the home of the Washington Conversion Unit (WCU), it was Marham's task to train all B-29 crews, and, like most such squadron re-equipment programmes, this tended to be done a squadron at a time. The WCU was commanded by Sqn Ldr F.R. Flynn, and in the early months included a large number of USAF personnel as instructors until sufficient trained RAF personnel were available.

First to acquire the new type was 115 Squadron, which re-equipped in June 1950, followed, in August, by 149 Squadron. The next unit to complete the conversion course was 90 Squadron in January 1951, although at the time they only had two aircraft on strength. New aircraft were arriving from the USA during most weeks, and by taking the next two of these, plus two from 115 Squadron, the squadron had the more respectable total of six and was able to concentrate on a training programme. Next out of the 'school' was 15 Squadron, but they moved to Coningsby, the second of the B-29 bases. Sqn Ldr Ken White, then Navigator Two (Nav II), started four weeks ground school and converted to the aircraft as part of the 15 Squadron build-up. He recalls:

First flight in WF411 as Radar Navigator on 13 December 1950. A full Washington crew comprised two pilots, two navigators (radar and plotter), one flight engineer, one signaller and three air gunners. The crew eventually flew their first crew solo on 22 January and following a final crew handling flight on 30 January, moved to Coningsby. The conversion course had included six sorties, a total flying time of 24 hr and 30 min.

Marham also ran the complete series of courses required for the various ground trades, and even had a 'touring' unit to provide additional tuition if required. The Washington was a very complex aircraft, and almost all of its equipment was completely different from anything the RAF tradesmen had seen before. Even the terminology in the manuals was different. The APQ-13 radar, fortunately a variant of the RAF's own H$_2$S system, was the heart of the blind-bombing capability, and as such had its own ground specialists.

Meanwhile, one of the RAF's most famous bomber squadrons had arrived for conversion; 44 (Rhodesia) Squadron. To assist the 'Brits' in the mammoth task of getting used to the intricacies of the new aircraft there were a number of American units, including the 301st Aviation Squadron and its Air Support Squadron, the 7513th.

The station was very busy, and even in these early days the flying effort was quite impressive – some 570 hr in January during 299 day and 178 night sorties. The only problem that seemed to occur regularly was that of engine failure, no fewer than five instances being recorded this month, three of which involved the No. 2 engine. During January five more aircraft arrived from the USA, three going to 15 Squadron, for its move to Coningsby, and two, as previously mentioned, to 90 Squadron. This gave Marham some 21 of the type, nine of which were with the WCU. As usual, the station operated a variety of other aircraft, the most common of which was the good old Oxford, or 'Oxbox', which performed a wide range of roles.

Among the other units stationed at Marham was 92nd Battery Light Anti-aircraft, (LAA), Royal Artillery, with seven officers and 122 other ranks. Equipped with the Bofors gun, the unit occupied a number of gun positions around the airfield. The increased American interest in Marham led to the arrival, on 8 March, of a US Army air defence unit, 'A' Battery, 4th AAA Battalion, to take over from the Royal Artillery.

The station armourers were kept very busy, both with practice bombs and, more especially, with the heavy demand for 0.5 in ammunition. In a typical month the air gunners would use between 15,000 and 25,000 rounds. Likewise, in a normal month the squadrons and the WCU between them would use more than 500 of the 25 lb practice bombs. It was almost farcical to see a huge B-29 dropping these very small bombs,

Boeing B-29 WW352 of 207 Squadron during the 1954 visit to Karachi. (Paddy Porter)

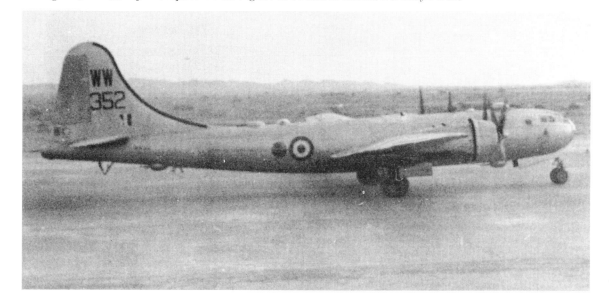

A 115 Squadron crew share a joke!

but 500 lb and 1,000 lb bombs were not readily available for training, although from time to time crews were sent off with a full weapons load which they salvoed on to one of the ranges. This was an impressive sight, especially when a for- mation performed a simultaneous release. With three air gunners and 12 0.5 in guns, the Washington packed a reasonable air-combat punch, as would be proved during many of the air defence exercises in the next few years. Paddy

A good shot of the Washington's four-gun front upper turret on a 115 Squadron aircraft.

A 27 Squadron Tornado at the SAC bombing competition.

MARHAM IN COLOUR

A Victor uses its centre hose on trials with the MRCA (Tornado).

Victor to Lightning refuelling.

The arrival of II(AC) Squadron, December 1991.

Above *A 27 Squadron aircraft takes off for a training sortie.*

Below *Tornado ZE553/JE of 27 Squadron over the Norfolk coast on return to Marham.*

Bottom *A XIII Squadron aircraft climbs out of low level.*

A Skyshadow pod on a 617 Squadron Tornado. This pod is part of the electronic warfare self-defence suite.

The last Victor air-to-air refuelling.

The Gulf LGB trio; Victor, Tornado and Buccaneer.

As part of the NATO hardening requirement, all of the Marham Tornado fleet is provided with hardened aircraft shelters and associated facilities.

The desert pink reappears for Operation Jural. (H. Evans)

A 617 Squadron aircraft being flown by a II(AC) Squadron crew during Operation Jural, October 1992. Note the TIALD pod on the left shoulder station.

Above *Flexibility means AAR from other types. Here, AJ-T awaits its turn to take fuel from a USAF KC-10.*

Below *Tornado AJ-L, airbrakes out, descends to low level over Saudi Arabia in October 1992.*

Bottom *A low-level reconnaissance pass over a Kuwaiti airfield during a training sortie, November 1993.*

Above *Arctic Express, March 1994. A Tornado GR.1A of II(AC) Squadron about to descend down into the wintry landscape.*

Below *A XIII Squadron line-up.*

Bottom *A 27 Squadron pair comes in to land.*

Porter, in an article in *FlyPast* magazine, explained the workings of the system:

> Another interesting installation was the Gunfire Control System. There were 12 0.5 in machine guns, four in the upper forward turret, two in the upper aft, lower forward, and lower aft turrets, plus two in the tail. The interlocking circuitry was such that it enabled certain gunners to be able to take priority over specific turrets. If a gunner's action switch was not depressed then an alternative gunner could take over the use of that turret. Likewise, the third gunner could take it over if neither of the other two were using it. This was referred to as primary, secondary, and tertiary control.
>
> Some aircraft were slightly different, in that the priority for the use of the guns had been programmed. It was usual for the mid-upper gunner to have primary control of the upper forward and aft turrets, with the nose gunner being able to take over the upper forward turret on a secondary basis, if it was not in use by the mid-upper gunner, or Central Fire Controller (CFC) as he was known.

By April, 57 Squadron had joined the ranks of those going through the WCU, with 207 Squadron the next to arrive, in June. Tragedy struck the base on 1 April when Oxford NM510 crashed into a Nissen hut after clipping the wind-speed indicator on the top of the runway caravan. The pilot, Flt Lt A. Brand, and his three airmen passengers on an air experience flight were killed.

While the building work around the airfield progressed and the 'students' flew their instructional profiles, the two operational squadrons, 90 and 115, were rapidly gaining experience with their aircraft, the daily routine being one of long-range navigation and bombing exercises. Targets were either declared as radar or visual attacks, and varied from factories to docks. The first major exercise took place on 24 May, when nine B-29s from Marham took part in Exercise *Ombrelle,* a major air defence exercise for the Western Union countries. As was to become the norm with most such exercises, the bombers were intercepted because they had neither sufficient speed nor altitude with which to evade the 'enemy'. However, in the ensuing combats they claimed a goodly number of the attacking fighters. Most of the B-29s now carried Gee Mk.II as part of a scheme to provide improved navigational aids to cover the primary operational theatre in Europe. Such modifications were, and still are, regularly carried out on all frontline aircraft, and there is usually some modification being made on most weeks, though most are of a fairly minor nature.

July saw WF437 undergoing a trial fit for a radio countermeasures (RCM) and Window system in an effort to improve the survivability of these

B-29 crews at briefing, March 1953.

A 149 Squadron crew with the Washington Conversion Unit, August 1950.

large bombers. The RAF had lost its confidence in the 'self-defending' bomber very early in the Second World War, and the American experience with their daylight raids had done little to alter the philosophy. Hence, although the Washington could be seen as a day bomber, to the RAF the night skies were still the most favourable, as long as you could find and hit your targets.

By the late summer of 1951 the bulk of the conversion task was complete, so the WCU disbanded, leaving the final unit under training, 35 Squadron, needing one operational flight and one conversion training flight. Each of the operational squadrons was given a monthly flying task of 320 hr, and it now became a matter of 'competition' between the squadrons of the Marham Wing to achieve the best all-round performance. In addition to this main flying task, the Marham Station Flight, with its mixed pool of aircraft, was expected to achieve 315 hr a month. All of this made for one very busy station. As the squadrons became more experienced and declared themselves fully operational, so they became involved in more and more exercises. The major exercise in late summer was *Pinnacle,* a large UK air defence exercise intended to push the defenders to the limit by mounting mass raids day and night. The B-29 units played a major part in all phases of this

exercise up to its termination on 10 October.

Such major training exercises, and especially the routine Bomber Command exercises such as *Bullseye* and *King Pin*, were intended to prove both the capability of the bomber force and the status of the air defences. The Washington's normal bomb load was either 500 lb or 1,000 lb bombs, all of Second World War vintage, and attack profiles had varied little since the mass raids of 1944/45, except in the scale of the effort. In order to achieve a similar effect, the Command sought accuracy rather than weight of bombs, and to this end most of the training was orientated around navigation to, and accurate bombing of, the targets.

Thus the day-to-day long-range navigation sorties, often lasting up to 8 hr, included both day and night phases, simulated radar and visual bombing, and the dropping of a few practice bombs on one or more of the various bombing ranges. Sorties often encompassed targets in Germany as well as in the UK, and at the end of the mission there would be a comprehensive debrief. In recognition of the critical part played by bombing accuracy, the new Command categorization scheme was based around this aspect. The idea behind this scheme was to have a sequence of levels of performance that crews

Probably the classic B-29 shot; a trio of 115 Squadron Washingtons.

aspired to achieve, the central element being the bombing accuracy of the crew in visual and radar attacks. In the categorization period, usually 12 months, a crew had to drop a given minimum number of bombs in each mode, and depending upon the 50 per cent bombing accuracy achieved

would be awarded a specific Command Category.

As part of the overall operational orientation for aircrew, the series of escape and evasion (E&E) exercises continued, including a few major examples such as *Cornflit,* held during 26–18 October 1951. Personnel from all four squadrons were

A formation of B-29s.

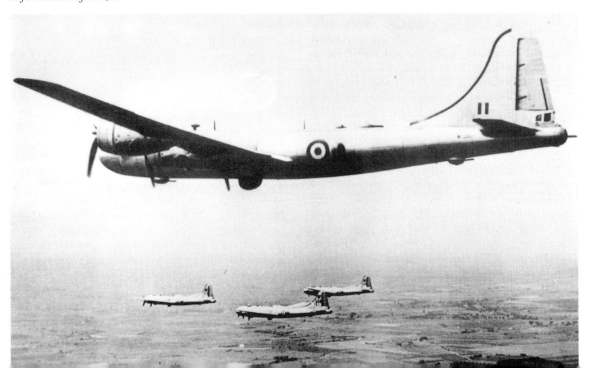

dropped off in various parts of Norfolk at 18:00 on the Friday evening and given 48 hr in which to 'escape'. This time the enemy was out in force, with the Norfolk Police and the Territorial Army actively looking for the evaders. Those who were caught, and most were, had to go through an interrogation session with personnel from AI.9, the specialist branch.

While most aircrew could certainly not claim to enjoy such exercises, they did recognize the need for such training. The number of E&E exercises actually increased into 1952, culminating in Exercise *Short Flit*, designed to find the best air-crew team to take part in the Bomber Command evasion exercise, *Moonraker*, in October. The evaders were given a few short rules: no dis-guises, no money, and no violence.

Moonraker itself took place during 17–26 October 1952, and, as the diarist records: 'all par-ticipants suffered considerable hardship over the period but many invaluable lessons were learned'. Sergeant Paxton of 35 Squadron man-aged to cover the whole 130 miles without being caught.

The introduction of the Washington had gone very smoothly, and in spite of the complex and, for RAF personnel, different nature of the aircraft there were very few problems. Serviceability was excellent, and the initial engine troubles seemed to have vanished. In fact the only accident at Marham during this period occurred to a Lincoln on weather diversion from Upwood, which crashed on radar approach to runway 06, all five crew being killed.

On 15 January 1952 the United States ensign was lowered for the last time with the final depar-ture of US personnel. Although this was to be the end of a permanent USAF presence, over the next 30 years they were to be regular visitors to Marham as the base maintained its close links with SAC.

In the early months of 1952 elements of 263 Squadron were attached to Marham, starting with 'B' Flight from 19 to 26 February. The Meteor F.8s of this squadron acted as both friendly (escort) fighters and 'bad guys' as part of this co-operative venture. Various Meteor squadrons undertook this fighter affiliation role throughout 1952. Another role performed by the Washingtons was Air Sea Rescue, and squadrons rotated as duty ASR unit. The requirement was for one aircraft on standby, with backup aircraft available at short notice. On Sunday 19 March, 19 Group called an alert to search for a Vampire fighter that was reported to have come down in the sea off Ramsgate. The duty aircraft was already in the air when a follow-up message was received that the distressed aircraft had in fact made it to Hawkinge. Such call-outs were not infrequent, and often had a much sadder outcome. In April, and again in June, the duty crews were scrambled to help in efforts to rescue F-86 aircraft. The 35 Squadron standby crew was scrambled in late July. Although Fg Off Stirrup set a new record of 11 min from alert to airborne, the crew were unable to find any trace of the Meteor pilot in the sea off Yarmouth.

Leading Aircraftman Gordon Dickie was one of the many National Servicemen on the station. He arrived in mid-1952, and received an almighty shock:

My trade training had been done on a Meteor, and I was suddenly confronted by this enor-mous four-engined piston aircraft that I was to work on, WW345/S. As an airframe mechanic this was to be my aircraft. The squadrons took it in turns to be Air Sea Rescue squadron, when a rigid metal lifeboat would be fitted to one of the bomb bays, the other one having Lindholme gear. We slept in our 'crew room' near the dispersal and would scrounge from the cookhouse – bread, butter, eggs and bacon – to cook over the tortoise-shell stove. When we were trying to sleep we would hear mice etc scuttling around the floor.

As one of the premier stations in the UK, Marham was considered to be a prime target both for sab-otage and for air assault. It was therefore consid-ered vital that the station develop a unified defence plan. The definitive version was issued in April, and included details of the defensive perimeter, vital points (there were five VPs: Defence HQ, Standby power supply, Armoury, Operations block, Main power sub-station and water supply system), and the arms issue to per-sonnel:

Aircrew	Revolver + 6 rounds
WO & SNCO	Sten gun + 2 magazines (100 rounds)
Airmen	0.303 Rifle, bayonet, 50 rounds
Defence Squadron	each Flight given two Light Machine Guns (LMG) + 12 magazines, five of which were anti-aircraft and

marked in white
25 grenades per squadron
Anti-sabotage Flight 3 LMG + 6 magazines

This was an appreciable amount of firepower. All station personnel were required to 'qualify' with their respective weapons, and the small-arms range was kept fairly busy. The regular station exercises now included ground play to test the effectiveness of the Defence Plan.

In June the Washington Conversion Unit was re-formed, and the training role performed by 35 Squadron reverted to the WCU.

The early part of the summer of 1952 was dedicated to practice for the Laurence Minot Trophy, the prestigious bombing trophy for which all Bomber Command units, plus invited American units, competed. The competition took place in July, and was won by 90 Squadron with an average bombing error of 150 yd. Nineteen squadrons had taken part, and the Marham units did very well, taking not only the first place but also 3rd (115 Squadron), 6th (35 Squadron), and 8th (207 Squadron). The trophy was presented by the Chief of the Air Staff, Sir John Slessor, during a parade on 18 October. At the same ceremony Marham also received the Avro Trophy, awarded to the Bomber Command station with the highest serviceability factor, an excellent achievement and testament to both engineers and the B-29. In September, 90 Squadron was involved in the SAC bombing competition at Davis Monthan Field. Competitions and trophies were a regular feature of operations; in the same month that 90 Squadron were receiving the Laurence Minot trophy, all of the squadrons were competing for the Sassoon Gunnery Trophy.

In July, 3 Group issued a new training directive to all of its units, calling for an emphasis on 'individual crew training to a high standard in both visual and radar bombing, and classification to Select, Combat, or non-combat status according to ability'. The crew classification depended upon achieving a given accuracy in each of the declared bombing methods with a certain number of bombs during the classification period. A crew could go up or down the system. Outside of exercise period, this became the primary daily routine for the bomber squadrons. The major problem with the system was that it was crew classification, and, with new arrivals, crews had to start again. With the large turn-over of personnel this meant a continuous effort. It was never easy for

squadron commanders to organize a training routine, as too many other inputs were made, such as fuel or hours restrictions through much of 1952. Furthermore, such events as the annual September Battle of Britain Flypast over London meant that precious time and effort was put into the rehearsals.

October's activities included the RAF's annual exercise, *Ardent,* which took place in three phases between the 3rd and 13th. During Phase I the B-29s operated on the 3rd/4th and 4/5th, with 20 aircraft from Marham airborne each time. On the first mission the crews flew night attacks on Glasgow and Manchester, followed by a day attack on Liverpool, all using simulated radar bombing. On the second night Glasgow was again the target, followed by a visual bombing run on the Redesdale range. Phase II entailed ten aircraft attacking a range of targets on the 9/10th; simulated bombing on Sheffield, London, and the Forth Bridge on the route between bombing

A navigator at work. The interior of the B-29 was luxurious compared with that of types such as the Lincoln.

ranges at Larkhill, Wainfleet, Luce Bay, and Redesdale.

The final phase of the exercise opened on the night of the 11/12th with a 14-aircraft wave flying a route out over France in order to run in and attack Bristol. Two aircraft 'carried' atom bombs and the other 12 Washingtons provided support. Meanwhile, two other aircraft flew decoy tracks and radar spoofing runs over the North Sea. The attack was made as seven pairs of aircraft, the A-bomb carriers being in the middle of the formation. The defending fighters rose to meet the attack and engaged the B-29s, including the two primary bombers. During the combats the fighters claimed over half of the bombers, while the latter made claims against 12 of the attacking Meteors and Vampires. The final raid of the exercise was a maximum effort daylight push to attack Tangmere airfield. The engineers at Marham performed marvels, and 32 B-29s took part in the mission.

After a busy but successful 1952, the year ended in tragedy with the crash of WF570 almost immediately after take-off on 14 December. Flight Lieutenant M. Creighton reported fuel leaking from a wing petrol cap, and shortly afterwards the Washington tumbled into a field at West Acre, killing four of the crew. Unfortunately the new year opened with another fatal crash. During the monthly *Kingpin* exercise on the night of 8/9 January 1953, WF502 crashed near Mold, North Wales, and Sqn Ldr W. Sloane, OC 90 Squadron, and his crew perished. This seemed to be a period of non-stop bad news, as in February Sgt Beer, an armourer on 115 Squadron, was killed in a bombing-up accident when a 500 lb bomb exploded.

February saw RAF units in East Anglia heavily involved in assisting with the problems caused by severe flooding all around the east coast. Gordon Dickie, along with most of 35 Squadron's ground-crew, was among those involved in the flood relief programme:

We went to Magdelen where the Ouse had burst its banks and a massive breach had been made in the bank. Thousands of acres were flooded. We had to cross a railway bridge on foot, all trains had stopped running, the bridge was swaying with the pressure of the water. We were filling sandbags and worked through the night, under floodlights, with the Salvation Army and NAAFI keeping us supplied with tea

etc. The floods are etched in my memory for ever – it was awful, bloated dead cattle and poultry, sewage, the smell was dreadful, the riverbank quaking under our feet. Nobody who worked on the floods will ever forget it. Others from Marham helped elsewhere and some weeks later a Church parade was held in King's Lynn, followed by a march through the town.

Exercise *Jungle King*, held on 16–23 March, was the largest air defence exercise since 1949, and the station went on to a full war footing. The theoretical situation was that West Germany had been overrun, and Bomber Command was tasked with neutralizing all major airfields. Air defence of the zone was provided by Allied Air Force Central Europe (AAFCE) fighters. The Marham units operated on five days, attacking Hamburg/Fuhlsbuttel, Wunstorf, and Gutersloh. Meteors, Mosquitoes, and Vampires intercepted most raids but, again, the Washington air gunners claimed several successes. A number of aircraft were equipped for electronic warfare, with Window fitted to most B-29s and 'Tinsel' jamming, the latter being a form of radio jamming of fighter R/T frequencies that had proved effective against the German night-fighter system.

Despite all of the operational activities, crews still found time to escape to the sun on Lone Ranger deployments. Number 90 Squadron sent Fg Off Conley and crew to Aden and Lagos (the first such deployment to Nigeria), the crew having just achieved Select status. The following month other overseas sorties went to Nicosia, Idris, and Habbaniya. However, most of the station's effort was being given over to formation flying rehearsals for the forthcoming Royal Review, scheduled for Odiham. Close formation in an aircraft like the Washington was no easy task, and to achieve the perfection required for this Royal event required hours of practice.

The Review took place on 15 July, the flypast being led by OC Flying Wing, Wg Cdr H. Wheeler, and each squadron putting up three aircraft. It was a most impressive sight as wave after wave of RAF aircraft flew over Odiham. On the ground a comprehensive static display included one B-29 from each of the Marham squadrons. Peter Morrey was one of the 115 Squadron crew that took WF562 down to Odiham: 'What was not often mentioned was the cleaning of aircraft using tins of "Duraglit" by air and ground crews before we went – only to fly through a rainstorm on the way down and having to do it all over again when we arrived!'

The Marham B-29 Wing was now an effective force, and the squadrons were happy with their aircraft. The luxury of the Washington, including such refinements as ashtrays, after the rustic interior of the Lincoln, made many aircrew keen to keep it in service. However, the type had been acquired under the MDAP purely as a stop-gap measure, and the V-bomber programme was proceeding at a reasonable pace. Thus, 1953 was also the year in which the run-down of Washington strength began. Op Order No. 3/53 gave details of Operation *Home Run* to 'return 37 B-29s, having become surplus to requirements, to the USA'. The plan was for 36 of the aircraft to go to Davis Monthan and the last one, WW347, to Oklahoma City.

With seven crew per aircraft, the planned route was Prestwick, Ernest Harmon AFB (Newfoundland) or Goose Bay, Dover AFB, and Davis Monthan. The schedule called for Flights of four aircraft to make the journey on various days from July to October. In the event the schedule was to be heavily modified, as aircraft were either not ready to go or the station was heavily committed with other tasks. Also, throughout this period the Washington squadrons had a number of important tasks to fulfil. The first series of returns went according to plan, the following waves departing Marham for the USA:

7 July – WW343, WF445, WF500, WF442;
22 July – WF437, WF498, WF443, WF546;
28 July – WF503, WF446, WF548, WF510.

Twelve more left in August, four each on the 11th, 18th, and 25th (WF571, WF504, WF501, WF492; WF494, WF512, WF511, WF507; and WF514, WF444, WF491, WF557).

That same month, three aircraft left Marham to position as support aircraft for the London to New Zealand Air Race, two going to Singapore and one to Negombo. The support schedule for this event was complex, as the RAF was determined that its Canberra entrants should have the best possible chance of winning. The requirement was for up to four Washingtons to be available at Shaibah, Singapore, Negombo, and Karachi for the period 1 September to 10 October.

Meanwhile, the round of exercises, such as *Momentum* and *Mariner* (a fleet interception exercise), continued to occupy much time. The Laurence Minot Trophy was retained by Marham,

the honours going this time to 115 Squadron, who duly received the Trophy from Lord Tedder in December. The station also retained the Avro Trophy. The RAF Marham report on Exercise Momentum provides a reasonable view of such exercise:

Exercise *Momentum,* 1953, was the annual Home Defence Exercise in which aircraft from Marham acted throughout in the role of attacking enemy bombers. Aircraft serviceability was good. There was no difficulty in meeting the aircraft commitments required but the limiting factor was the number of crews available, 8 crews being engaged on Operation 'Home Run' and 4 on leave. Every crew on the station flew on the operation on the 19th/20th.

Results

The only briefing materials available for blind bombing were $1/4$in topographical maps. This was most inadequate, especially for many targets that were in complex built-up areas, and therefore the bombing errors were rather larger than usual. The 50 per cent error for all the blind bombing attacks was 2,200 yd. The average error of four visual attacks, assessed by F24 camera photographs, was 330 yd.

It is appreciated that it will not always be possible to provide complete briefing material for attacks against tactical targets, which must often be ordered at short notice. However, this type of target would usually be an airfield, a bridge across a river, a small town, etc, which would give a fairly small and well defined radar response. An experienced radar operator should be able to attack such targets, without PPI photographs, with a reasonable degree of accuracy. Targets in complex built-up areas such as Birmingham or London are another matter. Such targets are not likely to be selected for tactical purposes. If they were, without proper briefing, a blind bombing attack against them would be ineffectual. The provision of briefing material would reduce the error manyfold and the saving in effort and expense of this increased accuracy would justify the most vigorous steps to obtain the best target information.

Combats

During the exercise the crews claimed 44 fighters. On 28 occasions the bombers were fired upon by the fighters. It should be borne in mind that the claims of fighter losses are made after the scanner merely sights and flashes an aldis lamp at the fighter before the latter flashes its lights. Were the scanners required to take aim at the fighters, using the gunsight, before claiming a kill, a process which might take several vital seconds, the claims of fighter losses would be less. Offset against this is the fact that the rear turret, the most suitable position for spotting an attack from the rear, cannot be used in most aircraft at high altitude because the Perspex panels frost over. The installation of an electric heater would eliminate this.

Tactics

The aircrew were remarkably enthusiastic during this exercise. This was due to the interesting and realistic routeing and the fact that on three days the aircraft stayed at bases in Germany. It is recommended that the latter tactics be used in future on simulated attacks against Great Britain. Although radar silence was ordered beyond 40 miles from the coast, it has been suggested that the use of radar may in future operations be restricted for protracted periods for tactical reasons. It might be of value to simulate these conditions on some future exercise to determine the effect on navigational accuracy.

Timing

The timing concentration point for each sortie was the target. As the navigation is assessed on the accuracy of this timing, the crew categories depend upon their being within very fine limits. To ensure reaching the target on time the navigators often have to keep several minutes in hand which they lose by dog-legging or reducing speed before the IP. This is unrealistic. Once inside enemy radar cover the bomber should go straight to the target. Doglegging or reducing speed increases the chance of a fighter attack. Furthermore, such preoccupation with timing at the target has an adverse effect on bombing accuracy. It is suggested that the concentration point should be positioned before the IP and after reaching it all aircraft should fly a predetermined speed to the target whilst adhering as closely as possible to the briefed track.

Even a brief examination of the above shows that the Command's tactics were, in general, still firmly based on those of Main Force, 1944. The bombing accuracy of 2,200 yd (almost 1.5 miles) sounds horrendous but, as the writer of the report stresses, this was largely due to the lack of target

preparation material. For a strategic and, especially, a pre-planned target, the crew would have radar predictions, offsets, and a whole wealth of material with which to achieve an accurate attack. This same basic policy existed throughout the later V-force period, the radar prediction being the most important element, allowing the radar navigator to compare this with his actual radar picture and thus deliver the weapons on target. As was often the case with these major exercises, the bombers were frequently seen as targets for the air defences, rather than as a central element of the plan. The B-29 Washington crews were convinced that they stood a reasonable chance against most Soviet fighters, which, rightly or wrongly, were still seen as being inferior to the NATO types. Thus, if they scored reasonably well against the NATO fighters, they would do even better against the Russians. They were also sure that, given reasonable conditions, they could reach and hit their targets.

On 19 September the station held its first Battle of Britain 'At Home' day since 1949. An impressive air and ground display was visited by over 10,000 people, and the flying display was most impressive:

14:00 Formation of four Canberras
14:19 Formation of nine F-86s
14:24 Formation of 24 Meteor F.8s
15:00 Hunter aerobatics
15:10 Formation of three Neptunes
15:15 Formation of 12 Meteor F.8s
15:25 Formation of four Canberras
Tea interval
15:55 F-84 aerobatics
16:00 Wyvern demonstration
16:05 Sea Hawk aerobatics
16:15 Demonstration GCA by four Meteor F.8s
16:23 Hunter aerobatics
16:30 Air defence – Canberra and Bofors
16:44 Formation of three Shackletons
16:55 Formation aerobatics by four Meteor F.8s
17:05 Hastings demonstration
17:15 F-86 demonstration
17:25 Canberra demonstration
17:40 Parachute drop by Rapide
17:45 Meteor T.7 aerobatics

It is strange that no Washingtons took part in the flying. The presence of the Canberras was, however, most appropriate, as it was with this aircraft that Marham was to re-equip upon the departure of the B-29. With the V-bombers still not due until the mid to late 1950s, it was essential that Bomber Command introduce the Canberra as soon as possible, both to give the Command experience with jet operations in readiness for the 'heavies' and to provide an interim improvement in overall capability. The Binbrook and Scampton Canberra Wings had already demonstrated the effectiveness of the English Electric bomber, although there were still many in the bomber hierarchy who regarded the role of these unarmed aircraft with concern.

A further three Washingtons were returned to the USA in October. As the numbers of B-29s dwindled, so the next generation arrived; the Jet Conversion Unit (JCU), commanded by Flt Lt D.H. Blomeley, was established at Marham late that same month. Responsible for converting squadrons to the Canberra, this unit used six Meteors to provide initial jet training. On 16 November the JCU accepted three pilots from 90 Squadron as the first Marham conversion course. A few days later Meteor VT282 landed wheels-up on runway 20, damaging both engine nacelles and wrecking a number of airfield lights. Jets were certainly very different from the B-29, and most pilots found it a great challenge – but also enormous fun. The Meteor was an excellent lead-in for the Canberra, as its widely-spaced engines enabled the demonstration and practise of asymmetric single-engined flying, the greatest Canberra handling problem.

Meanwhile, the departure of Washingtons to America continued apace, seven leaving in November and one in December. As January 1954 opened, Marham held 17 B-29s on strength; in the latter half of that month the first Canberras arrived, five B.2s being delivered (WH880, WH882, WJ731, WH870, and WJ995).

One of the most active units on the base was the Station Flight, which at this period was operating six Oxfords and a single Tiger Moth. In a typical month these aircraft would log well over 100 hr on communications duties and continuation flying for officers on staff appointments.

Operation *Home Run* had gone with hardly a snag, and during January a further 12 aircraft flew the Atlantic route home. Unfortunately, tragedy now struck. Flight Lieutenant Williams and crew left Marham in WF495 for the first stage to Prestwick. The aircraft left the Scottish base at 23:42 on 25 January. At 00:24 they sent the message: 'Fuselage vibration and severe icing, turning on to an easterly heading'. This was followed three minutes later by a garbled message that sounded like 'baling out'. Based on the expected flight plan, winds, timings, etc, it was calculated that the aircraft would have come down in the Morecambe Bay area. Marham launched three aircraft on search and rescue, a search that continued, along with other air and sea assets, for 30 hr in dreadful weather conditions. No trace of the seven crew was found. This was truly a tragic end to the Washington period. Peter Morrey was with 115 Squadron at the time: 'I was scheduled to be a member of that crew and had been issued with my kit, overseas bag etc and was delighted to have been chosen for the "jolly", but someone pulled rank and took my place, thus saving my life and losing his.'

By February all of the remaining B-29s at Marham were listed as with Disposal Flight. The final series of departures were made in February and March, the last aircraft, WF435, being ferried by a 35 Squadron crew on 30 March. A parade had been held two weeks earlier to mark the end of the period.

Canberra Wing

As a Canberra Wing base, Marham was designated as a night medium bomber station within Bomber Command's Main Force. The Command's original plan envisaged a force of 24 Canberra squadrons in six four-squadron Wings, the first of which had formed at Binbrook in 1952. After modification of the plan, Marham was the last of the Wings to re-equip, many of the others having given up the outdated Lincoln.

In the meantime, Canberra strength had been rapidly increasing, aircraft going to 90, 115 and 207 Squadrons. The JCU (now renamed Jet Conversion Flight (JCF)) had also increased its aircraft establishment to 12 Meteors as the pace of aircrew conversion accelerated. The Canberra squadrons were still declared as elements of Bomber Command Main Force, so the day-to-day training and exercise routine remained the same. Now, of course, the squadrons were much smaller. The Canberra carried a crew of three, compared with the Washington's ten, and the biggest postings problem was that of the air gunners, as with the demise of the Washington/Lincoln generation there was no longer a requirement for this trade. Crew classification was still the main driver of the squadron flying programme, although the main bombing techniques were now Gee-H and visual, as the Canberra was not radar equipped.

Above *A Canberra of 90 Squadron gets airborne for Exercise* Skyhigh.

Left *A fly-by of Canberras, led by a 35 Squadron six-ship.*

However, in all other respects it was great improvement over previous Bomber Command types. It could carry the same 6,000 lb bomb load as the B-29 Washington, but at a speed of 450 mph (Lincoln 290 mph and B-29 350 mph) and at a ceiling of 45,000 ft, some 10,000 ft better than that of the Washington.

As the final Bomber Command Wing, Marham received the standard four-squadron complement of B.2s, the official re-equipment dates being: 90 Squadron, November 1953; 115 Squadron, February 1954; 207 Squadron, March 1954; 35 Squadron, April 1954.

The Gee-H blind-bombing system was a development of the wartime version, and it continued to suffer many of the same problems of range and signal acquisition. A typical bomb run would require between 7 and 10 checkpoints equating to sighting angles for the bombsight. These, along with navigation checkpoints, were pre-calculated on the ground but often needed airborne amendment. When the system worked well the results were excellent, but this was often not the case. The 35 Squadron ORB records the generally held opinion:

> Considerable effort is being wasted on unsuccessful Gee-H attacks, both during exercises

and routine training. Much of this is caused by poor ground signals, the transmitter has on occasion only functioned at half power, and the inability of our ranges to plot the bombs.

Visual bombing, using the T2 to T4 series of bombsights, remained a standard technique, and Bomber Command Main Force employed the same general tactics that it had developed in 1944; an advance force of target markers dropping target indicators for the follow-on bombers to acquire. The majority of training sorties included both types of delivery, as the Canberras flew high-level sorties lasting about three hours. Statistical analysis of results showed that the Canberras achieved average errors of 575 yd (Gee-H) and 900 yd (visual) when bombing from 40,000 ft. The 1953 Bomber Command Classification Scheme called for crews to drop a minimum of 12 bombs visually within specified 50 per cent accuracy limits to achieve Combat, Select, or Select Star status. To achieve the same classification with radar bombing required up to 36 bombs.

The standard warload was six 1,000 lb bombs, and crews occasionally flew with this load to become familiar with aircraft handling and performance characteristics. In June 1954 two aircraft of 115 Squadron dropped a full warload on the Sandbanks range. The following April, during Exercise *Sky High*, a number of B.2s of 90 Squadron and 115 Squadron were each loaded with two 4,000 lb bombs which they then dropped on the range. This is one of the few recorded instances of this weapon being carried in the Canberra, and it was never declared part of the operational requirement. This does, however, prove how adaptable the aircraft could be.

In May 1954, 115 Squadron won the Bomber Command Efficiency Trophy, awarded to the squadron with the best all-round performance. During the assessment period the squadron had flown 3,480 hr, dropping 1,137 bombs using Gee-H and 1,148 using visual deliveries, the majority being 25 lb practice bombs. On a typical bombing exercise the unit was achieving averages of 102 yd when releasing from 30,000 ft. The engineers were able to carry out an Operational Turn Round (OTR) in about 20 min, and even that time was later improved upon as better ground handling equipment was introduced.

In its early years the Canberra suffered a number of problems, many of which were not the fault of the aircraft, but were due to lack of experience of high-powered-jet operations. Marham had its first accident with the type on 25 April 1954, when a Canberra crashed with the loss of Fg Off J. Wilkinson and his two crewmen. Five days later an aircraft returned with an undercarriage malfunction (no starboard main wheel), but the pilot was able to put it down on the runway with minimal damage.

Later the same year, on 3 December, WH906 of 207 Squadron crashed on approach to the runway, killing the three crew. Incidents were, nevertheless, few and far between considering the advanced nature of the aircraft's performance.

One of the rarer incidents occurred when WH905 lost part of its canopy while flying at 45,000 ft. In the ensuing explosive decompression the cockpit was filled with mist and the crew were blasted with oxygen. The pilot brought the aircraft back under control and made a rapid descent to a safer level before recovering to land at Kinloss.

Throughout the period the most common problem, and one that was to plague the aircraft throughout its career, concerned the tailplane actuators. There were a varity of failures, the most dangerous being a runaway tailplane which could cause a loss of control. At various times the Canberra force was grounded while modifications were made to the system.

Whilst disposing of some of its Oxfords, the Station Flight managed to acquire a number of de Havilland Chipmunks, the first, WF843, arriving in June 1954. The number increased during the early summer, but most of these were simply on loan for the period of the Air Training Corps summer camps. The Flight also acquired a Canberra T.4, WJ861, in early July (this aircraft has just returned to Marham; following the disbandment of 360 Squadron at Wyton in October 1994 it joined 39 Squadron).

By now the squadrons were well and truly operational and fully involved in major exercises. A typical example was Exercise *Dividend* in July, when the Canberras attacked the English Electric factory at Preston (where many of them had been built), a fuel store at Aldermaston, the Harwell ammunition factory, docks at Bristol, Liverpool, and Glasgow, and airfields such as Bruntingthorpe, Edzell, and Shawbury. All of these were typical of the strategic targets that Bomber Command had favoured since the 1930s.

Real proof that the new aircraft had established

Above *Julian Saker of 90 Squadron undertakes a spot of flight planning at Abu Sueir.*

Below *A rare shot of 90 Squadron Canberras. Note 'Golden Hind' motif on the fins.*

itself can be found in the hours total for a typical month. In July Marham flew 1,644 hr, 115 Squadron alone contributing 362 hr. The station's aircraft establishment was 34 Canberras, 7 Meteors, 3 Oxfords and 3 Chipmunks. Two months later the JCF disbanded, as all of the squadrons had a full strength of crews. Replacement crews would in future be provided by the new Operational Conversion Unit, 231 OCU, at Bassingbourn (this unit had formed in late 1951 and started No. 1 Course in May 1952). A number of the initial crews had in fact come through the OCU. In the case of 115 Squadron, for example, 10 crews were converted by the JCU from Washington aircrew, while a further seven pilots and seven navigators were 'imported' from 231 OCU.

The exercise tasks came thick and fast, a wide range of air defence exercises being flown throughout Europe; such names as *Coronet, Foxpaw, Phoenix, Marshmallow, Medflex Epic,* and *Green Pivot* feature in the squadron records. During most of these early 1950s' exercises the Canberras caused great difficulties for the defending fighters, few of whom were able to reach the operating heights being used by the bombers. Meteors, Venoms, and Sabres all struggled, much to the delight of the bomber crews: 'Against Sabres a steep climbing turn towards the fighter gave the Sabre great difficulty as it virtually stalled out of the turn. At height it was best to outrun it. Against the Venoms and Meteors, speed alone was sufficient.'

For most of the Canberra era the squadrons operated with an establishment of 10 aircraft, which usually meant that no more than six were available daily. However, serviceability was quite good, and crews were able to achieve reasonable flying hours. Most overseas trips, either exercises or Lone Rangers, were to Europe or the Middle East, the most popular venues in the latter case being Nicosia, Cyprus, and Luqa, Malta. Aircraft were frequently at Luqa for Exercise Sunspot. The squadrons tried to send one or two Lone Rangers away each month, although this very much depended on the exercise workload and the number of crews undergoing Classification.

As has already been seen, Marham was frequently plagued by fog, and this could have serious operational implications. A number of systems were tested to overcome this restriction, including renewing and redeveloping the wartime FIDO system, the basic concept of which was to burn fuel in troughs at the threshold and, in some cases, along the sides of the runway. The concept certainly worked, although it created its own problems, not least of which was the thermal effect from the fires and, if the fuel source was not clean, a veritable smog. In 1956 trials took place at Marham with a new system in an effort to make the procedure more effective, and cheaper. The records do not provide any more details, but FIDO was still in use many years later. In fact major work was carried out over the next five years, the station records detailing a number of tests on parts of the system, and expressing the expectation that the complete system would be working 'within months'.

V-Bomber Base

The Valiant, which made its maiden flight in May 1951, was the first of the V-bomber types to reach squadron service, going to 138 Squadron at Gaydon in January 1955. Powered by four Rolls-Royce Avon 204s, the aircraft had a crew of five, a bomb load of 21,000 lb (more than three times that of the Canberra), a top speed of some 560 mph, and a nominal range of over 4,000 miles. It was the kind of strategic weapon that the

bomber chiefs could understand!

The first of the Marham Valiant squadrons was 214 Squadron, its first B(PR).1s arriving in January 1956. The other two units had formed by the summer; 207 Squadron in April and 148 Squadron in July. Marham was one of the larger RAF stations, having a strength of 1,400 uniformed personnel, some 35 per cent of whom were National Servicemen. A large pig and arable farm was run by station personnel to provide raw materials for the Catering Squadron; pig farms were a common feature of RAF stations during this period.

The disposal of the Canberras was quite slow, there being 46 at the base in February, as Valiant strength gradually increased. That month became notorious in RAF history for the great Hunter farce, when the West Raynham Wing launched, expecting the foggy weather to improve. It did not, and of the eight Hunters diverted to Marham, where the weather was not a great deal better, only two landed safely, the other six crashing when they ran out fuel. Fortunately only one pilot was killed.

By April the number of Valiants had only risen to eight, and three of these took part in a flypast for the distinguished Russian visitors who flew

Bulganin and Khrushchev visit Marham, 23 April 1956.

into Marham on the 23rd. Marshal Bulganin and Mr Krushchev toured the station and were treated to displays by a Hunter and Canberra, in addition to the Valiant formation. Included in the Russian party was A.N. Tupolev; no doubt the Valiant would have appealed to this great bomber designer.

Just as 214 Squadron was getting to grips with its new aircraft they were grounded pending investigation into the loss of a Farnborough aircraft.

More of the squadrons were re-equipping, and, to bring the Canberra era to an end, 90 Squadron disbanded on 1 May 1956 and 35 Squadron moved to Upwood in mid-July. July also saw Her Majesty Queen Elizabeth visiting Marham to present 207 Squadron with a new standard. Part of the day's events included a fly-by comprising no fewer than 72 Canberras and 20 Valiants.

Throughout the summer the squadrons concentrated on familiarization with their new aircraft. A good deal of attention was devoted to formation flying, with a planned appearance at the 1956 SBAC display at Farnborough in mind. Unfortunately this participation was cancelled.

Without doubt, the most significant episode of this era was the station's involvement in the 1956 Suez War. The rising tide of Arab nationalism brought many problems to the British in the post-war Middle East, and from 1945 onwards there seemed to be one crisis after another. With the withdrawal of British forces from Palestine,

A V-bomber line-up, June 1964.

Jordan, and certain areas of the Persian Gulf, the centre of RAF activity became the air bases in the 'Canal Zone' of Egypt, the main ones being those such as Kabrit and Fayid, near the Suez Canal. However, the growing power of certain factions within Egypt, with their calls for the British to leave the country, was certain to create problems. The rise to power of Nasser, who became president of Egypt in 1956, led to direct confrontation.

Nasser's announcement on 26 July 1956 that the Suez Canal had been 'nationalized', and would henceforth be controlled by Egyptians, was the final straw for many politicians in Britain and France, and brought calls for military intervention to remove this 'Hitlerite dictator'. It was obvious, however, that no direct move could be made, as this would, without doubt, bring censure in the United Nations (UN). The solution adopted by the Anglo-French politicians was to enter into a secret agreement with Israel over military action in the event of an Arab-Israeli conflict. Such a conflict was never far below the surface.

War broke out with an Israeli attack in Sinai, and Britain and France called for *both* parties to withdraw from the Canal Zone to allow an international administration to take control of this vital economic waterway. When Egypt failed to agree to this demand, the Anglo-French military option, Operation *Musketeer,* was put into action. The major role envisaged for air power was the neutralization of the Egyptian Air Force, which, on paper, was quite powerful.

Within the overall air task force, Bomber Command contributed 11 Canberra and four Valiant squadrons. Among the latter were the three Marham units, even though they had only recently re-equipped. The Canberra forces deployed to Cyprus (B.2 variants) and Malta (longer-range B.6 variants), while the Valiants also went to Malta. Under Operation Albert the Valiants formed part of the Malta Bombing Wing in September 1956. On the 24th the Marham Station Commander, Gp Capt L. Hodges, arrived to become the force commander. By late October all of the Valiants (six from 148 Squadron under Wg Cdr W. Burnett, six from 207 Squadron under Wg Cdr D. Haig, and four from 214 Squadron under Wg Cdr L. Trent, plus eight from 138 Squadron) were in place, and bomb stocks had been prepared. Crews underwent a number of briefings on the threat posed by the Egyptian Air Force (which was not inconsiderable, as it had a reasonable number of modern jet fighters) and the nature of the likely targets, the leading one being that self-same air force. A postwar RAF study stated the major aims:

> The original plan called for destruction of the Egyptian Air Force as the first priority and it was considered that this might be achieved in about two days. The plan envisaged night bombing attacks to crater the runways, followed up at dawn by ground attack strikes to destroy the aircraft. Little opposition was expected. This phase of the operation went according to plan, in its final outcome, if not in its detailed execution.

The Valiants were to be targeted against five airfields, to counter the following Egyptian Air Force Order of Battle:

Fayid   – 9 Meteors, 12 Vampires
Kabrit   – 31 MiG-15s;
Almaza   – 24 MiG-15s, 4 Meteors, 21 Vampires, 10 Il-28s;
Cairo West – 9 Vampires, 16 Il-28s;
Abu Sueir   – 35 MiG-15s.

Marham Op Order 7/56, dated 11 October, had outlined the requirement to:

. . . deploy Valiant aircraft and support aircrew and servicing personnel to Malta on a rotational basis. Valiants to be fitted with full operational equipment, including:

4 x multi carriers
6 x light series bomb racks
NBS
Green Satin
T2/T3 sighting heads
5 x Mk.1 survival packs (desert)

This deployment was under a combined *Goldflake/Albert* requirement. One of the major problems with the Valiants at this stage was the state of their bombing equipment. The NBS was designed to integrate the H_2S Mk.9A with the Navigational Ballistic Computers (NBC), but production delays meant that many aircraft did not yet have the correct radar fitted. The fitting of an old T2/T3 visual bombsight was all very well, but this was not how the system was designed to operate. Trials had suggested that this temporary expedient was all right if the sighting angles were calculated on the run-in using Green Satin drift and groundspeed data. It was by no means ideal, but was probably workable if the target-area weather was good.

207 Squadron crews brief for a bombing sortie during the Suez crisis.

Marham Valiant crews debrief after a Suez mission.

On 30 October the BBC broadcast a warning to Egyptians to stay clear of all military targets, as these were likely to be bombed in the next 24 hours.

During the opening wave of attacks, on the night of 30 October/1 November, the Valiants bombed three of the airfields; Almaza, Kabrit, and Abu Sueir. Six Valiants plus 14 Canberras went to Almaza with a time over target (TOT) of 19:00z. The first flares from the markers went down over Heliopolis, and the TIs were dropped on the western hardstands some 1,000 yards from the nominated aiming point. A second marker dropped TIs closer to the aiming point and called the bombers to drop on the most eastern set of TIs. Bombing was scattered, the Valiants attacking from 42,000 ft with free-fall bombs and no truly integrated bombsight. Light AA fire was observed, but it was no threat.

During the attack on Almaza one of the bombers was intercepted by a fighter. Squadron Leader Trevor Ware made light of the incident: 'It was a Meteor NF.13. There was no actual shooting as he could not hold on to us. We climbed out of his range and he flew away below.' Because of the poor marking, the 50 per cent error circle was 1,550 yd, and only one runway was hit, suffering superficial damage. It was a similar story at the other two airfields; although the accuracy was better, damage was light.

It was airfields again the following night, attacks being made against Cairo West, Fayid, and Kasfareet. Damage was again light and at Cairo West, the major Il-28 base and therefore an important target, and the enemy bombers had already flown out to Luxor. On the night of the 2nd/3rd, seven Valiants attacked Huckstep Barracks, the same target being hit again two nights later, along with the coastal batteries on El Agami Island. On both of the Huckstep attacks the markers were well placed and bombing was reasonably concentrated, but at El Agami most bombers did not drop because the TIs were snuffed out, probably having fallen into the sea. Although many of the targets were defended by AAA, this was usually light and almost always well below the aircraft.

Pressure in the UN, at the instigation of the USA, led to a call for military action to be terminated, and the Suez War fizzled out.

The total Bomber Command effort during the campaign amounted to 49 Valiant and 278 Canberra sorties. In the post-conflict analysis the contribution of these aircraft was suggested to have been of limited value, the credit for the destruction of the EAF being given to the tactical fighter-bombers. This in its barest sense is a true assessment, but with the restrictions imposed upon the bombers, such as the use of 1,000 lb bombs at the maximum, meant that they were hardly likely to achieve great success in damaging airfield surfaces and facilities. By 8 November the squadrons had returned to Marham, but they continued to hold standby until the end of the month.

Although 115 Squadron did not join with the other Bomber Command Canberra squadrons, it did provide crews as part of Operation Alacrity. During November nine crews were made available each day as part of the Honington Wing, with a view to relieving aircrew of 10, 15 and 44 Squadrons should the need arise. This continued throughout the month, and then, in early December, orders came to deploy eight aircraft to Nicosia under *Reinforced Alacrity*, to be in place by the 18th.

Returning early in 1957, the squadron resumed its training and task commitments, the latter including exercise *Ratchet,* working with HMS *Girdle-Ness*, the Royal Navy's guided weapons experimental ship. The writing was on the wall for the disbandment of the squadron, but they managed one last 'good deal' with a deployment in May To Malta for *Medflex Epic* and *Green Pivot,* the main aim being to attack the American Sixth Fleet. Then came the end, recorded by the Squadron Commander, Sqn Ldr South:

> On return from Malta, the Squadron prepared itself for disbandment on June 1st. With the disbandment of the Squadron, Canberra operations from Marham will cease. The disbandment of 115 Squadron, which has such a close association with Marham, since the squadron re-formed here in 1937, is an occasion of great sadness. Let us hope then, that it will not be long before the Squadron is revived.

It was certainly true that, for much of their respective histories, the squadron and station had been closely connected.

Meanwhile, Marham's Valiant squadrons settled into the standard Bomber Command routine of conversion, standardization, station/Group/Command exercises, and a variety of overseas deployments. The aircraft were capable of toting a variety of bombs, and loading tests were frequent – including the biggest conventional bomb still in the inventory, the 10,000-pounder. A standard load comprised 21 1,000 lb bombs, but the Valiant could also take the latest nuclear weapons.

The annual SAC competition was always a high-profile event, and in 1957 the Valiants were invited to participate for the first time. They achieved a creditable 47th out of 90.

In the 1958 competition, held in October, the number of participants was up to 164 crews, of which 156 were American. Squadron Leader R. Richardson's crew came 9th, and Air Vice Marshal Cross commented:

> Last year we were regarded as welcome guests. This year we were thought of as very stiff opposition. The SAC has over 2,000 atom bomber crews to choose from and the 156 they choose are the pick of their crews. All our teams made a tremendous impression by their efficiency and organization on the ground and by the way they carried out their operations in the air. Several American Generals flew as observers in our aircraft and when I went out there to see them they were full of praise.

The competition entailed crews making three simulated A-bomb attacks in a single night on San Jose (California), Boise (Montana), and Batte (Montana), followed by an 800-mile cross-country route using astro navigation. The accuracy of the bombing was assessed by ground stations that monitored release signals generated by the bomber.

The major 'good deal' of 1957 was the goodwill visit to Ghana (Gold Coast) as part of the independence celebrations. It was appropriate for Marham to be involved, as it had been one of the wartime bases of 218 (Gold Coast) Squadron. The four Valiants departed on 6 March for Accra, accompanied by the AOC, Air Vice Marshal Keith Cross. A number of flying displays were given, and the visit was voted a huge success by all involved, on both sides. Aircraft were now ranging far and wide, frequent trips being made to the Middle and Far East. An example of the latter was Operation *Profiteer,* to Changi. Locations in Europe included just about every airfield; *Polar Bear* deployments often used Gardemoen in Norway, while Lone Rangers visited Ahlhorn, El Adem, and Idris (Libya), and countless other destinations.

The Valiant was also proving adept at picking up unofficial records, 214 Squadron laying claim to four during 1959:

The 207 Squadron Ranger to Ghana for the independence celebrations.

7 April   London to Nairobi, 4,350 miles in 7 hr 40
           min (Sqn Ldr B. Fern)
28 May   London to Salisbury, 5,320 miles in 9 hr
           42 min (Sqn Ldr J. Garstin)
18 June   London to Johannesburg, 5,848 miles in
           11 hr 3 min (Wg Cdr M. Beetham)
9 July   London to Capetown, 6,060 miles in 11
           hr 28 min (Wg Cdr M. Beetham)

In 1960, 214 Squadron, and the crew of Sqn Ldr J. Garstin in particular, took a number of distance and time records as part of this unit's growing air-to-air refuelling (AAR) role, 214 being the RAF's nominated AAR trials and development unit. At 18:00 on the evening of Wednesday 7 March this crew took off from Marham to fly an endurance sortie, the primary aim being to test the effects of such a sortie on aircraft and crew. The first AAR took place at midnight, and the crew settled into a routine of flying a route around the UK, meeting up with a Valiant tanker at a number of planned rendezvous. They landed back at Marham 18 hr 5 min later, having flown a route of 8,500 miles. The previous endurance record had been a 'mere' 11 hr 28 min. The same pilot was in the news again in June, with a record breaking flight to Singapore; 760 miles in 15 hr 35 min. Not

content with that, he also took the record for a flight to Aden, covering the distance in 7 hr 10 min on 17 November.

There was an increasing emphasis on alert and readiness exercises during the late 1950s and early 1960s. The three-day Exercise *Mayflight* in May 1959 had the aim of 'practising to the limit of the resources available the procedures for the Bomber Command Alert and Readiness (BCAR) plan, including the dispersal of aircraft'. It was the standard routine in 'time of tension' for vital assets to disperse to other airfields. In this instance, 207 Squadron sent aircraft to Filton and Yeovilton. In recognition of Marham's vital position in the Bomber Command deterrent network, the station was given a squadron of Bloodhound surface-to-air missiles (SAMs), 242 Squadron.

September 1959 brought the tragic loss of Valiant XD869 of 214 Squadron. After departing for a Nairobi ranger, the aircraft crashed shortly after take-off with the loss of all six crew.

There was never a shortage of competitions, and almost every month crews were either preparing for or taking part in such events. Typical of the regular ones was the Bomber Command Bombing and Navigation Competition '. . . to further the competitive spirit within the

Valiant mutual air-to-air refuelling from XD870 to WZ390.

Valiant WZ390, with the Bloodhound missiles of 264 Squadron in the background, June 1961.

medium bomber force and give recognition to the units and individuals who obtain the most accurate bombing and navigation results under certain defined conditions'. In the 1959 event the best Marham unit was 207 Squadron, who came fourth overall.

Operational strength was increased on 26 June 1961, with the transfer from Wittering of 49 Squadron. This unit had been operating Valiants since May 1956, and in October of that year WZ366 had carried out the first release of a British operational atom bomb during trials at Maralinga, Australia.

The station now had 35 Valiants on strength, three B.1s, four B(PR).1s, three B(PR)K.1s, and 24 B(K)1s, and all of the squadrons were operational. From 1961 onwards Marham's units held nuclear quick-reaction alerts (QRAs), and scrambles became a regular feature of life, to ensure that crews were able to get airborne within the critical few minutes available in the event of a pre-emptive ballistic-missile attack.

207 Squadron display the Laurence Minot Trophy and Armament Trophy in June 1960.

So the routine continued into the 1960s, until, in August 1964, serious metal fatigue was discovered in the Valiants' wing spars. In the following January, the ORB writer expressed 'The Valiant Story' very well:

The story of the decline and fall of the Valiant force began on 6 August 1964 and ended on 26 January 1965. Between these dates there had been a period of restricted flying and another in which the grounded aircrew drew on their experience alone for the ability to deliver their weapons in war. Inspection of WP217 after landing at Gaydon on 6 August showed only too plainly that the aircraft had suffered major damage. The fuselage skin below the starboard inner plane had buckled, popping the rivets; the engine door had cracked on the top surface of the mainplane between the two engines, the rivets had been pulled and the skin buckled. The primary cause of the damage was a broken rear spar on the starboard side. All Valiants of a similar age and life pattern were grounded forthwith. By 25 August a manufacturer's working party had been set up to discover the extent to which the Valiant fleet was affected by metal fatigue, and on 17 September XD818 was given an 'A' category, and by the 21st fifteen other Valiants had been categorized. Eventually all the Valiants were divided into three categories:

Cat A – flyable to 95 per cent of remaining fatigue life – 12
Cat B – flyable in an emergency – 19
Cat C – grounded – 5

For a time only the Valiants of Cat A flew again, but eventually some Cat B aircraft were also cleared for limited flying. Each aircraft was fitted with recorders and a most assiduous watch was kept on the readings in order, if possible, to relate fatigue co-efficient to heights and weather conditions. The SACEUR [Supreme Allied Commander, Europe] QRA commitment was maintained throughout. In the meantime two aircraft in Category B were given up to teams from 19 MU who literally hacked out with axes sections of the spars for further examination by metallurgical experts. After further inspection of these parts all the aircraft were grounded on 11 December 1964, from which date until January 1965 the QRA force continued but no flying took place. Aircrews embarked upon a period of intense and varied ground training and interest visits.

The AOC 3 Group, AVM M. Dwyer, briefs the crew for the Marham-to-Singapore flight of 25/26 May 1960.

On 26 January 1965 the long-awaited and much-postponed announcement was received at Marham – by permission of BBC radio and television. Not until 1730 hr, when most personnel had gone home for the night, was an official signal received. This authorized the disbandment of 214 Squadron, cessation of QRA and the ending of all Valiant training.

The official news and the MOD announcement

AVM D. Spotswood dedicates Valiant XD818 as a 'gate guard' at Marham on 25 May 1965.

The Valiant fleet meets the scrapman.

was numbing in both its effect on Marham and its matter-of-factness. Marham's contribution to NATO, which was by far the most powerful and reliable of any RAF station, was dismissed, and great play was made about the loss of tankers. There was no doubt at Marham or at SHAPE

[Supreme HQ Allied Powers Europe] which was the greater loss.

The first to go was 207 Squadron, which disbanded on 1 March; the other three squadrons followed on 1 May. Marham's role in the era of the strategic deterrent was over.

VICTOR
TANKERS

Although 214 Squadron had been pioneers in the AAR business, they were not the first unit to acquire the new Handley Page Victor tanker aircraft. The decision to retire the Victor from the bomber role and use it to replace the Valiant tankers was taken in the early 1960s, and it was one of these bomber squadrons, 55 Squadron, that received the first Victor B(K).1A conversions. The first of these two-point tankers entered service in June 1965, the squadron having arrived at Marham the previous month. Mid-1965 also saw the formation of a Tanker Training Flight (TTF) to provide crews for the planned Tanker Wing.

In May the 55 Squadron ORB noted:

The re-equipment with two-point tankers is an interim measure only and at a later date these aircraft will be withdrawn and replaced with the more versatile three-point tankers. The two-point tanker does not permit Victor to Victor refuelling operations and is a severe limitation to the squadron's long-range capabilities.

A few months later, in December, a second Victor squadron, No. 57, formed at Marham, the advance party of this squadron having arrived in mid-November and taken over No. 1 Hangar. They received the first examples of the three-

The first Victor tankers arrive, July 1965.

Victor XL513 after suffering a birdstrike on take-off, 28 September 1976.

point K.1 variant in January 1966. Conversion of the bomber aircraft to AAR capability was carried out by Avro at Woodford, who produced six B(K).1As, ten K.1s, and 14 K.1As.

As at 1 January 1966, Marham's role was defined as that of 'an operational base within Bomber Command', having two operational squadrons, 55 and 57, plus a Tanker Training Flight and Station Flight. The aircraft establishment comprised six B(K).1As (XH615, '620, '646,

'647, '648, and '667), eight B.1As (XH589, '591, '592, '593, '594, '614, '616, and '619), and three B.1s (XA930, '933, and '940), plus an Anson C.1 (VV964) with the Station Flight. With Gp Capt P.A. Kennedy, DSO DFC AFC as Station Commander, personnel strength stood at 208 officers, nine airmen aircrew, and 1,220 airmen.

One of the most frequent overseas exercises was *Forthright*, the standard name for a trail to the Mediterranean/Middle East region, with air-

Victor XH587 during the author's visit to Marham (as an ATC cadet) in the mid-1960s.

The first three-point tanker, XA937, arrives on 14 February 1966.

craft often deploying to Luqa or Akrotiri. The other common events were Western Rangers to Goose Bay and a fair smattering of Lone Rangers, the latter taking in a variety of locations, although the Middle East and Mediterranean appear most frequently, just as they had with the Canberras and Valiants.

Under *Forthright* the Victors also deployed British Aircraft Corporation aircraft to their destinations, and such was the case in July 1966, when *Forthright* 55 was used to take two Lightnings to the Saudi Air Force.

The AAR world was very much an expanding one, and with the new tankers came the requirement to conduct trials on techniques and suitability. One example was Operation *Jake* in February, concerning compatibility trials with the USAF F-100 Super Sabres at Lakenheath. The initial ground tests revealed no problems. This was only one of a number of trials that summer. On other occasions the Aeroplane and Armament Experimental Establishment (A&AEE) undertook tests at West Freugh to investigate the stability of the centre hose and, in September, XH168 was involved in trials with the Vickers VC.10.

The summer of 1966 also saw the Marham aircraft having to operate from Honington, as the runway was undergoing yet another resurfacing.

On 7 October the OC of 57 Squadron touched down in XA928 to 'christen' the new surface. Movements of Lightnings provided major tasks for the Victors, and almost every month there was a squadron to move from one place to another, the short-ranged fighter needing a tanker to go almost anywhere outside the UK. Codenames for these operations varied, a typical example being the deployment under Exercise *Horwich* 1 and 2 of Lightnings to Masirah in November.

Meanwhile, the third and final squadron for the Marham tanker Wing, 214 Squadron, received the first of its new aircraft in July. Most of the crews had already served on the Valiant squadron, and were experienced in AAR. The routine of deployments and training continued into 1967, with the three tanker squadrons carrying out a similar range of tasks. The major events for the year were Jake 67 (the F-100s working with the K.1As), Operation *Hydraulic* to deploy 13 Lightnings to Tengah in June, Exercise *Fawn* to deploy 111 Squadron to Rygge in Norway, *Malayan Litex*, and *Levant Litex*. The major trial that year was Exercise *Pint Vessel*, in which two aircraft detached to Edwards AFB in July to work with the YF-4K Phantom along with McDonnell Douglas. This detachment, led by Wg Cdr Hall, OC 57 Squadron, arrived at Edwards on 6 July and, after the usual ground compatibility tests, undertook a number of air-to-air sorties, all of which went without a hitch. The only other change to Marham's status during 1967 was its transfer to No. 1 Group, No. 3 Group having disbanded on 1 November.

Tanking by day is a tricky enough business, but doing it at night is a whole new ball game; the fast jet materializes out of the pitch black into the lit world around the tanker. Perspectives are very different, and the first sortie is, to say the least, interesting. The night AAR trials with the Lightning took place in January 1968, and most pilots soon adjusted to the new techniques. Most British fast jets were equipped for AAR, so the Victors were involved with a variety of types, all of which undertook regular training using the AAR areas in various parts of the UK. Regular training was essential, so that when it came to a long-range deployment or fighter intercept the crews were proficient in the techniques. Exercise *Recast* in April 1967 saw the deployment phase of naval aircraft involved on Exercise *Crayon*, 12 Sea Vixens of 893 Squadron and nine Buccaneers of 801 Squadron being involved. So the year progressed, with the workload always being high. July was a typical month for Marham, with the following major tasks:

Forthright 82, 83 and 84;
Malayan, Island, and *Levant Litex*;
Western Tankex Ranger;
Far East Air Force (FEAF) Tankex Ranger;
Operation *Magic Palm* 1 and 2 (deployment of BAC Lightnings to Saudi);
Western Ranger;
Exercise *Heartease* (deployment of 29 Squadron to Grossetto, Italy).

These were the routine matters, but with the increasing appreciation of the complexity of the NATO task, the station was involved in more and more 'war' exercises. As one of the Class A airfields with bomber facilities, Marham was a dispersal base for elements from other stations, including Waddington's Vulcans. During major alerts such as *Mickey Finn*, four of the delta-winged bombers would appear at Marham to hold nuclear readiness from the ORP. The station also received dispersed reconnaissance assets of Victors and Canberras from Wyton. One of the major tasks for the home-based units was to provide K.1As for Airborne Command Post (ACP) duties.

There were no appreciable differences in the routine in 1969. The only special event for the year was the support provided for the *Daily Mail* Transatlantic Air Race. This event was organized

XH672 at Marham in August 1993.

to commemorate the 50th anniversary of the original non-stop crossing by Alcock and Brown. Training started in April, with Victors working with the Royal Navy's F-4 Phantom entry, code-named 'Royal Blue', and the RAF's Harrier entry, codenamed 'Blue Nylon'. Both required the use of a high-speed drogue, the fuel transfer being planned for Mach 0.88. The F-4 approached the rendezvous at Mach 1.5 – somewhat faster than the usual join-up. All of the procedures were rehearsed, and the control ship HMS *Nubian*, which would be stationed in mid-Atlantic to help effect the join-up, was brought into the training routine. On 28 April the Victors took the Harrier that was to make the west-to-east attempt over to the USA, using the opportunity to run through the techniques that would be used during the actual race.

The first race, the east-to-west stage, took place on 5 May, and the Harrier flown by Sqn Ldr T. Lecky-Thompson won with a time of 6 hr 11 min 57 sec. Eight tankers were involved in this stage of the race; four from 214 Squadron, three from 57, and one from 55. The west-to-east race four days later was more closely contested. The Harrier flown by Sqn Ldr G. Williams lost by a mere 30 sec to a Victor SR.2 (with a time of 5 hr 49 min 58 sec).

While this was an interesting venture, it was of limited operational value in the NATO sense. With Exercise *High Noon* in July 1969, Marham was called upon for the first time to generate tanker assets as well as the ACP. The integration of the tanker force into the 'war plan' was to play an increasingly important part in the day-to-day life of the squadrons. Operation *Dragonfly* in October called for two aircraft to deploy to Leuchars to hold readiness. The same type of exercise was extended under the title *Dragonfly Mobile* to test the flexibility of the tanker forces. Typical of the latter requirement was that of 27 February 1970:

On 27 February, Flt Lt G. Mason in Victor XA936 was tasked for Operation *Dragonfly Mobile* whilst receiver training with Flt Lt G. Farlam in Victor XA937, both of 214 Squadron. Flight Lieutenant Mason took all available fuel from Flt Lt Farlam and proceeded north to RV with a pair of Lightnings under control of Buchan. Having made the RV the formation was vectored well out over the North Sea where successful interceptions were effected, thus successfully completing the operation before returning to Leuchars, where the tanker as well as the Lightnings landed.

Without an airborne fuel station, the operational radius and time on station of the Lightning was

Initial checks on XH669.

very poor. In the air defence scenario of Russian bombers approaching over the North Sea to launch stand-off weapons it was thus essential that the twin elements of fighter and tanker be able to work together at all times and at short notice.

Major deployments required a complex trail plan. The movement of ten of 54 Squadron's Phantoms to Tengah, Singapore, for Exercise *Bersatu Padu* in May 1970 involved the setting-up of a tanker chain, nine Victors deploying to the airfields at Akrotiri, Masirah, and Gan; three to each location. The first pair of F-4s departed at midnight on the 6th, carrying out a number of AAR brackets to land at Masirah. The second and third pairs flew direct from the UK to Singapore as part of the demonstration that, even with the British withdrawal from the Far East (the disbandment of FEAF being planned for 1971), the RAF could have combat aircraft in theatre in a matter of hours.

That same month the TTF disbanded, but re-formed the same day as 232 OCU.

The standard routine continued through the early 1970s, each of the fast-jet types being given its own 'Trail' designation: *Panther Trail* (Lightning), *Ghost Trail* (Phantom), *Leopard Trail* (Jaguar), *Hawk Trail* (Harrier), *Pirate Trail*

(Buccaneer), and *Storm Trail* (Tornado) (1980s). All of them, apart from the Lightning, are pretty obvious.

Panther Trail N96 of February 1973 was typical:

> To deploy one Lightning F.6 from Binbrook to Akrotiri on 9 February completed on schedule. Two tankers took off to support this operation. One tanker gave two fuel transfers to the fighter and returned to Marham; the second tanker gave a third transfer and landed at Akrotiri where it remained for a planned *Levant Litex*. Subsequently it was also used as a reserve for Phantom Trail N72, recovering to Marham on 23 February.

The Lightning was a thirsty beast, and needed a high degree of tanker support. Moving four F.4s to Luqa later in the month only took two tankers.

A great deal of time was spent undertaking AAR training on the various refuelling towlines around the UK. The tankers spent many hours on mutual tanking, as well as providing a service for a multitude of fast jets.

A press release of 1974 described a typical mission:

> Dotted around the shores of the United

Victor servicing.

Kingdom are six 'towlines', imaginary patterns drawn on a map which are used for refuelling exercises. The sortie is going to use towline 6 and the RV time is 1600 hr . . . Flying clothing is checked, the crew have a pre-flight meal and go out to the Victor about one hour before take-off. The Air Electronics Officer is first into the aircraft and he checks all the electrical systems on board. About 20 minutes before take-off the four Rolls-Royce Sapphire engines thunder into life and are warmed up. Air Traffic Control gives clearance to taxy to the end of the runway.

"100 per cent – call me 93 per cent." As the power rises through the 90s, the Captain does a pre-rolling check.

"93 per cent", says the co-pilot, the Captain checks that the brakes are holding.

The co-pilot sets 100 per cent and checks that the engines are within limits. "100 per cent – engines checked."

"Brakes off – rolling," replies the Captain.

"60 knots."

"90 knots."

"Decision."

"Rotate" – and the Victor is airborne.

. . . The Victor arrives on the towline and awaits the arrival of the Lightnings. As the receiver closes with the tanker, the Captain confirms the details of the type of RV, flight level and speed. The Lightnings appear below the tanker.

"Delta 61; visual contact with the tanker."

"61 clear to join on the port."

The two Lightnings, call-signs Delta 61 and 62, join the tanker on the left side.

"61 cleared astern the starboard . . . 62 cleared astern the port."

The Lightnings move into position behind the trailing hoses as the Victor radar navigator watches them through his periscope.

"61 clear contact starboard, wet to full."

The Lightning edges forward until its probe clicks into the basket and fuel starts to flow. The same procedure is followed by Delta 62. Both remain in contact until their tanks are full.

"61, 62 – clear to break."

The Lightnings drop back clear of the drogues and move to the port side of the Victor before clearing the area.

It sounds a very simple procedure, and at times it can be simple. Pull up behind the basket and stick the probe into the drogue, take your fuel

A superb airborne study of the front half of a Victor.

The first Victor K.2 touches down, 7 May 1974.

and go away again. Some pilots seem to have nat-ural ability when it comes to jousting with the basket, others find it the hardest task they have to face, and some simply cannot do it at all. The good book says that the approved technique is to establish a good 'waiting position' behind the basket and, when cleared for contact, ease the aircraft forward, using reference points on the tanker and NOT looking at the basket, with just the right amount of overtake to make a solid con-tact. Too hard a push and there is a great danger of the hose bending and, in an extreme circum-stance, breaking, with all sorts of possible dire consequences. Fast jets have been known to return home with a basket and piece of hose attached to their probe. Too soft a hit on the bas-ket and the fuel will flow around the probe and not into it; spectacular to watch but not very effective. It can be great sport to sit out on the wing of the Victor, having taken your own fuel, and watch the next guy having a good joust.

With the air defence aircraft holding 'Q' (QRA) it was essential to have tankers ready to go to their support at a moment's notice. This was the pur-pose of the *Dragonfly Static* and *Mobile* exercises that we have already outlined. The Soviet long-

Geoff Parnell, an ex-214 Squadron Stirling rear gunner, adapts the tail of a Victor, May 1974.

A chariot race during the September 1975 Families Day was won by 214 Squadron.

range forces regularly visited the UK airspace to test the air defence reaction, and were always met by a fighter. Typical of such events in 1974 was that on the night of 16/17 May. Flight Lieutentant Thomas and crew of 55 Squadron were scrambled at 22:06, met up with the fighter and went off over the North Sea, but with no result. Just over an hour later, Flt Lt Barrett and crew of 214 Squadron went on a similar mission, resulting in the interception of a Bear 'Delta' and Bear 'Foxtrot'. At some stage in the late 1970s the codename for this standby was changed to Tansor.

A short-notice requirement to deploy Phantoms to Akrotiri arose in July 1974 as a result of the invasion of Cyprus by Turkish forces. The first aircraft flew out of Marham on the 22nd. The Phantoms were brought back to the UK in early September.

October saw the last flight by the Victor B.1As of 232 OCU when XH592 and 593 were delivered to Cosford.

March 1975 was clouded by the loss of an aircraft over the North Sea on the 24th. Four of the crew were killed, but the fifth crewman, Flt Lt K.

A picture taken during the Royal College of Defence Studies visit in June 1975 shows the 'waterfront' to good effect. Of the 12 types on show, six are now out of service.

57 Squadron Victor on Tansor. (Paul McKernan)

Handscomb, managed to bale out.

November saw the disappearance of the Victor SR.2s and a series of trials with the new BAC Multirole Combat Aircraft (destined to become the Tornado and, in that guise, to play a major role in the Marham story). It was a busy month with a number of special tasks. October brought Exercise *Sea Trek*, an intensive session with US Navy pilots from the USS *Independence* who were working up for Exercise Ocean Safari. The same month brought Magic Sword and work with the Buccaneers from HMS *Ark Royal*.

The tired Victor K.1As were retired in this same period, being replaced by the more powerful K.2 variant for service with 55 Squadron, which had officially 're-formed' as a K.2 unit in July. The new variant had been converted from the Rolls-Royce Conway powered B.2s, the tanker modification including a reduction of wingspan to 113 ft to improve fatigue life. Although the K.2s were not seen as a long-term solution to the AAR requirement, other types being under consideration by the MoD, this was a wise move, as the type was to serve for another 20 years and take part in two conflicts.

The next major change, however, was the disbandment of 214 Squadron on 28 January 1977. The demise of this pioneering unit was greatly regretted.

Canberras Return

After a break of 20 years, Canberras returned to Marham once more with the arrival, in January 1976, of 100 Squadron from West Raynham. In

AVM P. Lagesen, AOC 1 Group, meets the Marham Bull on 27 April 1976; good material for a caption contest!

Canberras of 231 OCU depart Cottesmore for Marham, July 1982.

fact the first aircraft, WH666, had arrived on 26 December the previous year. The squadron had formed out of 85 Squadron as a target facilities unit, and was equipped with eleven Canberra B.2s, two E.15s, two T.4s, and two T.19s. These numbers were to change later in the year with the acquisition of four more E.15s and the departure of four of the B.2s.

The following month Marham acquired the Canberras of 231 OCU when they moved from Cottesmore on 18 February to allow that airfield to prepare for the Tornado Training Unit. Life for the OCU continued as normal at Marham, the unit running short and long courses using four T.4s and two or three B.2s, two of the latter being B.2T variants with enhanced navigation equipment in the form of Green Satin Doppler and

Ground Position Indicator (GPI) Mk.IV. There were, however, fewer courses and fewer students, reflecting the continued run-down of Canberra strength with the withdrawal from the Near and Far East. The demise of the interdictor force in RAF Germany resulted in a reduction in low-level training, and the OCU no longer taught weaponry.

The author attended 231 OCU in 1977 to undergo the long course before posting to the Canberra PR.9s of 39 Squadron at Wyton. The first flight was exercise C1 in T.4 WT483, with Flt Lt Dave Lord as captain for a sortie lasting 2 hr 10 min. The ground school gave the basic technical details of both the airframe and its equipment (not much on the navigation side). There was no simulator, so pilots used a very basic cockpit pro-

100 Squadron arrives. Wg Cdr Harvey and Sqn Ldr Sweeney are met by Gp Capt Parry-Evans.

Canberra WK118 of 100 Squadron, March 1982.

cedures trainer and navigators 'flew' the Dead Reckoning Trainer (DRT). The latter comprised a series of cubicles with basic instrumentation; when the navigator wanted to take a position line or fix, he told the instructor the basic details and a piece of paper with the fix details would be passed through the back of the cubicle.

Students were crewed together and flew most sorties together. Exercise C28 concluded the author's course after a total flight time of 53 hr 20 min, 9 hr of which had been at night. Eleven of those sorties were flown in the B.2, and the remainder in the T.4, a type that few aircrew liked. The most inspiring of the B.2 trips were those flown at low level, when the navigator could lie in the nose to map read. At this time the Canberras of the OCU and 100 Squadron were very much a low-key element of the station's activities, as the tanker role for which Marham had already established a reputation was far more important.

On 15 August 1977 Canberra E.15 WH948 of 100 Squadron got into trouble on a training sortie, and the crew, Sqn Ldr Tony Gordon and Flt Lt Roy Smith, had to eject. The aircraft crashed near Oulton.

The aircraft of 100 Squadron were kept very busy in the target facilities role, the primary task being that of banner towing for air-to-air gunnery by NATO fighters. The overseas Armament Practice Camps (APCs), usually to Cyprus or Sardinia, were looked on as the highlight of the banner-towing calendar. The 'flag' or banner was a 30 ft x 6 ft piece of material with a large black aiming spot on it, the material being held tight by a spreader bar. This was attached to the aircraft by a 30 ft strop and 900 ft of nylon rope. The target tower would fly race-tracks or figure-of-eight patterns within the air-to-air range; Lightnings preferred the latter pattern as it meant they could put two aircraft on the banner at the same time. Each aircraft used bullets with a different colour of paint on the tip so that the holes, if any, could be credited to the right pilot.

For the initial sorties of an APC the fighters were only allowed cine guns, to ensure that their approach, and opening and closing (of fire) positions were safe before they were let loose with real bullets. The Canberra crew could hear the fighters' cannon; the distinctive 'vroom-whoosh' of the Phantom's Gatling gun and the more staccato note of the Lightning's Aden. Sometimes the bullets seemed to pass all too close to the Canberra, a fact that was on occasion confirmed by the gun film – after which the fighter crew would face a hefty bill in the bar. Banners were frequently adorned, as on one 92 Squadron shoot, when the banner carried a picture of a Sepecat Jaguar in 'appreciation' of the recent shooting down of a Jaguar by a Phantom in Germany. At other times trophies consisted of such items as female clothing. On returning to the airfield the Canberra flew along the runway to drop the banner for recovery by groundcrew, ready for the *post mortem* on pilots' shooting abilities.

Canberra WJ753 of 100 Squadron crashed on the runway threshold on 19 June 1978.

While Akrotiri was without doubt the favourite routine deployment, the squadron was kept busy with frequent NATO tasking and exercises, plus Lone Rangers whenever they could be fitted into the hectic schedule. The target towing role was not purely confined to air-to-air work, and banners were towed for a range of ground systems, guns, and SAMs. In 1980 the squadron said farewell to its T.19s. The bread and butter of UK flying was the Practice Intercepts (PIs) for the fighter units. Most of these were flown with the Canberra acting as a dumb target, flying race-tracks over the North Sea to allow the ground-controlled interception (GCI) sites and fighters to have a live target for intercepts. These sorties, along with the night *Coffee Charlies*, were viewed by most crews as the most boring aspects of the squadron's job. One way of livening up the procedure was to allow the navigator to fly the aircraft. To many others it was a good time in which to catch up with paperwork. Tasking also included calibration duties for airfield radars, which, at least, often had the advantage of including overseas locations, RAF Germany being the most frequent user.

Marham was still proving that it was the best station in the UK, receiving the Stainforth Trophy in May. This was awarded to the station within Strike Command that achieved the highest marks in tactical evaluation (TACEVAL).

Returning from a weekend away on 19 June 1978, Canberra WJ753 of 100 Squadron crashed on the threshold at Marham, injuring three of the crew. Ian Roberts was sitting in one of the rear seats, and remembers the awful moment before the aircraft impacted; one wing hit the ground and the aircraft fortunately fell on its belly rather than on its upper surface. The Canberra broke at the bulkhead just behind the crew compartment, and he staggered from the wreckage and stumbled across the grass before collapsing, his broken ankles now making themselves felt. The crew were very lucky, the worst injuries being the broken legs suffered by the pilot.

That same month four Boeing B-52 Stratofortresses from SAC were present for the now familiar routine of training and participation in the bombing competition. July saw Marham fall quiet as the squadrons 'boltholed' just up the road to Sculthorpe. This old American bomber base had been superbly kept under care and maintenance, and proved to be an excellent temporary location while the Marham runway was being resurfaced.

Marham had at some time acquired the description 'El Adem with grass', a reference to the RAF airfield in the middle of Libya that had not been a favoured location. It was a distinct insult, but reflected (and still does) the opinion of many when posted to this Norfolk 'backwater'. It was perhaps more justified in earlier years, when the station's remoteness was a major problem, although in those days, as we have seen, Marham personnel thought nothing of walking down to Narborough to catch a train or bus to the bright lights of King's Lynn. Expectations change. Like

Yet another B-52 detachment arrives; 14 April 1977.

most major bases, the station has endeavoured over the years to provide social and sporting facilites for its 'inmates', and the ORBs are full of references to such matters; the opening of schools, shops, a cinema, etc. – even a NAAFI petrol station (although this caused local petrol station owners to complain about privileged RAF personnel).

The day-to-day life on the base continued as normal, all of the flying units remaining very active and frequently being away on detachment. The station support facilities, all too often forgotten, but a vital element of the smooth running of the organization, underwent many changes over the years to match the changes in, and demands of, the squadrons. In any month there is always construction work of one kind or another taking place.

Canberra B.2 WH667 was taking part in an APC on 11 November 1980 when it suffered an engine failure at a critical stage of take-off. The aircraft crashed with the loss of both crew, Sqn Ldr G. Thompson and Fg Off M. Wray.

With the demise of 7 Squadron at St Mawgan, five of that unit's TT.18s were transferred to 100 Squadron in December 1981, increasing both the role and capability of the squadron. The TT.18s had primarily been involved in working with the Royal Navy on 4.5 in gun and SAM firings. With all the types the squadron now possessed, a typical month's tasking would look something like

this: 104 PIs, 2 Army tasks, Bloodhound liaison, 22 navy tasks, flight checking (Gibraltar), TACE-VAL support, banner for the Coningsby Qualified Weapons Instructor (QWI) course, Joint Maritime Course support, and Rangers.

With the continuing reduction of the Canberra force, it was inevitable that the OCU itself would continue to shrink. The Canberra force took another blow in 1982 with the disbandment of 39 Squadron at Wyton, and the decision was taken to move all remaining non-trials Canberras to Wyton. Number 100 Squadron moved to the Cambridgeshire base in January 1982, followed by the OCU in July. This latest shuffling of squadrons not only consolidated the Canberra force, but also allowed Marham to become the second UK base to operate the strike/attack variant of the Panavia Tornado. The station also said goodbye to its last Valiant when XD818 was taken to pieces for the move to the RAF Museum at Hendon, to become an exhibit in the Bomber Command Hall. However, as these changes were being made, Marham was put on full alert. The Victors would soon be going to war.

Falklands Conflict

The Argentinian invasion of South Georgia and the Falkland Islands on 1 April 1982 caught the British Government by surprise, and presented the military with the very tricky problem of how to undertake a successful military operation some

6,000 miles away from the home base and with no friendly land base within thousands of miles. In the absence of air bases, traditional air power wisdom relied on two alternatives; sea-based air power using aircraft carriers and the air-to-air refuelling (AAR) of land-based aircraft.

Defence reductions and policy changes had left the military somewhat lacking in the first of these, though HMS *Invincible* and HMS *Hermes*, with Sea Harriers, provided the core of the air assets. At the time, the sole in-flight refuelling capability of the RAF rested with the 23 Victor K.2s of 55 and 57 Squadrons at RAF Marham, a number of which were getting long in the tooth and were due for retirement. Furthermore, the RAF's standard doctrine was that only short-ranged aircraft such as fighters and attack types required AAR, as there would always be a base near enough for the larger types to use. It was not so in this case. During the Falklands Conflict Marham's Victors played a crucial part in supporting the missions of most of the other aircraft types involved.

The Government decision to use military force caused frenetic activity at all UK bases. Marham became a hive of activity, with renewed interest in AAR for all the likely combat aircraft, some of which had no in-flight refuelling capability. However, the squadrons were also instructed to

Ascension detachment; a cricket match for relaxation, Cliff Carter bowling. (Paul McKernan)

carry out maritime radar reconnaissance (MRR) training. The Vulcans of 27 Squadron had specialized in this role until the unit was disbanded in March 1982, and it had since been taken on by the Nimrod force. But at this stage only the

A small part of the Victor line-up at Ascension. (Paul McKernan)

Victors had the refuelled range to operate as far south as the Falklands, and MRR of the vast sea areas in which the naval task force would operate would be essential in providing an accurate intelligence picture. Another new role for the aircraft was that of low-level photographic reconnaissance, three aircraft being fitted with nose cameras and sent off to Scotland in mid-April to try out their skills. Most aircraft received various equipment modifications, ranging from radar enhancements for MRR to revised navigation kit (such as Carousel inertial navigation) to increase accuracy over remote sea areas.

Ray Biddle recalls the 'buzz and excitement' in a busy and hectic schedule that brought round-the-clock working as the Victors underwent a mass of modifications: 'There was always something going on, 3 Hangar was open all the time – but we were glad that it was "over there" and not "over here".'

On 18 April the advance party and five aircraft (XL163, XL189, XL192, XL511, and XM715) left Marham for Wideawake Airfield on Ascension Island. This remote lump of volcanic rock off the west coast of Africa was still some 3,800 miles from the Falklands, but it was to be of vital importance in the air operations to follow, and was the main operating base for the Victors. Four more aircraft (XH671, XL164, XL188, and XL232) arrived the following day, along with Gp Capt J.S.B. Price, Marham's Station Commander, who now became Detachment Commander at Ascension. The detachment settled into the dismal surroundings at Wideawake and adopted standby, ready for the first missions.

The island, with its Exiles Club and general ex-patriot atmosphere, struck the Victor personnel as somewhat 'colonial'. Accommodation was initially in the American all-ranks Volcano Club, officers then going into the US Transit Aircrew block at up to four to a room, although the situation was eased by taking over two bungalows at Georgetown. The groundcrew went into tents at Two Boats, but after a quick rethink everyone was put into 'Concertina City' as it was erected, complete with noisy generators guaranteed to prevent a night's sleep. Sleeping pills and earplugs became essential. The most notable thing was that every round of drinks, no matter what it comprised, seemed to cost $2. Most of the officers tended to migrate to the Exiles Club in Georgetown for a spot of snooker as well as an assortment of draught beer; it made a change

from the surroundings at Wideawake.

Other relaxations were swimming, although there were only a couple of reasonable swimming locations, and sports, such as cricket, against local teams. There were a number of remote sites around the island that were always happy to see visitors, and a fishing trip by boat was usually a good way to spend a day. For the really adventurous there was always a trip up Green Mountain. With its stand of pines (planted to provide replacement ships' masts in the 19th century) and reservoirs (for ships' water), it was a pleasant location. However, the workload was high enough to prevent the majority from getting bored; the AAR tasking involved very complex flows and detailed planning.

The first operational sortie was an MRR flown on 20 April by Sqn Ldr John Elliott and crew in XL192. Operation *Corporate* was under way. The aircraft took off at 04:00Z and, in company with four other Victors serving as tankers, headed towards the South Atlantic. Having reached the target area, the aircraft descended from its transit height to around 18,000 ft, and for the next 90 min carried out a radar sweep of some 150,000 square miles of sea. With the task completed, it regained altitude and rendezvoused with another group of tankers on the way home. The 7,000-mile sortie had taken 14 hr 45 min.

Similar missions were flown on 22/23 and 24/25 April. The primary purpose of all three sorties was to provide data on surface shipping, ice conditions and so on to HMS *Antrim*, the lead ship in Operation *Paraquat,* the recapture of South Georgia (accomplished on 26 April). The complex planning of the AAR drop-off trail, whereby tankers gave fuel to each other in sequence so that there was always a tanker ready to top-up the mission aircraft at the right time and place, was a major achievement, especially, as shall be seen, on some of the later missions, when many more aircraft were involved.

The need to deploy aircraft south led to the home-based elements of the Marham Victor wing being almost as busy as the operational detachment. Vulcans were rapidly refitted with re-fuelling probes (a team even removed the probe from the Vulcan on display at the RAF Museum), and intensive training was the order of the day. It was the same story for the Fleet Air Arm's Sea Harriers, as many of these would be flown to Ascension Island to join their ships. Perhaps the most startling tasks were those involving the

Nimrod and Hercules, aircraft which were not AAR capable before the Falklands Conflict. The first Nimrod MR.2P was given a ground test from Victor XL231 at Woodford on 28 April, followed by successful flight trials the next day. Then, at Boscombe Down on 30 April, it was the Hercules C.1P's turn for a ground test, with the air test on 1 May. The modifications to the two types may not have been very aesthetic, but they certainly worked.

By 30 April six more Victors had deployed to Ascension, bringing the total to 14 (XM715 had returned to the UK in the meantime). On 29 April two Vulcans (XM598 and XM607) had been tanked from Waddington to Ascension, followed on the 30th by a batch of Sea Harriers. The latter were to join the container ship *Atlantic Conveyor* for the trip south, during which time one Sea Harrier was kept on deck alert, with Victors flying tanker support from Ascension 'just in case'. Meanwhile, at the end of its flying career, the Vulcan had gone to war.

At 23:50Z on the night of 30 April two Vulcans and 11 Victors left Wideawake, destined for Port Stanley airfield, the intention being for one Vulcan to drop its load of 1,000 lb bombs across the runway, denying its use to the Argentine Air Force. Each Vulcan crew included an experienced AAR instructor from Marham. The primary bomber, XM598, had to turn back, leaving Flt Lt Martin Withers and crew in XM607 to carry on with the mission. One of the Victors also had to return, and its place was taken by one of the two airborne spares. Nothing being left to chance in this complex operation.

The drop-off plot worked well until the stream was down to one Vulcan and three Victors. Flt Lt A. Skelton in XL512 had just given his fuel offload when the aircraft developed a fuel leak. He turned back towards Ascension, but it was soon obvious that the aircraft was not going to make it without help from another Victor. The two remaining Victors went through a final mutual exchange, Sqn Ldr Bob Tuxford in XL189 topping-up the Vulcan and then giving all spare fuel to Victor XH669, piloted by Flt Lt Steve Biglands. However, during the latter operation the probe on '669 broke before sufficient fuel had been transferred. The crews decided to change roles, with Bob Tuxford going on with the Vulcan, but first he had to take back the fuel he had just given. Some 3,000 miles south of Ascension the last refuelling bracket took place. Tuxford had to give more fuel than planned, leaving his aircraft with insufficient fuel to return to base. The need for radio silence at this critical stage of the mission meant that he could not call Ascension and arrange for another tanker meet him on the way back, although there should have been enough time from the Vulcan coming off target (at 07:46 with a call of 'Superfuse' to indicate success) to make the call.

The Vulcan duly dropped on the airfield, scoring at least one hit on the runway, and turned away to pick up the first of its return tankers. All aircraft recovered to Ascension safely, and *Black Buck 1* was declared a success. Bob Tuxford was awarded the Air Force Cross for his part in the mission, and the remainder of his crew (Sqn Ldr E.F. Wallis, Flt Lt M.E. Beer, Flt Lt J.N. Keable, and Flt Lt G.D. Rees) each received the Queen's Commendation for Valuable Service in the Air (QCVSA).

Black Buck 2, a similar bombing mission, went ahead on 3 May, this time without any drama. On the 7th the two Vulcans were tanked back to the UK, the initial bombing raids having been considered to have achieved their aim of demonstrating British political will (and damaging the Port Stanley runway). In the interim the Victors ferried out the next batch of offensive aircraft, the Harrier GR.3s of 1 Squadron, ready for loading on to ships at Ascension Island.

The AAR fit in the Nimrod was now ready for operational employment, and the first Nimrod MR.2P mission was flown on 9 May by Flt Lt D.J. Ford and crew of 206 Squadron in XV227. This mission was supported by three Victor tankers. From then on, almost daily Nimrod MRR or ASW patrols were flown into the South Atlantic, that of 15 May setting a new 'record' with an 8,300-mile mission (19 hr 5 min) which needed the support of 12 Victors. A week later, on the 20th/21st, an even longer sortie was flown, supported by 14 Victors. The Victor aircrew were certainly working hard. In a single month Paul McKernan clocked up 99 hr 45 min flying; had he realized, he would have made the pilot loiter for another 15 min.

A *Black Buck 3* planned for 16 May was cancelled, but on the same day the first AAR-supported flight by a Hercules C.1P took place. Flight Lieutenant Harold Burgoyne and crew of 47 Squadron flew XV200, supported by three Victors, to drop essential material to HMS *Antelope* in the Total Exclusion Zone (TEZ). These Hercules missions became a regular feature of RAF operations until the Argentinian surrender on 16 June.

It is worth stressing the 'behind-the-scenes' work that is always essential to operational flying. With only a pool of some 14 aircraft and a requirement to have 12 or so tanker sorties in support of a single mission, the groundcrew at Ascension worked long and hard to keep the fleet of Victors serviceable. Likewise, the Marham elements of the squadrons had to undertake most of the deployment sorties while supporting the Ascension detachment. Serviceable Victors were at such a premium that, when XL231 went to St Athan for major servicing on 12 May, a routine that usually took months, it was returned complete within three weeks. A similarly rapid turn-round was given to XM717 when it went into the shed at St Athan.

Because Wideawake airfield was essential to the British military operations, it had to be provided with air defences to counter any possibility of Argentinian air attack. With the departure of the Harriers to the South, it was decided to deploy three Phantoms of 29 Squadron from RAF Coningsby, and these aircraft were duly tanked over by Victors on 24 May (XV484 and XV468) and 25 May (XV466). These aircraft held QRA and were yet another potential drain on the limited Victor resources.

A few days later, on 28/29 May, the Vulcan was back in action again, this time in a Suppression of Enemy Air Defences (SEAD) role, equipped with the Shrike missile. *Black Buck 4* was aimed at the AN/TPS-43 surveillance radar in the Port Stanley area, but the mission had to be curtailed halfway through when a Victor went unserviceable. However, on 30th/31st *Black Buck 5*, supported by 18 Victor sorties, reached the target area and launched two Shrikes, causing limited damage to the radar.

Two additional Harrier GR.3s were tanked from Ascension to the TEZ on 1 June, to join HMS *Hermes*. The Vulcan was back in action on 2/3 June, tasked against the same radar. The radar could not be detected, but the crew did pick up a Skyguard fire-control radar which was duly destroyed by Shrikes. The return trip was going smoothly until, in one refuelling bracket, the Vulcan (XM597) broke its probe. Unable to reach Ascension, it had to divert to Rio de Janeiro in Brazil. Only one more Vulcan raid was flown, XM607 carrying out *Black Buck 7* to bomb Port

Stanley airfield on 11/12 June. Throughout that month, however, the tankers were kept fully occupied with Nimrod and Hercules support. During the conflict the two Victor squadrons logged an amazing 1,980 hr 30 min (1,105 by 55 Squadron), an incredible total, but one that took its toll of the airframe lives of the Victors.

The Argentinian surrender on 14 June did not bring an end to the Victor operations, as Nimrod and Hercules missions continued at the same pace for some time, the last of the Nimrods not leaving Ascension for the UK until mid-August. This, plus the reopening of Stanley airfield for use by Hercules and the introduction of six Hercules fitted for the AAR tanking role (with hose-drum units in the fuselage and a drogue out of the back), enabled a reduction in the deployed Victor force. It was not before time, as the aircraft had been worked at many times their normal rate for some months. Nevertheless, the limitations of the Port Stanley runway meant that it could not take long-range jet traffic, so the Victors continued to be tasked with deployment support. This task only came to an end with the opening of the newly-built full-scale airfield at Mount Pleasant in May 1985. Thus, on 10 June 1985, Wg Cdr Martin Todd, OC 55 Squadron, flew the last Victor (XL163) out of Ascension and back to Marham.

Black Buck 1: Victor Details

Ascension to Stanley

XL163	Sqn Ldr F. Milligan	1 hr 10 min
XL192	Flt Lt N.J. Brooks	4 55
XL232	Sqn Ldr J.G. Elliott	4 15
XH672	Sqn Ldr M.D. Todd	4 20
XM717	Sqn Ldr B.R. Neal	4 20
XL511	Wg Cdr C.C.B. Seymour	4 40
XL162	Flt Lt S.P. Hamilton	5 20
XL512	Flt Lt A.M. Skelton	8 10
XL188	Sqn Ldr A.M. Tomalin	8 30
XH669	Flt Lt S. Biglands	12 15
XL189	Sqn Ldr R. Tuxford	14 5

Stanley to Ascension

XL163	Sqn Ldr F. Milligan	1 hr 25 min
XL192	Flt Lt A.J. Barrett	2 55
XL233	Sqn Ldr M.D. Todd	3 25
XH671	Flt Lt S.O. Jones	5 20
XL511	Wg Cdr C.C.B. Seymour	5 40
XL232	Sqn Ldr J.G. Elliott	6 10
XH672	Sqn Ldr B.R. Neal	9 20

CHAPTER 5

TORNADO FORCE

The first Tornado unit for Marham was 617 (Dambusters) Squadron, an ex-Vulcan unit and probably the most famous bomber squadron in the RAF. This squadron officially re-formed on 1 January 1983, although the first eight aircraft had arrived the previous summer, the first on 23 April. The Squadron took over the north-eastern hardened aircraft shelter (HAS) site in October, although the Personnel Briefing Facility was not ready until November. The other event in July was the four-ship fly-by of Canberras as 231 OCU said farewell and moved to Wyton.

The arrival of their noisy but smaller brethren did not distract the mighty crescent-winged Victors. However, one of their number, XL232, was lost in spectacular fashion on 16 October 1982. One witness recalls: 'I heard it revving up ready to take-off and I saw the tail section moving past a hangar, but suddenly the engines cut out and the next thing I saw was black smoke pouring from the plane'. Another who saw the aircraft's demise was Ray Biddle:

> I heard the station tannoy announce 'aborted take-off, engine fire', and looking down the road saw a pall of black smoke. By the time I got to 4 shed there was quite a large crowd watching the fire engines tearing down the runway. All the crew had made it out OK, but the aircraft was burning well, with clouds of black smoke billowing into the clear sky. It was quite a still day and the plume rose high up. There was no great explosion from the full fuel load, just a constant flame – plus small explosions as oxygen bottles went flying through the air. The CO ordered everyone to keep clear as it was obvious that the aircraft could not be saved. By the time it was all over there was quite a hole to repair in the runway.

In November 1982 Wg Cdr J.B. Grogan, OC Designate of the third Tornado squadron, had received the message: 'you will be pleased to

Construction of the hardened aircraft shelter (HAS) complex, 1980.

know that your new squadron will be numbered 27 Squadron and will re-form on 1 May 1983.' The first crews for the new unit arrived at Marham in March 1983, having completed the conversion courses at Cottesmore and Honington. Some of the engineers had been there since the previous December, preparing the squadron site. However, the first Tornado GR.1s did not arrive until May, ZA609, ZA604, and ZA613 coming out of storage and ZA542 and ZA553 being acquired from the Tornado Weapons Conversion Unit (TWCU) at Honington. Wing Commander Grogan flew the first sortie on the 28th, the aircraft now carrying the squadron's green elephant insignia, preserving a tradition that extended back to the First World War, plus a red bar and, on the forward fuselage, a green arrowhead.

A further four aircraft were 'donated' by the TWCU in June, including a trainer version, ZA549. The summer months were hectic for the squadrons as they settled into operating from HAS sites and began to work up to combat-ready status, in preparation for declaration to NATO as strike-attack squadrons. The presence of the two Tornado units meant that, with its well-established tanker force, Marham now boasted a world-wide deployable composite wing. However, this was not the adopted operational policy, although, as events were to prove, it was to become very much the operational stance of the RAF in the Middle East crises of the early 1990s.

With the HAS sites complete and the Tornado squadrons declared to NATO, Marham effectively became the premier strike/attack base within No. 1 Group. As part of the continued efforts to improve the base's operational status, 2620 (County of Norfolk) Regiment Squadron, Royal Auxiliary Air Force, was formed in April 1983. With a small nucleus of permanent staff, but with its strength primarily comprising local 'part-timers', this enthusiastic unit was created to bolster the airfield's defence forces.

Between 28 January and 8 February 1984, 27 Squadron deployed to Thumrait airfield in the Sultanate of Oman. This was the first RAF Tornado venture into the Middle East, and provided an excellent opportunity for crews to operate in this very different region. The emphasis was on low-level flying, but appearances were also made at Abu Dhabi and Dhahran, Saudi Arabia. While the deployment was without doubt excellent value for the Tornado crews, and for the

tanker crews who supported the deployment, it was also very much a 'sales drive' to encourage Middle Eastern nations to buy the Tornado. Oman was planning to acquire a number of GR.1s, but owing to funding problems this order was later cancelled. Saudi Arabia, however, became a major customer for the type.

The detachment included an event referred to as the 'Dhofar Handicap', a navigation and bombing exercise against the local Hunter and Jaguar units. With an element of suspicion that the rules had been 'arranged' in favour of the single-seat aircraft that were, after all, operating in their own backyard, the Tornado squadron nominated crews and joined the fray. The competition was flown on 2 February and was extremely testing, with a number of low-level 'gates' to achieve on time and a selection of targets, including a range, to attack, plus Rapiers as a ground threat. The squadron was delighted when it came first in both the individual and team results.

In the summer of the same year the Dambusters sent a high-profile detachment to America to participate in the SAC bombing competition. This was to be the first Tornado involvement, and as such the spotlight was very much on how the aircraft would perform. It was a great success, the squadron scooping a host of prizes.

One basic operational *raison d'être* of the Tornado was its ability to operate 'hands off' at low level at night and in bad weather, using its terrain following radar (TFR). In view of the problems with low-level training of this nature, the Tornado squadrons continued the old Vulcan tradition of deploying to Goose Bay, Canada, to undertake both TFR and operational low flying (OLF) training. Number 27 Squadron deployed for its first *Western Vortex* to Goose Bay in July, and during the deployment ZA494 was lost in an accident. Recovering to the airfield with a flap problem, the aircraft went out of control on the final approach. The crew ejected safely, but the aircraft crashed on the airfield.

It was not to be a good year for the squadron. In November it lost a second aircraft when the crew ejected from ZA603 during a training sortie in Germany. The Martin-Baker rocket-powered ejection seat proved equal to the task on both occasions, none of the crewmen suffering serious injuries.

March 1985 saw Marham aircraft participating in the Electronic Warfare (EW) training exercise, *Green Flag*, at Nellis AFB, Nevada. The squadron took over from IX Squadron in what was to prove a very valuable deployment, this being the first time that RAF aircraft had been invited to participate in this EW variant of the well-known *Red Flag* exercises. It was also the first real test for the aircraft's self-defence suite of Skyshadow and the BOZ chaff and flare dispenser, both of which worked remarkably well. The ability to operate in a hostile electronic environment was deemed to be the key in any future conflict, and it was therefore essential that the training routine contained appropriate sortie profiles. The UK facilities for such training in the early 1980s were distinctly limited, and only the large American training areas had the range and type of equipment necessary.

The RAF had been involved in *Red Flag* for some years, and although this was essentially an attack exercise it also contained a high degree of both EW and fighter threat routines. The basic NATO concept for major air employment is that of the package, whereby an appropriate selection (package) of aircraft is sent against a given target. Such a package would usually include a fighter escort, EW support (stand-off jamming such as the EF-111 Raven and suppression of enemy air defence (SEAD) support from the F-4G Wild Weasel), plus the actual 'strikers' themselves. It is not easy to co-ordinate these packages, especially in the face of 'live' opposition from fighters, missiles, guns, and weather. The *Red* and *Green Flag* concept is to provide the training in such co-ordination, a mutual understanding of procedures. Most NATO exercises of any size now employ this concept.

In April 1985 27 Squadron began its work-up for Exercise *Prairie Vortex*, the USAF SAC bombing competition succeeding *Giant Voice*. This was to be the Tornado's second outing in this competition, and much preparatory work was required, although the experience gained by 617 Squadron in their very successful participation proved invaluable. The competition comprised long, involved sorties with air-to-air refuelling, strict timing tolerances, and medium- and low-level bombing. The tanker support was to be provided by 57 Squadron, making it very much a Marham 'show'. The detachment left Marham in August and returned on 30 October with a string of awards.

Two teams each of two crews had been entered, and they were able to fly a limited number of familiarization sorties over the Nevada ranges in preparation for the three-week competition. Each crew had to complete two daytime and one night-time mission during the competition, each one lasting an average of six hours and including two air-to-air refuelling brackets. Scores for bombing were based upon delivery accuracy, which the Tornado crews managed to average out at less than 30 ft for the low-level attacks, and on time of bomb strike, in which they achieved the awesome accuracy of +/− 2 sec during a sortie exceeding six hours' duration. Bombing was carried out on the Forsythe, Belle Fourche, Lemmon, Bismarck, and Eureka ranges.

Add to this the requirement to survive both air and ground threats, the latter involving a run through the 'heavily-defended' Powell Electronic Warfare Training Range, and one starts to get some feel for the nature of the task. The support given by the Victor crews was absolutely vital to the mission, as it would have been all too easy to lose time during the refuelling brackets. It was essential for the tankers to be in the right place at the right time, and to stay flexible to the needs of the Tornado crews. This they did in their usual style. It was not all work, of course, and the detachment were very well hosted by the Americans and managed to find ways in which to enjoy any well-deserved leisure time.

Thirty-four teams took part in the competition, and in the three major awards 27 Squadron was placed first (98.8 per cent) and second (98.4 per cent) in the Le May Trophy, second (97.2 per cent) in the Mathis Trophy, and first (94.97 per cent) and second (90.75 per cent) in the Meyer Trophy; an incredible achievement and slightly better, by one place in the Meyer, than 617 had managed the previous year. Needless to say, Wg Cdr John Groggan was delighted: 'We have never doubted its most impressive capability. Our successes in the last two year's competitions merely serve to reinforce our view that the Tornado is clearly the best in the world.'

Perhaps the most amazing aspect of the successes in 1984 and 1985 was the fact that the aircraft had been in operational service with these squadrons for only two years. The Tornado was rapidly proving that it was more than capable of carrying out the tasks for which it was designed. It was truly the first all-weather day/night attack aircraft that the RAF had employed; others had claimed the title before, but none had been truly capable.

In addition to supporting events such as the

American deployments, the two Victor squadrons were kept very busy with the 'routine' series of fast-jet deployments to various parts of the world, plus the usual Lone Rangers and assorted tasks. The increased importance of AAR as the so-called 'force multiplier' had been emphasized during the Falklands Conflict, and the tasking level for 55 and 57 Squadrons reflected this change of philosophy. While the RAF sought ways to increase its tanker strength, partly to cater for the impending demise of the ageing Victors, those same Victors had to keep on going; an increasingly testing problem for the engineers.

In May 1984 the first of the Vickers VC.10 tanker conversions had been delivered to 101 Squadron at Brize Norton, to be followed in 1985 by AAR-capable Lockheed TriStars for 216 Squadron. This eased the burden on the Victors and allowed the older K.1 and variants to be phased out. On 1 July 1986 57 Squadron carried out a final fly-by with their aircraft at the unit's disbandment. It was a sad end to a great squadron that had contributed much to developing the AAR role. With only a single Victor squadron remaining, it also made sense for the OCU to disband, so after a 31-year existence, during which it had trained some 2,000 aircrew, 232 OCU was closed down on 5 April 1986.

It was also deemed appropriate, in view of the Victor's history at Marham, to use one of the 57

Squadron aircraft as a gate guard, and the decision was taken to position the aircraft, XH673, facing the Station Headquarters building. It was moved into No. 4 hangar and dismantled into more manageable portions before being placed on a Queen Mary transporter for the short trip to its new home. A number of trees had to be cut down to make the move possible, and on the day in question a very precarious load eased its way around the station, until the driver had to brake to avoid a car. The Victor's fuselage shifted to the edge of its trailer, causing hold-up number one.

Eventually XH673 arrived at the car park for reassembly, and all was going well, the wings being put into position and held with trestles. Overnight, however, the trestles of the starboard wing collapsed, creating hold-up number two. Similar problems reoccurred, but at length an aircraft tractor was attached to the towing arm and the aircraft was manoeuvred towards its plinth. At that moment the tractor ran over one of the heating ducts, now hidden by the gravel around the plinth, and promptly sat on its tail as the back wheels went down. That, fortunately, was the last of the many problems, and the Victor now sits proudly on its plinth.

Meanwhile, both Tornado squadrons were kept very busy, not only with routine training, but with a range of exercises and overseas deployments.

After some difficult moments while getting it into position, Victor XH673 now guards the Marham gate.

Some of the latter were of a routine nature, such as the Goose Bay jaunts and, in due course, the use of the APC facility at Decimmomanu, Sardinia. The squadrons of RAF Germany had been using the range at 'Deci' for years, but it was only when the RAF acquired additional range slots that the UK-based units joined in.

For most periods of the year this is an excellent location for the squadrons to undertake intensive weapons training, the array of targets at Capo di Frasca range allowing a wide variety of attack profiles, including medium-level bombing and high-angle (45°) dive, profiles that are often hard to achieve in the UK's somewhat unpredictable weather. This is the time when the squadron QWIs sharpen their knives and acquire reputations as 'fatherless individuals' for their hard-hearted approach. There is intense competition among crews not to acquire too many 'pigs', and thus to reach the end of the detachment in a position to win the bombing competition. 'Pigs' are awarded for a variety of misdemeanours, such as forgetting to film the attack; even if the camera in a particular aircraft is broken, it still counts against the crew.

Most sorties last less than an hour, the transit from the airfield to the range taking only a few minutes, carrying a usual fit of two Carrier Bomb Light Store (CBLS), each with four practice bombs, usually one with 3 kg and one with 14 kg, their use depending upon the attack profile. Profiles vary from the standard hands-off full computer-aided laydown delivery, through radar bombs (no computer), to a range of dive attacks with such names as 'Hornet Pop'. The latter are favoured by the pilots, who seem to enjoy approaching the target steeply and at a high rate of knots! It is superb training, and a chance to practise delivery techniques that would otherwise not be possible, thus exploring the full spectrum of the aircraft's capabilities.

Deci is also an air combat manoeuvring instrumentation (ACMI) range, for use in air-to-air combat training. Detachments often mix the training, with a week or so of bombing and a week or so of combat, if a suitable 'enemy' is present at the same time. With an appropriate instrumentation pod fitted to one underwing pylon stub, and an AIM-9L acquisition round on the other, the aircraft is ready for battle. The instrumentation pod relays all data to the ground computer that tracks the battle and determines the validity of any missile shots. There is, of course, time for the odd social event, be it a session in the 'pig and tape' bar, a pizza down-town, or even a stroll along the seafront at Cagliari.

OC 27 Squadron, Wg Cdr Bob Hounslow, and Sqn Ldr Pete Batson brief Defence Secretary Rifkind for a low-level sortie. Marham frequently hosts political visits.

The daily routine of the fast-jet squadrons is orientated around flying training, both for 'Convex' crews and for the combat-ready (CR) personnel. Having arrived on a squadron from the training unit at TWCU, the pilot and navigator have to undergo a defined conversion course (Convex) to learn the operational procedures used by that unit, and to qualify as combat ready in both the strike (nuclear) and attack (conventional) bombing roles. The Convex package is structured to take the 'new boys' through all aspects of the routine, from fairly simple singleton missions up to a four-ship co-ordinated attack with a 'bounce'. The latter is usually provided by the squadron, and the aim is to disrupt the formation's plan and try to shoot down as many as possible before the target is reached. However, achieving the magic CR status and downing the 'op pot' does not end the training routine. Low-level flying requires constant practice; every sortie has to be analyzed to see what went right, or wrong, and how it could be improved next time.

The test of the squadron's overall performance comes with the regular station exercise, usually referred to as *Mineval* or *Maxeval,* depending on how many days it lasts. This is when the station 'goes to war' to test all of its procedures and, as with squadron training, to correct any faults that are found. The arrival of the NATO Taceval (tactical evaluation) team is the ultimate test of such war procedures, and every station is examined by this organization periodically. At the end of the three or so days of 'war', the unit is given a set of marks relating to various aspects of its performance, and these marks are closely examined by commanders from Group right up to the highest NATO echelons. These events are, therefore, of critical importance in the life of the unit and its squadrons, the principle being that if you are ready at all times for war (the slogan being 'Train for war, not for Taceval'), then you are not going to be caught out. It has been proven in many conflicts that if you are not ready on Day One, your chances of seeing Day Two are greatly reduced.

On 13 January 1988 HM Queen Elizabeth the Queen Mother presented 617 Squadron with their new standard, an occasion also attended by two of the squadron's most famous veterans, Leonard Cheshire and 'Bill' Tate. Her Majesty said: 'Today, nearly 30 years later [referring to the previous presentation ceremony], it has been my pleasure to present your new standard – years during which the squadron has most worthily maintained its high reputation in the forefront of RAF offensive operations.'

In the middle of 1988, with the runway at St Mawgan being resurfaced, the Nimrods of 42 Squadron operated out of Marham for a few months.

Operating fast jets is always a risky business, and losses for a variety of reasons are inevitable. Sadly, 617 Squadron lost another aircraft in August 1988.

Over the next two years the station's squadrons kept up the busy routine of training and deployments to various parts of the world. There was never a dull moment for aircrew and groundcrew. All too often the part played by the long-suffering engineers is forgotten. The Tornado requires a range of highly-trained experts to ensure that its systems are kept in good order. A typical major deployment involving eight or so aircraft would require just over 100 ground personnel in support.

After the RAF had spent almost 10 years rehearsing for the envisaged war in central Europe, which its deterrent stance was intended to help prevent, the whole picture changed with the collapse of the USSR and the Eastern Bloc. While the Service was considering its future structure and posture, it was called upon to take part in a crisis in the Middle East. The Gulf Conflict proved to be a testing time for all concerned.

The Gulf Conflict

On 2 August 1990 Iraq invaded the oil-rich state of Kuwait, claiming that it was restoring a province of Iraq to its homeland. The Kuwaiti resistance was fierce but shortlived, and within days the Iraqis had upwards of 50,000 troops on the border of Saudi Arabia and were consolidating their hold on Kuwait. There seemed to be a real possibility that the Iraqi president, Saddam Hussein, would order his jubilant forces to continue their southward advance into Saudi Arabia and the Gulf States, threatening the West's oil supplies. This galvanized the West, and the United Nations, in an almost unprecedented response, universally condemned the Iraqi conquest and called for a withdrawal. To lend muscle to the words while a Coalition was being formulated, American and British air assets moved to the region, the initial RAF element comprising Tornado F.3s that had been on exercise in Cyprus. As Operation *Desert Shield*, the build-up of Coalition forces accelerat-

Above *The Gulf War; a Victor among a selection of transports. (via Paul McKernan)*

Below *Tornado 'FG' at low level over the desert. (via Paul McKernan)*

Bottom *A pair of 'desert pink' Tornadoes get airborne. (via Paul McKernan)*

Victor XL164 plus Tornado 'G' Hello Kuwait G'Bye Iraq *with LGBs; the Marham Gulf team. (via Paul McKernan)*

ed throughout the summer.

It was obvious that the Tornado's unique capabilities would be needed in the event of any offensive action, and the Marham squadrons went into an intensive training routine, concentrating on 100 ft Operational Low Flying (OLF) flying and co-ordinated attacks using the JP233 anti-airfield weapon. This was carried only by the Tornado, and would form a vital part of the Coalition arsenal for attacks on Iraqi airfields, which were massive and very well equipped, their size making Heathrow look like a regional airport.

The major operational bases were provided with the latest-generation hardened structures, and much thought was put into providing multiple runways. In any counter-air operation they would prove to be difficult to 'shut down'; JP233 was able to help redress that balance. It was obvious that the Tornadoes' task would include night deep penetration sorties to attack such airfields. The Iraqi military machine was organized and equipped on Soviet lines, so the years of NATO-orientated training would be applicable. As a Soviet-style system it was also very well provided for in the SAM and AAA departments, and crews could be assured of a very hot reception at their

targets. Training in the UK and Germany thus included great attention to EW aspects.

Low level being the name of the game, it was necessary to paint the aircraft in a more appropriate manner. The chosen colour, officially described as Alkali-Removable Temporary Finish (ARTF), was more commonly known as Desert Pink, although it seemed to come out in a variety of shades.

Ray Biddle's workshops were responsible for repainting the aircraft, and he recalls:

We sprayed 13 jets in 36 hours using the ARTF. They were taken into 2 shed, masked up and then off to 1 shed to be sprayed. The ARTF was good material, easy to use and it adhered pretty well except on the underwing tanks, as the material that these were made of had absorbed fuel and so did not give a good surface on which to paint. We had to try and degrease them using vinegar. The theory of this paint was that it would steam clean off, but it was meant to be only a temporary cover and in the Gulf it was left on so long in the hot conditions that it virtually baked on, so we eventually had to use detergent to remove it.

Gulf readiness; shark-mouthed and armed with 1,000 lb bombs, Sidewinders, and guns.

Tornado 'D', Snoopy Airways.

Under Operation *Granby* the RAF rapidly increased its strength in the Gulf, the major offensive contribution being the Tornado GR.1 squadrons from Marham and RAF Germany, along with the Jaguars from Coltishall.

In August 1990 the first crews left Marham to join the Tornado detachment forming at Muharraq, Bahrain. This first Tornado unit was to be a composite squadron, with aircraft and personnel from five squadrons, including 27 and 617. The concept was to have an offensive capability at readiness should the Iraqi forces decide to push into Saudi Arabia or down the Gulf towards the other Gulf states. Muharraq was a civil airport (although it had been an RAF base in the days of RAF Persian Gulf) and had no military accommodation, so detachment personnel had to 'rough it' in the local hotels. This was no problem, as the tourists and businessmen had, for some reason, decided to leave the area.

Training was the order of the day, crews flying sorties to prepare for low-level missions over desert terrain. The training areas over Saudi Arabia proved ideal for acclimatization to the dangers of ultra-low-level operations over seemingly flat desert, where optical illusions waited to trap the unwary. What appeared to be flat desert might well have a sneaky sand dune that blended in and became invisible. A Jaguar was lost during the work-up phase, and one or two Tornado crews were chastened by seeing their No. 2's aircraft and shadow become almost the same size, a sure indication that there was not much ground clearance. Crews used various bombing ranges in Saudi to sharpen their weapon delivery.

Back in the UK, other crews continued the Gulf work-up, concentrating on ultra-low-level, day and night AAR and long sortie profiles including co-ordinated attacks. During September one of 27 Squadron's aircraft was lost in the North Sea, Gp Capt Bill Green and Sqn Ldr Neil Anderson being killed.

By early October the decision had been taken to form a second Tornado GR.1 detachment in theatre, and a number of crews from both Marham squadrons moved to Tabuk in northern Saudi as part of this new force. The delights of Bahrain were soon forgotten in this less-than-hospitable piece of desert. Tents and portacabins were the order of the day here, although the aircrew did manage to commandeer some far from luxurious villas. Training started immediately, and was voted a great improvement over that available in Bahrain; the variation in landscape allowed far more realism (and fun) than the somewhat boring 'desert and more desert' of the eastern side of the country. The terrain included some very inspiring valleys that proved very popular with the Tornado crews. In a recent history of 617 Squadron, Steve Hillier, one of the 27 Squadron detachment, recalled a typical training sortie:

After take-off, the formation would check in with the ever watchful AWACS aircraft, before transiting at medium level to the RV with the VC.10 tanker for air-to-air refuelling. The join with the tanker and the refuelling would be conducted in radio silence to maintain tactical surprise, all details having been agreed between aircraft before take-off. Even on training sorties, the Tornadoes would practice being 'cast-off' by the tanker at a precise position and time – an essential element of the refuelling procedure which ensures that all the various formations of the attack package can form up before 'pushing' into enemy territory. Descending to low level, the formation would move into tactical formation. Low flying on the route to the target area would typically be around 100 to 150 ft, a height that allowed both pilot and navigator to look out for potential fighter threats – which on a training sortie might be provided by Tabuk-based F-15s, US Navy F-14s from carriers in the Red Sea or, perhaps, another Tornado. But when threatened by a fighter, or when in a high ground threat area, the Tornadoes would rapidly accelerate, dip down to as low as 50 ft and hug the terrain. Simulated targets that were representative of what might have to be attacked in Iraq were somewhat scarce, and typically an ancient fort which last saw service with Lawrence of Arabia would find itself the object of the Tornado's co-ordinated attacks. Much more interesting were the occasional attacks flown against the US Navy Red Sea Fleet.

Victors of 55 Squadron deployed to Muharraq on 14 and 15 October. Air-to-air refuelling was to prove an essential element of the strategic air operations; the scale of the Coalition air effort, with more than 2,000 aircraft in theatre, meant that air bases were in short supply, and aircraft had to be based throughout Saudi Arabia and the Gulf States. The Victors were initially dedicated to supporting the Jaguars and Tornado F.3s, the

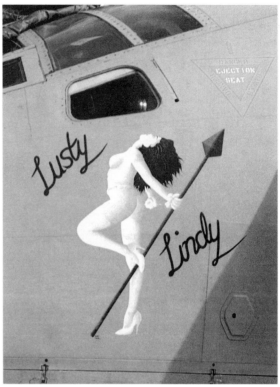

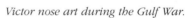

Victor nose art during the Gulf War.

strike/attack Tornado force using the VC.10 tankers of 101 Squadron. It was, however, a question of staying flexible, and the years of NATO exercises now came into their own, as the Victors had to be ready to tank any and all probe-equipped aircraft – British, Canadian, French and US Navy.

The complex nature of the air co-ordination plan gave each tanker a towline, and height, and a time bracket in which to refuel its nominated 'chicks'. Reality, however, meant that there were frequent changes. Aircraft needing more fuel, a change in the timing of the package, or a re-routeing might mean that the original plan was no longer viable, or another tanker might go unserviceable, bringing extra trade; there was never a dull moment. As high-value assets (HVAs) the tankers were given their own area fighter protection; had the Iraqi Air Force decided to fight rather than sit on the ground, these vulnerable aircraft would have been important targets. The 'phoney war' that developed in the second half of 1990, as the Iraqis attempted to unbalance the Coalition in the belief that the UN forces would not actually go to war, gave the squadrons plenty of time to rehearse their procedures and become familiar with operating in the desert conditions.

The training routine continued until the Marham detachment was replaced in November by crews from RAF Germany. With the rotation at Tabuk, 617 Squadron returned home in December. However, this proved to be only a short respite, as the increased tension with the approach of the UN deadline in early January led to a strengthening of the Tornado detachments. On 5 January crews left the UK to join the Muharraq composite squadron, the crews being:

Wg Cdr Nigel Elsdon/Flt Lt Max Collier; Sqn Ldr Jon Taylor/Sqn Ldr Graham Thwaites; Sqn Ldr Frank Waddington/Flt Lt Mal Hammans; Flt Lt Mark Ruddock/Sqn Ldr Jim Crowley; Flt Lt Graham Beet/Flt Lt Stu Osborne; and Flt Lt Dave Waddington/Flt Lt Robbie Stewart. Additional crews arrived over the next few days.

As all but one of these crews had already had a training period in theatre, the work-up was rapid and all were convinced that the shooting war would soon begin. On the afternoon of 15 January crews were told that the war was only hours away. Final preparations were made and the initial pre-planned missions were given the finishing touches.

On the eve of the first missions 55 Squadron had six Victors and eight crews at Muharraq, supported by 99 groundcrew. At 22:50Z two Victors refuelled the first Tornado GR.1 attack package on the Olive Trail. The Tornado detachment flew its first operational missions on 17 January, attacking airfield targets at Al Jarrah and Shaibah, in south-east Iraq.

A four-ship JP233 attack was planned against Al Jarrah airfield, with a time on target of 17:57. The four Tornado attack aircraft were supported by VC.10 tankers for AAR on the outbound and return legs, four F-15Cs for fighter cover, and four F-111 attack aircraft, with SEAD provided by four F-4G Phantom Wild Weasels and two EF-111 Ravens.

During the initial tanking phase the No. 3 had to return to base with equipment problems. Having refuelled twice to ensure that tanks were as full as possible for the mission, the remaining three aircraft descended to low level *en route* to the target area. Shortly after crossing the border, aircraft 'Mike' was locked on by a Roland missile system. Nige Ingle spotted the missile, and went into an evasive manoeuvre while Paul McKernan operated the self-defence suite ('chaffing like a bastard!') as the aircraft made good its escape. The remainder of the ingress was uneventful, and the target became visible from some way out, the SEAD support having engaged the defences. Splitting up for their attack runs, the Tornadoes flashed across the desert at 150 ft and 540 kt, each aiming at its own target area on Al Jarrah airfield. During the run-in, Ingle's aircraft was hit by what the crew thought was AA fire (it subsequently turned out to be a birdstrike), but the attack was continued and the JP233 munitions released. The escape from the target was smooth, although the blanket AAA continued to light up the sky well after the aircraft had departed. Total mission time was 4 hr 10 min.

The crews for the Al Jarrah mission were:

Flt Lt Beet/Flt Lt Osborne (27)	A
Flt Lt Ruddock/Sqn Ldr Crowley (27)	D
Sqn Ldr Waddington/Flt Lt Hammans (27)	I
Fg Off Ingle/Flt Lt McKernan (617)	M

Steve Hillier gives the following graphic account of a mission:

Each airfield had around 40 emplacements for anti-aircraft guns, and each gun was now blazing skywards, throwing up a wall of waving bright tracer. It was unaimed fire, but the canopy of light it produced over the target made it visible from over 30 miles away. This gave the crews of the approaching Tornadoes three to four minutes to contemplate the sight, and the fact that they would soon have to fly right through this curtain. Closing in toward the target at 200 ft and 540 kt, short, terse comments between pilot and navigator confirmed that the target had been accurately marked with the radar, all switches were live for weapon release, a final check that the radar warning receiver was clear (of threats), then into the thick of the tracer. The sound of the furious battle raging is lost to the crew cocooned in their cockpit, but the sight of the tracer is enough – and there is only one tracer round in every seven bullets being fired. The weapon aiming computer automatically determines the precise moment for weapon release, the aircraft feels like it is driving over a cobbled road as the JP233 ejects hundreds of munitions in a few seconds, the underside of the aircraft glows as the cratering munitions explode into the runway. An even bigger thump as the canisters blow off the aircraft at the end of the stick of bombs, and then it's out the other side. A sudden bright flash and a fireball across the desert floor as one of the 27 Squadron aircraft crashes – the first RAF casualties of the war.

During this mission ZA392, flying No. 3 in Norwich formation, was lost and the crew, Wg Cdr Nigel Elsdon (the squadron commander) and his navigator, Flt Lt Max Collier, were killed. This first loss was greeted with deep shock by the other crews, but all were kept very busy and had little time to dwell on the causes.

On the following day, 18 January, prime minister John Major explained Britain's position in the UN operations:

We are acting with the authority of the United Nations and on behalf of the whole world. It is a just cause. It is right that we in Britain should play our part; and we shall, I promise you, bring our own forces back home just as soon as it is safe to do so.

On 19 January an additional Victor was taken to Muharraq to ease the workload, as the squadron was flying an average of 14 sorties a day.

The eight aircraft of Belfast formation left Muharraq at 14:57z on the 19th to attack the major operational airfield at Tallil in central Iraq. Four of the aircraft were tasked with suppression of the airfield AAA defences, while the others used JP233 to attack the airfield surfaces. Having refuelled from the VC.10s, the formation dropped to low level for its route through Iraq to the target. All remained quiet until the first bombs went off, then all hell broke loose, with streams of tracer everywhere. The JP attacks went well, but at some point during the attack the No. 2 aircraft, 'Foxtrot', was shot down, probably by a Roland missile. Flight Lieutenants Dave Waddington and Robbie Stewart ejected safely, although the latter suffered major leg injuries. Both were to become POWs. Nige Ingle and Paul McKernan were at the back end of the formation. Their cockpit voice tape of the attack expresses so much:

Pilot: A few explosions ahead. No AAA so far.
Nav: Happy with the first offset . . . 15 miles to run . . . five late . . . 13 miles . . . nothing on the RHWR . . . 567 knots . . . nine miles . . . corner's painting . . . good mark . . . chaffing . . . one mile . . . nothing on the RWHR.
Pilot: Over release.
Nav: It's going, it's going . . . there go the canisters.
Pilot: Yeehah!
Nav: We are the boys!
Pilot: Let's get ourselves away. They're still firing, look. That was a brilliantly successful attack . . . they didn't know we were coming.
Nav: They're all asleep. They're all in their little beds. SAM out on the left hand side but it's just looking.

On the following night the target for the Muharraq crews was the dispersed operating base (DOB) of Al Najef, with a medium-level attack planned. Refuelling this time was from two Victors. The mission went with hardly a snag and, in conjunction with the effects of a B-52 raid, caused significant damage to the DOB.

It was the turn of Jalibah airfield on the night of the 21st, eight Muharraq aircraft leading a large package against this heavily defended target. Weather over the target was good, although patches of ground fog obscured some detail of the HAS site desired mean points of impact (DMPIs).

Two nights later the target, Mudaysis airfield, was covered by cloud, but the navigators had good radar returns and were able to deliver the bombs with reasonable accuracy.

The standard weapon load was now eight 1,000 lb free-fall bombs, and the range of targets now including barracks, ammunition dumps, and industrial installations (oil and power stations) as well as airfields. Six aircraft, two having aborted the mission owing to unserviceability, attacked the Al Zubayr oil pumping station on the 23rd, witnessing secondary explosions from the target area. The troposcatter site at An Nasiriyah was the target for the Muharraq force, although a spate of unserviceabilities meant that only three aircraft actually bombed the target. To make up for that, nine out of ten attacked the petrol storage site at An Najef on the 28th.

The last mission of the month, on 30 January, was an eight-ship attack on the Al Jahrah commando camp and SAM facility. Take-off for this short trip (less than two hours) was planned for 18:00, and there was just time for a quick squadron song to celebrate Sqn Ldr John Taylor's birthday before the out-brief and the walk to the aircraft.

Petro-chemical sites were on the menu for 1 February, eight aircraft being tasked to attack the site at Al Aziziyah, that at Al Hillah being the reserve for the second element should the first four-ship formation destroy the primary target. Shortly after the first bombs went down there was a vast secondary explosion that the second four-ship could see from their trailing position some distance away. They went for the secondary target.

A guidance system is needed to ensure consistent accuracy in this scenario, and at the time the only exponents of this art were the Lossiemouth Buccaneers. A detachment deployed to Muharraq to undertake target marking for the laser-guided bombs (LGBs) carried by the Tornadoes. Attacks would now have to be carried out in daylight from medium level, to allow the 'spiker' Buccaneer a clear view of the target. The basic principle behind the LGB is that a laser is fired at the target, the aiming point being signified by cross on the navigator's screen. Once he is happy that the target has been correctly identified, he fires the laser and the bomber releases its weapons. The bombs then pick up the reflected laser energy and 'home' on to the target. A direct hit (DH) is virtually guaranteed. The standard procedure was for one Buccaneer to spike for two Tornadoes, each of which carried three LGBs.

The first operation was flown from Muharraq on 3 February. This was a standard arrangement of two three-ships, with two Tornadoes and one Buccaneer in each formation. Practice with Pave Spike (the airborne laser designator used to direct the LGBs) had been carried out in the days leading up to this, to perfect the techniques and inter-crew co-operation. The target was the railway bridge at Muftal Wadam, with a time on target of 12:00. The first pair achieved a good hit on their end of the bridge, but the second pair missed the other end.

For the next ten days it was a mix of standard eight-ship attacks interspersed with LGB attacks. Seven aircraft dropped 56 1,000 lb bombs on the Tall Al Lahm ammunition storage site on the 3rd, the main target being a group of 100 storage bunkers to the east of this huge complex. The following day it was back to LGBs against the An Nasiriyah railway bridge. Nasiriyah was the target again on the 5th, the thermal power station being visited by four aircraft. Another eight-ship was up on the 6th to attack a variety of targets on Al Jarrah airfield, scene of the first Tornado mission. Al Basrah petrol production and storage site was next on the list, eight Tornadoes each dropping five 1,000 lb bombs into the complex. As with most targets, there was still a fair amount of AAA, but almost all of this was well below the Tornado attack heights. Although a number of SAM radar indications were picked up by the radar warning equipment, it was becoming increasingly rare actually to see any missiles.

Another oil installation was targeted on the 8th, eight aircraft attacking Al Zubayr for the second time. The storage tanks at Bayji South were the subject of an LGB attack on the 9th; this target was in the north of Iraq, a lengthy trip for the four Tornadoes and two Buccaneers. The LGB tactic was employed again the following day against one of the road bridges at An Nasiriyah, both ends of the bridge being hit. That same day, six aircraft took 1,000 lb bombs to the Al Basrah oil refinery.

Al Jarrah was revisited on the 11th.

The Muharraq crews had a hectic schedule right up to the last day of the conflict, all but one employing the medium-level LGB option.:

12 Feb. 6 aircraft. Lafiya SSM facility.
14 Feb. 4 aircraft. Al Taquaddum airfield. LGB.
15 Feb. 4 aircraft. Kut Al Hay East airfield. LGB.
15 Feb. 4 aircraft. Kut Al Hay East airfield. LGB.

16 Feb. 4 aircraft. Amara airfield. LGB.
18 Feb. 4 aircraft. Jalibah airfield. LGB.
18 Feb. 4 aircraft. Jalibah airfield. LGB.
19 Feb. 4 aircraft. Shaibah airfield. LGB.
19 Feb. 3 aircraft. Shaibah airfield. LGB.
20 Feb. 4 aircraft. Kut Al Hay airfield. LGB.
21 Feb. 4 aircraft. Qalit Salih airfield. LGB.
22 Feb. 4 aircraft. Kut Al Hay airfield. LGB.
23 Feb. 4 aircraft. Qalit Salih airfield. LGB.
24 Feb. 4 aircraft. Tallil airfield. LGB.
25 Feb. 4 aircraft. Shaykh Mazhar airfield. LGB.
26 Feb. 4 aircraft. Shaykh Mazhar airfield. LGB.
27 Feb. 4 aircraft. Taqaddum airfield. LGB.
27 Feb. 4 aircraft. Shaykh Mazhar airfield. LGB.

The weather caused problems for the spikers on some missions, but overall the results were good. During the 26 February attack on Shaykh Mazhr airfield a number of transport aircraft were seen on the airfield, so the back pair, Flt Lt Cobb/Fg Off Wilson and Flt Lt Byford/Flt Lt Morris, decided to go down and strafe these targets. They claimed one damaged.

The Tabuk detachment had been equally busy, with three crews of 617 Squadron operating on most days from 30 January. The two thermal-imaging airborne laser designator (TIALD) crews and one bomber crew, a split crew operating with a 13 Squadron pilot and a 16 Squadron Navigator, were: Wg Cdr Bob Iveson/Flt Lt Chris Purkiss; Flt Lt Gareth Walker/Flt Lt Adrian Frost; (Sqn Ldr Greg Monaghan)/Flt Lt Harry Hargreaves; Flt Lt Al Monkman/(Flt Lt Paul Smyth).

The first sortie from this base to involve Marham aircrew took place on the 30 January, when Al Monkman and his 16 Squadron navigator, Paul Smyth (who was ex-27 Squadron), took part in an attack on the Rufhah Fuwad Scud missile testing site. This same crew flew six more bombing missions during the first week of February.

Meanwhile, the 617 Squadron element at Tabuk was about to give the RAF's newest piece of kit, the TIALD pod, a live test. The TIALD was still in the pre-production stage when it was called up for service in the Gulf, and in early February two pods, which soon acquired the names Sharon and Tracy (after two comic characters), were in theatre. After one quick training sortie the two 617 crews, Wg Cdr Bob Iveson/Flt Lt Chris Purkiss and Flt Lt Gareth Walker/Flt Lt Adrian Frost, who had only just arrived in theatre themselves, declared that they were ready to go.

The first operational mission with the new system was flown on 10 February. The targets were HASs on the H3 Southwest airfield, and the 617 TIALD aircraft acted as designators for the Tabuk bombers.

The same routine was followed for the remainder of the war, and TIALD rapidly proved how good it was. Missions were flown on the 11th (Hachama road bridge), 12th (Ruwayshid airfield), 13th (Al Asad airfield), 14th (H2 airfield), 15th (Mudaysis and H2 airfields), 16th (H3 and Jalibah airfields), 17th (As Samwah bridge), 18th (Fallujah bridge), 19th (Al Jarrah airfield), 20th and 21st (Shaibah airfield), 22nd (Al Jarrah airfield), 23rd (Wadi Al Khir airfield), 24th (Tallil airfield), 25th (As Samawah bridge), 26th (Habbaniyah airfield), 27th (Al Asad airfield), and, finally, the 27th (Habbaniyah airfield). In total the 617 Squadron crews flew 30 TIALD operations (with very few kit problems despite the newness of both the equipment and its operators), seven with 1,000-pounders, and six using LGBs.

At Muharraq on 28 February, crews were briefed and ready for a cluster bomb unit (CBU) attack on an airfield when the mission was scrubbed. They sat down to watch the news broadcast by US president George Bush, announcing a ceasefire.

The ceasefire came into effect on the morning of the 28th and operations were brought to an end, although it was still regarded as a 'wait and

Crews visited Kuwait after the ceasefire. Nige Ingle and Paul McKernan 'admire' a crater. (Paul McKernan)

see' situation, rather than a definite end to hostilities. With the news broadcast over, it was back to the hotel and a party with the TV AM crews, with whom a good 'working relationship' had been established. The detachments held readiness for another couple of weeks, but a return to home bases was then authorized.

The crews of 27 Squadron flew a total of 89 missions during the conflict, and 617 Squadron notched up a similar number. The Victors were proud of their 100 per cent success record, totalling almost 300 sorties. Despite ill-informed media criticism, the Tornado had proved to be a great success in the Gulf. The gaining of air superiority after the first 10 days of the conflict meant that medium-level tactics became viable; hence the introduction of LGBs and TIALD. Marham's units had once again proved themselves.

With the conflict over, everyone settled in. Back at Marham it was back to the normal routine – after a short period of leave.

There are three aspects to the programme followed by the station's Tornado squadrons: operational deployments, major exercises, and routine training.

The most appropriate way to look at these is to describe one or two examples of each in detail. As it is an operational requirement, the

The Russians are here! An exchange of gifts following one of the inspection visits by a Russian team.

MENU

Smoked Venison and Redcurrant Jelly

*****

Scallops Mexican Style

*****

**Tournedos Cordon Rouge
Rissolee Potatoes
Bouquet of Green Beans
Grilled Tomato**

*****

Blackcurrant Delice

*****

Coffee and Rum Truffles

*****

English Cheeseboard

*****

Chef Flight Sergeant Gordon Bruce MacGregor

A menu from the Gulf War commemoration dinner held by the Marham squadrons. (Paul McKernan)

Operation *Jural* commitment is by far the most significant. With the changes being made to the RAF's structure in Germany, another Tornado unit, II (AC) Squadron from RAF Laarbruch, equipped with GR.1As, was moved to Marham. The squadron had been heavily engaged during the Gulf Conflict, flying hazardous singleton reconnaissance missions at night throughout Iraq, and acquiring the epithet 'Scud-hunters' for their work in tracking down the elusive missile launchers. Their arrival in December 1991 heralded the station's future role as a reconnaissance base.

A line-up of II(AC) Squadron on 'Alpha' dispersal, with 55 Squadron dispersal in the background.

Operation Jural

The hoped-for change in the Iraqi leadership did not take place, and within months of the end of the conflict Saddam Hussein was using his armed forces to reimpose his authority on dissident areas in the north and south of Iraq. In the north the Kurdish population had been seeking independence for many years, and had suffered severe repression. In the aftermath of the war, and in the hope that the Iraqi military had been

Decorative Victor; XH672 sports a good selection of artwork, including petrol pump mission symbols from the Gulf and an 'I ran Offutt' cartoon, August 1993.

A fly-by marks the end of an era (and the Victor's passsing) as 55 Squadron disbands.

weakened, they made yet another bid. The response was swift and vicious. Consequently the UN declared a number of safe havens and imposed a 'no-fly' zone north of the 36th parallel. Coalition aircraft, including RAF Jaguars, deployed to bases in Turkey to enforce this policy.

Once again the ranges involved meant that AAR was required and, once again, the tired but irreplaceable Victors were called out. In early September 55 Squadron sent a detachment to Akrotiri to work with the Jaguars flying out of Incirlik, in southern Turkey. This commitment, alternated with the VC.10 tankers, continued for the next two years. Meanwhile, in the south of Iraq, the Shi'ite Muslims rebelled against the

The scrapmen take control of the Victor fleet. Fortunately, a number were flown away for preservation.

Baghdad regime, and were soon on the receiving end of the attentions of the Republican Guard. The UN imposed a second 'no-fly' zone, and Marham's aircraft once more went into the sheds to be given pink skins.

Aircraft of 617 Squadron and II (AC) Squadron deployed to Dhahran in Saudi Arabia, and within hours of their arrival were airborne as part of the Coalition force enforcing the no-fly zone.

December saw the Victors involved once more in the Gulf, operating from their old base at Muharraq and taking over from the VC.10s to work with the GR.1 detachment at Dhahran. This rotation between the two types continued for the next year or so, the last Victor leaving the theatre on 15 October 1993 in order to be back at Marham in time for the squadron to disband.

After almost 30 years at the forefront of the AAR world, and with an impressive operational record, the Victors were pensioned off with the disbandment of 55 Squadron on 15 October. All aircraft come to the end of their useful life-spans, but to see the Victors being cut up for scrap on the far side of the airfield was very sad. Fortunately a few were saved, and one even comes to life from time to time with a 'fast taxy' down the runway at Bruntingthorpe.

The Jural mission

The attempted revolt in the areas around Basra, primarily by the Marsh Arabs, was an attempt to break free of the rigid control exercised by Baghdad in the years before the Gulf conflict. However, once again the Iraqi military showed that it was by no means impotent following the Gulf War, and strong forces moved into the marshes to quell the revolt.

This is, however, a very difficult region in which to operate a modern military machine. One of the greatest assets is air power, especially tactical air power, and in the face of combined arms operations the Marsh Arabs rapidly lost ground. The Iraqi leadership adopted a policy of virtual extermination, razing villages to the ground.

Once again the Coalition stepped in and imposed a 'no-fly' zone to cover the area, extending over the whole of Iraq south of the 32nd parallel. The major difference between this and the northern zone was that no Coalition ground forces were involved and no safe havens established; it was purely a case of 'don't fly in this area, or else'.

To enforce this policy a Coalition air force was assembled. Southern Watch, the major element of this air arm, is provided by the USA, the two primary elements being the 4404th Composite Wing (provisional) USAF forces, plus a naval task force centred around an aircraft carrier in the Persian Gulf. The Allied contribution is provided by France and Britain, in addition to certain types of missions flown by Arab air forces over their own airspace.

The RAF contribution received a great deal of publicity when first announced in August 1992, the spotlight falling on the Tornado force deploying from RAF Marham. As the primary task was to be reconnaissance, the intial deployment comprised three Tornado GR.1As from No. II (IAC) Squadron and three Tornado GR.1s from 617 Squadron. Crews came from the respective units, although in due course the GR.1As were replaced one-for-one by GR.1s.

The only other in-theatre operational element

The author (right) and his pilot, Flt Lt 'Taff' Evans, on Operation Jural; note combat vests.

was provided by VC.10 tanker support from 101 Squadron. As usual, however, the Air Transport (AT) force has played, and continues to play, an immense part in both deploying and supporting the detachment. An HS.125 of 32 Squadron provides in-theatre transportation for the RAF Air Commander, although it also performs a range of other tasks.

When the Tornado detachment arrived at Dharhan it did not know what to expect. What type of missions would be required, and would the Iraqis react to the presence of Coalition aircraft? The first task was to set up a base, as there was little other than a bare patch of desert and a few tents, plus temperatures of 50°C and a healthy population of camel spiders and scorpions. Meanwhile, the first operational sortie was flown within hours of arrival in theatre, proof once more of the inherent advantages of air power over other forms of military intervention.

While the 'desert pink', or more accurately Alkali Removable Temporary Finish (ARTF), aircraft adapted themselves to the heat, the detachment personnel constructed their shanty town using a mixture of formal and informal acquisitions. The Americans, as ever, provided excellent support.

The primary aim of the Coalition forces is to deter repression of the civilian population and impose the 'no-fly' zone, but, as with the northern operation, the systematic monitoring of Iraqi military activity in the area provides a useful secondary task. Tasking follows a standard pattern whereby a list of areas to be overflown is put together by the planners and given as a mission to a package commander. The package commander is provided with a set of resources with which to achieve the aim of policing the airspace in the no-fly zone.

A typical package comprises fighters, reconnaissance aircraft and defence suppression aircraft; for example, F-16/F-15/F-14/Mirage 2000 fighter CAP and/or escort, F-15E/F-14/A-6 Intruder/Tornado reconnaissance, F-4G/EF-111/EA-6B Prowler defence suppression. The size of the 'package' is decided by the tasking agency, but the employment of the package, within the constraints of the task, is the job of the package commander. Additional support is provided by a variety of AAR resources plus AWACS via Grumman E-2 Hawkeye aircraft. The 'mix and match' of these assets is very variable, packages varying from less than ten aircraft up to 40 plus.

The primary aim of the RAF mission is reconnaissance, and the detachment includes a Reconnaissance Interpretation Centre (RIC) run by skilled Photographic Interpreters, whose task it is to examine the returned film and decide what elements of interest can be found.

At the time of writing this is an ongoing deployment, so much of what it entails must remain 'under wraps'. There is little future in revealing details of operational employment and tactics, even though certain sections of the media think they have a right to know every little detail.

At present, all sorties are flown at medium level, although RAF crews maintain their low-level proficiency by flying sorties in Kuwait. It is saddening to fly around Kuwait. Large expanses of desert are black with oil, and it will no doubt be years before nature restores the balance. Most of the destroyed Iraqi armour and other vehicles has now been cleared into compounds, and these provide excellent reconnaissance training for crews. However, in some areas one still finds a lone T-72 tank or D-30 artillery piece. Major structures have yet to be repaired; their level of destruction is testimony to the ferocity and effectiveness of the air campaign.

The Kuwaiti Air Force re-established itself at Kuwait City International Airport (KCIA), and operates a good selection of combat aircraft, including an increasing number of F-18s. The A-4s and Mirages remain an important element in the KAF Order of Battle (ORBAT), as do the Puma and Gazelle helicopters.

An A-4 pilot recently discovered that ejecting safely from a stricken aircraft was only the start of his problems. Having made a good parachute descent into the desert he was somewhat amazed and unnerved to find that he had landed in the middle of a minefield. It took some hours for a rescue party to free him. Mines remain a major hazard in Kuwait. The Iraqis laid millions of anti-personnel and anti-tank mines, and clearing them is a slow and dangerous task.

The question of mines occupied one RAF crew when they were volunteered as participants in a Combat Rescue exercise taking place in the Kuwaiti desert. A briefing on how to recognise a variety of mines and unexploded ordnance (much of it from Coalition aircraft), did little to put their minds at rest. However, the actual rescue by MH-53 was described as 'awesome', as the helicopter appeared out of the night sky to pluck the 'survivor' from the clutches of the 'enemy'.

This was yet one more example of how well the Allied co-operative effort worked.

Co-operation between all of the participating air forces is the key to the success of such ventures, as was proved during the war. The fact that the main participants have been involved in NATO exercises, and especially such major events as Red Flag, has proved a major factor. A typical Southern Watch mission follows the same basic precepts from planning through to execution and debrief as any Red Flag exercise. This does not mean that the whole thing is routine and easy. Far from it. Each mission requires careful planning from the initial intelligence assessments down to the debriefing of every small element. If something has gone wrong, it needs to be highlighted so that it does not go wrong the next time.

Because of the distances involved, with missions operating over Iraq from the main Coalition bases, AAR is an essential part of any task. The Tornado force tends to work with its own VC.10 tankers, but if these are not available the USAF KC-10s provide an excellent secondary 'gas station'. With a fixed time to cross the border incorporated in the mission task, any pre-task tanking becomes the first critical point, and all aircraft must take on board the required amount of fuel in the planned time. Any delays will create a ripple in the plan.

It is all too easy for a tanker to appear with one of its hoses not working, thus halving availability because as all aircraft have to take it in turns on the remaining hose. It may well be that some other trade is already at the tanker, taking up part of someone else's slot. These are elements that the formation leader must juggle to ensure that his formation is in the right place at the right time, and with enough fuel to complete the task. Any major variations have to go through the package commander, as they may affect the entire mission.

Once the force is over the border the balancing act continues, keeping a mental picture of who is on station, ensuring that the necessary cover is available and, if it is not, revising the plan. Iraqi airspace is potentially hostile both from the air and from the ground, so it is no place to relax. The Coalition has warned Iraq not to operate aircraft or helicopters in the area, and that is why the Coalition air forces patrol there.

Having returned from the sorties the crews carry out an extensive debrief, both on what they observed over Iraq and on how well the mission went. The crews work a six-day week, flying on average twice every three days, although this rate is largely dictated by the rate of tasking. Missions can be tasked at any time, day and night, the latter having the advantage of crewing-in when the temperature is somewhat lower. Until or unless

Number 27 Squadron became 12 Squadron with the change to a maritime role for the Tornado, before departing to Lossiemouth. Here, a departing Buccaneer and a Tornado, displaying both squadrons' markings, visit a Victor.

One of Marham's newest arrivals, a Tornado of XIII Squadron, with Victor XL512.

The Royal Review aircraft line-up, April 1993.

there is some major change in either Iraqi or Coalition policy, it seems likely that the RAF will be maintaining operational deployments to cover both of the 'no-fly' zones.

With the impending demise of the maritime Buccaneers at Lossiemouth, the decision was made to replace them with two Tornado squadrons. The two Marham GR.1 squadrons were designated for this change of role and the consequent move to Scotland. The first to 're-equip' with the GR.1B (GR.1s modified to carry the Sea Eagle anti-ship missile), was 27 Squadron. Throughout the summer of 1993 the squadron undertook initial training in the new role, although none of the modified aircraft were yet available. No more flashing around at low level overland in four-ship formations; they now faced the complex task of planning co-ordinated attacks of up to six aircraft at ultra low level over the sea. As usual with major changes in the RAF's structure, some squadrons have to renumber, and 27 Squadron took on the ex-Buccaneer numberplate of 12 Squadron. The move to Lossiemouth was made in October 1993. Meanwhile, 617 Squadron had also been exploring their new role, and this unit moved to Lossiemouth in April 1994.

A few months before that, however, Marham's strength had been increased by the arrival of two more reconnaissance units. In December 1993 the Canberra PR.9s of 39 (1 PRU) Squadron arrived from Wyton, thus opening the station's third Canberra period. The PR.9s remained part of No. 18 Group, lodging on this No. 1 Group Station. Then, the following February, the RAF's other Tornado reconnaissance unit, XIII Squadron, came from Honington. Marham was now the home of a major reconnaissance wing, the most significant collection of reconnaissance assets in the RAF.

Besides operational commitments in the Gulf, and in common with all RAF units, the Marham Tornado units are kept very busy with major exercises outside the UK. These take two forms; routine detachments such as the Deci APCs and the OLF training at Goose Bay (Western Vortex), and major NATO or alliance exercises in various parts of the world. In recent years such tasking has included *Arctic Express* (Norway), *Distant Frontier/Cope Thunder* (Alaska), *Distant Thunder* (Turkey), *Desert Sword* (Gulf States), and *Red Flag* (Nevada).

Most of these have the same basic aims of allowing RAF crews to operate in other geo-

The Royal Review on the RAF's 75th Anniversary, a major event held at Marham. Marching on the Squadron Standards.

Royal Review 1993; Her Majesty the Queen meets local children.

At 617 Squadron's 50th Anniversary, the parade is inspected by Flt Lt Ken Brown.

graphical regions, with other air forces, to develop mutual understanding and commonality of procedures. The American package concept is the usual basis for the exercise. The involvement of II (AC) Squadron in Exercise Arctic Express in March 1994 was typical of such deployments, and serves to illustrate them.

Exercise Arctic Express 94

The northern part of Norway was always seen as a vulnerable yet strategically vital area of the NATO defensive perimeter, and as such it became the scene of regular, often large-scale, 'reinforcement exercises'. *Arctic Express* is one of the series of deployment exercises designed to provide in-theatre training for elements of the Reinforcement Forces allocated to this region, and includes land, sea, and air elements.

In March 1994 the scenario was an amphibious assault force landing in the region just to the north of Bardufoss airfield. Air assets play a vital role in the defensive strategy for this region, and for this exercise the RAF deployed a number of fast-jet units; Harriers and Jaguars to Bardufoss,

and the Tornado GR.1As of II(AC) Squadron to Bodo. Bodo Air Station, the largest operational airfield in Norway, is home to two F-16 squadrons and a number of other units. In addition to the Tornado deployment of eight aircraft, Bodo also hosted Dutch F-16s and F-5s, plus Norwegian F-16s from bases in southern Norway. A variety of other air assets moved into nearby air bases such as Andoya, Evenes, and Bardufoss.

Seven GR.1A reconnaissance aircraft and one GR.1(T) of II (AC) Squadron deployed to Bodo for three weeks in March 1994. The first afternoon was devoted to extensive briefings by the host nation. It was still very much winter in north Norway in mid-March, and the average temperatures during the detachment ranged from +2° to −15°C, although with a wind of 15 kt the 'apparent' temperature was much lower. Such low temperatures provided a host of problems, not least to the groundcrew, although in this instance all aircraft were housed in HASs. For the aircrew it becomes more a problem of how to survive in the event of ejecting and ending up either in the freezing waters of a fiord or stuck on a mountainside. The snow-covered conditions also give rise to the problem of 'white-out', in which white cloud and snow-covered rock merge into a single white mass, with potentially fatal consequences for the unwary. An additional hazard to flying in Norway is that of wires strung across the all-too-attractive fiords. Most fiords have them, and they are almost impossible to see. With such words of wisdom the briefings ended, and the tasking for the first few days began to arrive.

The initial sorties were designed as familiarization profiles, most missions being to the south of the exercise area and the approaching amphibious task force being a favoured target. The weather was its usual variable self, changing from 20 miles' visibility and almost no cloud to nil visibility in a snow shower in a matter of seconds. Most sorties were tasked as singleton reconnaissance missions or as attack pairs/four-ships, the former often serving as pre-attack reconnaissance for a follow-on F-16 anti-shipping mission.

While the fleet made its way north, the ground troops in the exercise area were in a training and deployment phase, the Forward Air Control (FAC) parties proving particularly keen to receive trade. All missions to the exercise area were likely to be engaged by the defending fighters, primarily F-16s, including, in the second week, a number of USAF aircraft armed with advanced medium-range air-to-air missiles (AMRAAMs).

The AWACs aircraft were airborne on most days, providing information to friend and foe alike. Such 'bogeydome' information was invaluable to the attack mission trying to thread its way at low level through the threats; the idea being to avoid combat and reach the target unharmed. However, on most occasions this was not to be, and the F-16s appeared out of the clouds, intent on closing for an AIM-9 kill. The performance of this agile aircraft was such that, once the raider was found, it was hard for him to make a fight of it. By going fast and low, and trying to hide behind mountains, the intended victim could only hope to make his attacker's life as difficult as possible, and perhaps force him to seek easier prey. It was, however, an advantage to have one's own AIM-9, and during the exercise the squadron claimed a number of 'kills' against F-16s.

Having avoided the fighters and settled down to deal with the ground targets, there was no time to relax. First came the problem of finding them; black dots of vehicles among the black dots of the background or hidden under the trees. With

an attack speed of 500 kt plus, and with the target intent on shooting its attacker down with SAMs or anti-aircraft fire, it made for an exciting few minutes. The Tornado reconnaissance system, with its heat-sensing infrared and real-time cockpit display, ideal for finding camouflaged troops and vehicles, demonstrated its ability during Arctic Express. Having flown over the target area, the crew could then relay accurate target information to either a follow-on attack force, a concept known as Recce-Attack Interface (RAI), or to base operations.

On return to Bodo, the aircraft's reconnaissance tapes were downloaded and sent to the Reconnaissance Intelligence Centre (RIC) for detailed examination by the Photographic Interpreters (PIs). The PI and mission aircrew worked together to analyze the tapes and extract the maximum information. At a later stage the PIs made a more detailed examination of the other areas covered on the tape. The crew, meanwhile, took the chance to grab a quick meal from the field kitchen before picking up the next task to plan. Out in the HAS the aircraft had been re-fuelled and, if appropriate, bombed-up for the next task.

As the exercise progressed, so the missions became a little more complex, with increased, albeit small-scale, use of attack packages. For example, the Tornado pair or four-ship might be given an F-16 escort and limited defence suppression support. Having a pair of F-16s to sweep ahead of the formation was a definite bonus, as they could engage the 'enemy' Combat Air Patrol (CAP) long enough to eliminate the threat. On the way to and from the tasked target it was essential for crews to keep a look-out for targets of opportunity; a frigate hiding in a fiord, perhaps, or a group of helicopters disgorging troops on the edge of a clearing. Such information was essential to help the intelligence staff keep an accurate plot of the theatre of operations.

During the last few days of the exercise the weather turned particularly bad, the airfield at Bodo frequently vanishing under a few centimetres of snow in less than an hour, and missions were delayed or cancelled. Nevertheless, by the end of the final week the squadron had accomplished the majority of its tasks, and could look back on *Arctic Express* as a useful training period, during which it had operated from a deployed base in harsh weather conditions and flown missions with other NATO air forces. On the social

Hardened aircraft shelter 47, with a GR.1A of II(AC) Squadron carrying out engine runs. Note the debris guard. The arrival of 39 Squadron's Canberra PR.9s completed the Marham reconnaissance wing.

side, there was time for the expert and not-so-expert skiers to take to the 'idiot boards' on the various local slopes, plus a chance to take in the local sights, such as the world famous Saltstrumen maelstrom.

Bosnia

The break-up of Yugoslavia into ethnic conflict returned that region to its late 19th century troubles, amounting to 'inter-tribal' warfare. Having been censured in the UN, the various factions, and in particular the more powerful Serbian elements, were reluctant to achieve a peaceful solution. The UN therefore decided to deploy a humanitarian force to try and relieve some of the suffering of the beleaguered towns. To support the NATO ground forces (for it was NATO that picked up this European task), air task forces were deployed to the region. The RAF's major contribution took the form of Jaguars from Coltishall and Tornado F.3s.

Although the Tornado reconnaissance force was not called upon, the Canberra PR.9s, with their wide range of photographic sensors, have been extensively employed.

At the time these final words were written, December 1994, one of Marham's units, XIII Squadron, was back on Operation *Jural,* and the PR.9s of 39 Squadron were still active around Bosnia. All of the units have a hectic schedule planned for 1995. Marham is also likely to increase in size, following the recently announced decision to move the Red Arrows from Scampton to Marham during the year.

Even in these times of major defence changes, the future of RAF Marham looks secure. Since its origins, Marham has been at the forefront of the operational side of the RAF, and this seems set to continue.

APPENDIX A

STATION COMMANDERS

1916	Maj H. Wyllie
1916	Maj F.E. Baker
1917	Maj H. Wyllie
1918	Maj H.L.H. Owen
	Station closed
1937	Gp Capt A.P.V. Daly AFC
1939	Gp Capt H.P. Lloyd MC DFC
1940	Gp Capt C. Hilton-Keith
1940	Gp Capt V.E. Groom OBE DFC
1941	Gp Capt A.C. Evans-Evans
1941	Gp Capt A. McKee DSO DFC AFC
1942	Gp Capt W.H. Kyle DFC
1945	Air Cdre G. Spencer
1947	Air Cdre W.E. Staton CB DSO MC DFC
1949	Gp Capt P.W. Stansfield DFC
1951	Gp Capt B.A. Casey OBE
1952	Gp Capt O.R. Donaldson CBE DSO DFC
1955	Gp Capt R.C. Ayling OBE

1956	Gp Capt L.M. Hodges CBE DSO DFC
1959	Gp Capt W.J. Burnett DSO DFC AFC
1961	Gp Capt I.R. Campbell AFC
1964	Gp Capt P.A. Kennedy DSO DFC AFC
1967	Gp Capt D. Roberts DFC AFC
1970	Gp Capt J.E. Smith AFC
1972	Gp Capt V. McNabney GM
1974	Gp Capt H.A. Caillard
1975	Gp Capt D. Parry-Evans
1977	Gp Capt B.J. Jackson BA
1979	Gp Capt M.A. Sutherland MBE
1980	Gp Capt J.S.B. Price CBE ADC
1983	Gp Capt R.P. O'Brien OBE ADC BA
1985	Gp Capt P.C. Norriss AFC ADC MA
1987	Gp Capt D.F.A. Henderson OBE ADC
1990	Gp Capt G.E. Stirrup AFC ADC
1992	Gp Capt N.R. Irving AFC ADC
1994	Gp Capt J.A. Broadbent DSO ADC

APPENDIX B

MARHAM AIRCRAFT

This list is compiled from entries in the Operational Record Books (Public Record Office Air 28 series for RAF Marham and Air 27 series for the individual squadrons). Although such documents are without doubt the best primary research material available, they do contain errors and omissions. So much depends upon the style in which the compiling officer put together the monthly entry. All too often they include only the barest of detail, and so raise more questions than they answer. Aircraft disposals/fates have been cross-checked with the Air-Britain series of publications on British military aircraft serials, and with the record cards for individual aircraft. There are a number of serial errors in the ORBs, the wrong letter or number combination often giving an aircraft of the wrong type. Where these could not be resolved they have been left in place, but with a note of the actual aircraft type. Nevertheless, this list will provide a good starting point for those wishing to look at aircraft details and losses in greater depth.

The original intention was to provide casualty details where appropriate, but space has precluded this. However, the History Room officer at Marham has been provided with a print-out of the list with these details for those who wish to research this subject.

Abbreviations

AAEE – Aeroplane & Armament Experimental Establishment; AAS – Air Armament School; AOS – Air Observers School; BATF – Beam (originally Blind) Approach Training Flight; BDU – Bombing Development Unit; CGS – Central Gunnery School; CU – Conversion Unit; DBR – Damaged beyond repair; Di – ditched; EANS – Empire Air Navigation School; EWS – Electrical & Wireless School; FL – forced landing; FSCTE – Fire Services Central Training Establishment; FTR – failed to return; FTU – Ferry Training Unit; ME – Middle East; METS – Middle East Training School; MTU – Mosquito Training Unit; MU – Maintenance Unit; NTU –

Navigation Training Unit, Pathfinder Force; OTU – Operational Training Unit; PEE – Proof & Experimental Establishment; RAE – Royal Aircraft Establishment; SD – shot down; SFU – Signals Flying Unit; SOC – Struck off Charge; SoTT – School of Technical Training; WO – written off; TFU – Telecommunications Flying Unit.

First World War Aircraft

Royal Aircraft Factory F.E.2b

4871	
4890	
4980	
A5519	
A5520	
A5523	
A5532	
A5548	
A5549	
A5551	
A5584	
A5723	
A5724	
A5729	
A5753	
A5758	
A5778	
A6465	
6521	B.E.12?
6531	B.E.12?
7021	
7676	
7680	Crashed Tibbenham 28.11.16
7817	F.B.9?
9121	
9125	

Avro

?3030	
?3032	
?3033	

504A	A3365		I	L4305	to 5 MU
504A	A3367		I	L4306	to 214 Sqn
	?3501		I	L4307	to 38 Sqn
	?3502		I	L4317	to 23 MU
	?3505		I	L4318	to 8 MU

Fairey Hendon, 38 Squadron, May 1937 – January 1939

			I	L4319	to 5 MU
	K5085	to 1 EWS/1614M	I	L4321	to 8 MU
	K5086	to 1564M	I	L4323	to 8 MU
	K5087	to 1565M	I	L4324	to 10 MU
	K5088	to 1 EWS/1615M	I	L4325	to 10 MU
	K5089	to 1616M	I	L4333	to 8 MU
	K5090	SOC 29.8.39	I	L4334	to 8 MU
	K5091	Crashed Marham 26.5.37	IA	L7774	to 214 Sqn
	K5092	to 1 EWS/1617M	IC	L7796	to 9 Sqn
	K5093	to 1566M	IC	L7798/S	to 218 Sqn
	K5094	SOC 22.1.39	IC	L7801/H	to 4 MU
	K5095	Crashed Marham 25.2.38	IC	L7810/F /R	FTR 23.2.41. Boulogne
	K5096	to 1 EWS/1618M	IC	L7812	to 149 Sqn
	K5097	to 1 EWS/1619M	IC	L7845/U /W	to 4 MU
	K5098	to 1567M	IC	L7854/S /X	to 29 OTU
			IC	L7895/E /G	to Vickers
			IC	N2755	to 18 MU

Handley Page Harrow, 115 Squadron, June 1937 –

			IC	N2756/U	to 38 Sqn
I	K6941	to 8 AOS	IC	N2759	to 38 Sqn
I	K6943	to RAE	IC	N2760/R	to 27 OTU
I	K6944	to 75 Sqn	IA	N2875	to 33 MU
I	K6962	to 75 Sqn	IA	N2876/D	to Bassingbourn
I	K6963	to 75 Sqn	IA	N2877/B	to 75 Sqn
I	K6964	to 8 MU	IA	N2878	to 38 Sqn
I	K6965	to 215 Sqn	IA	N2884	to 38 Sqn
I	K6966	to 75 Sqn	IA	N2885	to 4 MU
I	K6967	to 75 Sqn	IA	N2899/U /N	to 23 MU
I	K6968	Crashed Aldergrove 9.11.37	IA	N2900/E	to 38 Sqn
I	K6969	to 75 Sqn	IA	N2901	to 75 Sqn
I	K6970	to 215 Sqn	IA	N2902/T	to 23 MU
II	K6971	to 215 Sqn	IA	N2947/J	to 4 MU
II	K6972	to 215 Sqn	IA	N2948/A	Hit trees on t/o 24.2.40
II	K6973	to 6 MU	IA	N2949/H /J /G	SD Shipping. 7.4.40
II	K6983	to 4 MU	IA	N2950/J	Crashed on t/o 23.3.40
II	K7012	to 5 MU	IA	N2987/O	Crashed nr Huntingdon 19.3.40
II	K7013	to 215 Sqn	IA	N2988	to 23 MU
II	K7014	to 215 Sqn	IA	N2989	to 23 MU
II	K7015	to 24 MU	IA	N2990	to 23 MU
II	K7019	Crashed Speke 21.10.38	IA	P2524	SD N. Sea 7.4.40
II	K7020	to 215 Sqn	IA	P9207	to 218 Sqn
II	K7028	to 215 Sqn	IA	P9224/F /I	to 311 Sqn
			IA	P9226/I /D	to 4 MU

Vickers-Armstrongs Wellington, 115 Squadron – September 1942

			IA	P9227/A	FTR 19.7.40 a/c factories
			IA	P9229/S	Crashed nr Rouen 15.5.40
I	L4221	to 10 MU	IA	P9230/R	to 311 Sqn
I	L4295	to 10 MU	IA	P9235/G	to 311 Sqn
I	L4299	to 5 MU	IA	P9236/B	Burnt out 11.7.40
I	L4300	to 8 MU	IC	P9271/O	belly-landing 11.4.40
I	L4301	to 23 MU	IC	P9283/U	FL Oulton 27.10.40
			IC	P9284/J	SD 11.4.40. Stavanger
			IC	P9285/T	to Brooklands

IC	P9286/K	SD 17.11.40. Hamburg
IC	P9290/K	to Brooklands
IC	P9291	to 9 MU
IC	P9292	to 75 Sqn
IC	P9296	to 218 Sqn
IC	P9297/F	FTR 21.5.40 Bridges
IC	P9298/H	FTR 20.5.40. Guise-Cambrai
IC	P9299/O /P /T	Crashed Wittering 17.11.40
IC	P9300/Q	to 4 MU
IC	R1004/U	Crashed Cambridge 12.2.41
IC	R1033/D	to 38 Sqn
IC	R1034/J /R	to 22 OTU
IC	R1063/T /D	FTR 5/6.7.41. Munster
IC	R1084/Q	SD nr Swaffham 11.2.41
IC	R1094	to 9 MU
IC	R1179/W	to Brooklands
IC	R1219/D	to Brooklands
IC	R1221/F	Crashed East Winch 23.2.41. Brest
IC	R1222/H	FTR. 17.4.41. Duisberg
IC	R1238/A	Crashed Finningley 12.2.41. Hannover
IC	R1269/F	to Czech training unit
IC	R1280/H	Crashed Oakington 4.5.41. Brest
IC	R1332/X	FTR 26/27.9.41. Emden
IC	R1379/B	FTR 10.5.41. Hamburg
IC	R1468/G	Crashed West Raynham 28.8.41. Mannheim
IC	R1469/Q /V	to 149 Sqn
IC	R1470/H	SD over Wash 4.4.41. Brest
IC	R1471/V /T	FTR 5/6.8.41 Mannheim
IC	R1474	to 149 Sqn
IC	R1496/A	
IC	R1500/K	Di 14/15.8.41. Osnabruck
IC	R1501/X	Crashed on t/o 27.6.41
IC	R1502/W	FTR 13/14.7.41 Bremen/Borchum
IC	R1505/U	to 101 Sqn
IC	R1509/P	FTR 29/30.6.41 Hamburg/Bremen
IC	R1517/Z	Crashed on t/o 17.6.41
IC	R1570/J (5710)	
IC	R1721/U	Crashed on landing 13.6.41. Hamm
IC	R1732/X	
IC	R1772/M	FTR 7/8.9.41
IC	R1798/B	FTR 15/16.7.41 Trout (7/8.9.41)
IC	R1805/T	Crashed Manby 29/30.6.41 Hamburg/Bremen
IC	R3150/E	to 37 Sqn
IC	R3151/D	to 46 MU
IC	R3152/J	Crashed nr Le Havre 20.5.40
IC	R3153/V	to 218 Sqn
IC	R3154	Crashed N.Yorks 1.5.40. Stavanger
IC	R3155/P	to 4 MU
IC	R3156	to 75 Sqn
IC	R3157	to 75 Sqn
IC	R3158	to 75 Sqn
IC	R3159	to 75 Sqn
IC	R3160	to 75 Sqn
IC	R3195	to 37 Sqn
IC	R3198/R	to 22 OTU
IC	R3202/J	FTR 2/3.8.40. Hamburg
IC	R3213/S	FTR 17.11.40. Hamburg
IC	R3232/K	to 4 MU
IC	R3237/D	
IC	R3238/H	Crew baled out 12.2.41
IC	R3276/B	Crashed Norfolk Mannheim
IC	R3278/D	to Malta
IC	R3279/X	FTR 3.3.41. Brest
IC	R3288/J	
IC	R3291/F	to 38 Sqn
IC	R3292/F	FTR 1.10.40. Osnabruck
IC	R3232/K	
IC	T2465/O	FTR. 29.12.40. Hamm
IC	T2466/C	FTR. 12.12.40. Mannheim
IC	T2506	Crashed Bircham Newton 16/17.11.40
IC	T2507/Q	to 38 Sqn
IC	T2509/W	Di 15.11.40. Hamburg
IC	T2511/P	Crashed on landing 23.1.41. Dusseldorf
IC	T2520/A	Crashed Wales 9.12.40. Bordeaux
IC	T2549/K	FTR 1.10.40. Osnabruck
IC	T2551	to 38 Sqn
IC	T2560/E	Crashed Wroughton 23.4.41. Brest
IC	T2563/J /D	SD crashed Scotton 12/13.8.41
IC	T2606/H	Crashed Bircham Newton 16.11.40. Hamburg
IC	T2613/R	Crashed Langley 30.10.40
IC	T2713	to 20 OTU
IC	T2742/B /V	to 38 Sqn
IC	T2803	to 99 Sqn
IC	T2805	to 75 Sqn
IC	T2887/B	to 218 Sqn
IC	T2963/A	FL Moat House Farm 23/24.6.41. Kiel
	W2509/W	Di 15.11.40
II	W5449/Q /V	to 218 Sqn
II	W5459/L	FTR 29/30.6.41. Hamburg/Bremen
II	W5526	to 218 Sqn
II	W5566	to 305 Sqn
IC	W5684/G	Bale out, Horra Bridge 3/4.9.41. Brest
IC	W5710/J	Bale out, Cromer 27.8.41. Mannheim
III	X3341/W	FTR 28/29.4.42. Lubeck

III	X3342	to 23 OTU
III	X3343/Q	to 23 OTU
III	X3344/V /Z	to 419 Sqn
III	X3345/T	to 156 Sqn
III	X3348	to 9 Sqn
III	X3351/Y	(SD minelaying 31.12.42)
III	X3354	to 27 OTU
III	X3364/Y	to 51 MU
III	X3365	to 20 OTU
III	X3391/Q /O	to 8 MU
III	X3392/K	to 9 MU
III	X3393/R /G /H	(SD Turin 9.12.42)
III	X3394	Crashed Swaffham 11.11.41
III	X3397	to Vickers
III	X3402/P	to 57 Sqn
III	X3408/H /M	to 75 Sqn
III	X3412/D /L	Di 26/27.7.42. Hamburg
III	X3413/S	to 9 MU
III	X3414/L	to 103 Sqn
III	X3416/F	to 419 Sqn
III	X3417	to 156 Sqn
III	X3419/T	FTR Essen 8/9.3.42
III	X3423/W	to 9 MU
III	X3424	to 9 MU
III	X3445/S /Q	to 17 OTU
III	X3446/F	to AAEE?
III	X3447/G /F	to 16 OTU
III	X3448/E	to 48 MU
III	X3450	to 48 MU
III	X3464/Y /L /B	FTR 28/29.8.42. Nuremberg
III	X3466/N	FTR 6/7.5.42. Stuttgart
III	X3471/J	to 16 OTU
III	X3472	to 101 Sqn
III	X3488/X	to 75 Sqn
III	X3539/W	to 75 Sqn
III	X3540/J /K	Di 29.10.42. Essen
III	X3554/Q	Di 26.6.42. Bremen
III	X3555/W	Di 22.6.42. Emden
III	X3560/K	FTR 13/14.7.42. Duisberg
III	X3561/X	FTR 21/22.7.42. Duisberg
III	X3565/Y	to 30 OTU
III	X3584	to 57 Sqn
III	X3589/F	FTR 26/27.3.42. Essen
III	X3591/S /R /K	FTR 6/7.5.42. Stuttgart
III	X3592	to 419 Sqn
III	X3593/C	FTR 29/30.4.42. Ostend
III	X3596/B	FTR 12/13.4.42. Essen
III	X3597/Q	(FTR minelaying 17.11.42)
III	X3601/V	FL Marham 13.8.42. Mainz
III	X3602/Q	Hit mast? 11.5.42
III	X3604/Y	FTR 26.3.42. Essen
III	X3633/G /H	SD 27.4.42. Rostock
III	X3635/Y	FTR 25/26.4.4.42. Rostock 4.1.42 Bremen?
III	X3639/A /K	FTR 28.4.42. Cologne
III	X3644/A	FTR 17/18.5.42. Minelaying
III	X3647/A	FTR 28/29.8.42. Nuremberg
III	X3655/H	101 Sqn?
III	X3662/P	to 20 OTU
III	X3666	to 23 OTU
III	X3669/K	101 Sqn?
III	X3675/F /D	FTR 28/29.8.42. Nuremberg
III	X3718/Q	FTR 18/19.9.42. Minelaying
III	X3721/F /H	FTR 2.6.42. Essen
III	X3724/T	Crashed N. Sea 2.6.42. Bremen
III	X3726/A	FTR 21/22.7.42. Duisberg
III	X3749/D	FL Marham 4.6.42. Bremen
III	X3750/T /B	FTR 22.7.42. Duisberg
III	X3878/J	to 15 OTU
III	X3924/B /T	to 26 OTU
III	X3946/Q	(FTR minelaying 18/19.10.42)
III	X3989/V	FTR 20/21.8.42. Minelaying
IC	X9616/W	to 26 OTU
IC	X9632/F	to Brooklands
IC	X9663/R	to 149 Sqn
IC	X9671/F	to Brooklands
IC	X9672/U /F	Bale-out, Norfolk 28.8.41. Mannheim
IC	X9673/Z /B	FTR 29/30.4.41. Stettin/Hamburg
IC	X9677	to 218 Sqn
IC	X9733/E /L	to 311 Sqn
IC	X9742/F	to 215 Sqn
IC	X9751/A	to 218 Sqn
IC	X9755/H	to 218 Sqn
IC	X9826/D	SD M. Heath. 29/30.8.41. Mannheim
IC	X9831/K	to 1505 BATF
IC	X9837/K	(no serial)
IC	X9853/J	OTU ac
IC	X9871/R	to 215 Sqn
IC	X9873/P	FTR 31.11.41. Bremen
IC	X9875/J	to 23 OTU
IC	X9877/Q	to 311 Sqn
IC	X9888/T	FTR 15/16.11.41. Kiel
IC	X9909/F	to 40 Sqn
IC	X9910/Y	FTR 29/30.9.41. Stettin/Hamburg
IC	Z1069	to 218 Sqn
IC	Z1070/S /B	to 218 Sqn
IC	Z1084/N /A	to 99 Sqn
III	Z1563/G	Crashed in circuit 15.1.42
III	Z1572	to 75 Sqn
III	Z1574/A /C /S	W/O BD 22/23.10.42. Genoa
III	Z1605/R	FTR 28/29.7.42. Hamburg
III	Z1606/J	FTR 25/26.7.42. Duisberg
III	Z1607/T	Crashed Norfolk 29.8.42. Nuremberg
III	Z1614/R	SD 31.5.42. Cologne
III	Z1624/D	FTR 28/29.7.42. Hamburg
III	Z1648/A	to 23 OTU
III	Z1657/R	to CGS

III	Z1663/J	SD 28.9.42. Lingen
III	Z1874/S	(no serial)
III	Z3445/D	306 Sqn?
III	Z8339/Z	305 Sqn?
II	Z8375	to 405 Sqn
II	Z8399	to 305 Sqn
IC	Z8779/X	to 20 OTU
IC	Z8788/H	FTR 21/22.7.41. Chub A
IC	Z8796	to 20 OTU
IC	Z8799/R	to 20 OTU
IC	Z8802/W	to 20 OTU
IC	Z8804	to 20 OTU
IC	Z8809/Y	to 20 OTU
IC	Z8830/O	to TFU
IC	Z8835/U	FTR 18/19.8.41. Essen
IC	Z8841/Z	to 20 OTU
IC	Z8844/S	FTR 14/15.10.41. Nuremberg
IC	Z8846/V	to 20 OTU
IC	Z8848/V /H	FTR 15/16.11.41. Kiel
IC	Z8852	to 20 OTU
IC	Z8853/H	to 218 Sqn
IC	Z8857	to 20 OTU
IC	Z8863/G	Crashed March 24.11.41
III	BJ589/X	to 156 Sqn
III	BJ595/S	Di 23/24.7.42. Duisberg
III	BJ615/G	FTR 26/27.7.42. Hamburg
III	BJ624/D	12 OTU?
III	BJ658/P	424 Sqn?
III	BJ660/H	(FTR Essen. 29.10.42)
III	BJ663/N	FTR 4/5.9.42. Bremen
III	BJ670/K /W	Di 27/28.7.42. Bremen
III	BJ688/R	FTR 28/29.8.42. Saarbrucken
III	BJ692/D	FTR 21/22.9.42. Minelaying
III	BJ693/J	FTR 14/15.9.42. Wilhelmshaven
III	BJ706/B	to 22 OTU
III	BJ710/L	FTR 27/28.8.42. Kassel
III	BJ722	to TFU
III	BJ723/B	Di 27.7.42. Hamburg
III	BJ724/P	Crashed Norwich 6/7.9.42. Duisberg
III	BJ770/Y	to 18 OTU
III	BJ771/L	FTR 4/5.9.42. Bremen
III	BJ796/H	Di 29.6.42. Bremen
III	BJ797/M	to 17 OTU
III	BJ832/F	to 29 OTU
III	BJ833/C	to 26 OTU
III	BJ842/W	SD 23.11.42. Stuttgart
III	BJ879/X	to 26 OTU
III	BJ880/W	to 82 OTU
III	BJ893/C	FTR 1/2.9.42. Saarbrucken
III	BJ898/C	FTR 6.12.42. Mannheim
III	BJ962/D	FTR minelaying 21.9.42
III	BJ965/V	to 12 OTU
III	BJ990/N /X	to 17 OTU

Vickers-Armstrongs Wellington, 38 Squadron, November 1938 – November 1940

I	L4128	to 15 OTU
I	L4219	to 15 OTU
I	L4230	to 75 Sqn
I	L4231	to 75 Sqn
I	L4234	to 20 OTU
I	L4235	to RAE
I	L4236	to 148 Sqn
I	L4237	to 148 Sqn
I	L4238	(to 1625M)
I	L4239	Crashed, hit tree, Broughton 5.11.39
I	L4240	Crashed on landing, Debden 11.8.39
I	L4241	to 20 OTU
I	L4242	to 148 Sqn
I	L4243	Caught fire, Marham 15.2.39
I	L4245	to 15 OTU
I	L4248	to 15 OTU
I	L4295	to 115 Sqn
I	L4296	to 20 OTU
I	L4307	(to 2772M)
I	L4335	to 215 Sqn
I	L4339	(Crashed 14.4.41)
IC	L7808	(SOC 20.2.41)
IC	L7809	FTR 11.9.40
IC	L7810	to 115 Sqn
IC	L7854	to 115 Sqn
IC	N2740	(SOC 1.42)
IC	N2756	(FTR 14.7.41)
IC	N2759	(Crashed 15.1.41)
IC	N2760	to 115 Sqn
IC	N2855	(FTR 2.5.41)
IA	N2878	to 12 OTU
IA	N2879	to FTU
IA	N2880	to 311 Sqn
IA	N2881	to CGS
IA	N2884	to 20 OTU
IA	N2900	to 20 OTU
IA	N2910	to 221 Sqn
IA	N2951/D	FTR 21.2.40. Heligoland
IA	N2952	to 150 Sqn
IA	N2953	FTR 14.6.40.
IA	N2954	to 15 Sqn
IA	N2956	to 99 Sqn
IA	N2957	to 99 Sqn
IA	N2858	to 99 Sqn
IA	N2963	to 1 AAS
IA	N2995	to 11 OTU
IA	N2996	to 103 Sqn
IA	N2997	to 103 Sqn
IA	N2998	to 103 Sqn
IA	P2526	Crashed (out of petrol) 21.2.40
IA	P9207	to 115 Sqn
IA	P9220	to 1 AAS

IA	P9226	to 115 Sqn	IC	R1183/N	to 18 OTU
IA	P9227	to 115 Sqn	IC	R1210/O	Bale out, Tebay 12.2.41
IC	P9249	Crashed on landing 16.6.40	IC	R1339/J	
IC	P9250	(Crashed on t/o 6.2.40)	IC	R1346/B	to 16 OTU
IC	P9265	(Dest. on ground 3.2.41)	IC	R1368/F	Bale out, King's Lynn 23.4.41
IC	P9269	FTR 12.4.40 (.41)	IC	R1400	to 22 OTU
IC	P9284	to 115 Sqn	IC	R1401	to 27 OTU
IC	P9285	to 115 Sqn	IC	R1436/N	to 20 OTU
IC	P9286	to 115 Sqn	IC	R1442/D	SOC 1.5.41
IC	P9287	FTR 7.10.40	IC	R1448/N	to 20 OTU
IC	P9290	to 115 Sqn	IC	R1496/R	(SOC 19.11.41)
IC	P9291	to 115 Sqn	IC	R1497/H	to 311 Sqn
IC	P9292	to 115 Sqn	IC	R1507/V	FTR 25.4.41
IC	P9293	(FTR 7.1.41)	IC	R1511/E	FTR 11.10.41
IC	P9294	to 108 Sqn	IC	R1536/G	FTR 16.7.41
IC	P9295	to 1 AAS	IC	R1594	to 311 Sqn
IC	P9296	to 115 Sqn	IC	R1596/A	(SOC 1.7.44)
IC	P9297	to 115 Sqn	IC	R1597/N	to 23 OTU
IC	P9299	to 115 Sqn	IC	R1601/H	to 1505 BATF
IC	R1018	to 148 Sqn	IC	R1713/V	SOC 30.6.41
IC	R1034	to 115 Sqn	IC	R1719/K	to 22 OTU
IC	R1180	(SOC 18.11.41)	IC	R1726/O	SOC 31.7.41
IC	R1182		IC	R3153	DBR 16.9.41
IC	T2465	to 115 Sqn	IC	T2739/J	to 311 Sqn
IC	T2507	(SOC 31.10.43)	IC	T2801/E	to 15 OTU
IC	T2551	to ASR Flt	IC	T2806/T	FTR 29.6.41. Bremen
IC	T2570	to ASR Flt	IC	T2815	to 108 Sqn
IC	T2580	(DBR 3.3.42)	IC	T2885/D	
IC	T2614	to 108 Sqn	IC	T2887/W	(Crashed Bingham 21.12.42)
IC	T2704	to 2 METS	IC	T2958/T	Crashed Marham 25.4.41
IC	T2742	(FTR 13.2.41)	II	W5400	to 99 Sqn
IC	T2743	(Crashed 3.11.40)	II	W5434	to 57 Sqn
IC	T2838	to 148 Sqn	II	W5445	to 9 Sqn
IC	T2839	to ASR Flt	II	W5447/C	to 305 Sqn
IC	T2843	to ASR Flt	II	W5448/L	Crashed Downham Market
IC	T2849	(SOC 17.7.41)			18.5.41
IC	X3168	to 37 Sqn	II	W5449/Y	Crashed Barton Bendish 8.9.41
IC	X9685	(Crashed 15.9.41)	II	W5457/Z	FTR 19.8.41. Duisberg
IC	X9686	(Crashed 12.12.41)	II	W5526	to 305 Sqn
IC	X9693	(to 37 Sqn)	IC	W5727/V	to 3333M, 5.42
			IC	X3217/E	to 18 OTU

Vickers-Armstrongs Wellington, 218 Squadron, November 1940 – February 1942

			IC	X9663	to 16 OTU
I	L4293	to 1505 Flt	IC	X9670	FTR 12.9.41. Frankfurt ??
IC	L7797/F	to 20 OTU	IC	X9672	to 115 Sqn
IC	L7798/S	FTR 23.4.41. Brest	IC	X9673/Z	FTR 30.9.41?
IA	N2844/M		IC	X9674/H	to 99 Sqn
IA	N2937	SOC 1.5.41	IC	X9677/V	Di 11.10.41
IA	P9207	Crashed on t/o 15.1.41	IC	X9678/R	to 22 OTU
IC	P9291	to 2 METS	IC	X9679/D	to 99 Sqn
IC	P9296	to 11 OTU	IC	X9745	to 311 Sqn
IC	P9299/R	to Czech OTU	IC	X9747/E	Bale out 3.8.41
IC	R1008/A	FTR 14.8.41	IC	X9751	to 304 Sqn
IC	R1009/L	Crashed Swaffham 25.2.41	IC	X9753/E	FTR 15.8.41. Hannover
IC	R1025/B	to 16 OTU	IC	X9755/K	to 25 OTU
IC	R1135/N	FTR 16.11.41. Emden	IC	X9757/E	to 20 OTU
			IC	X9785/O	Bale out 16.12.41

IC	X9787/S	to 99 Sqn
IC	X9788	to 25 OTU
IC	X9810/K	SD 2.9.41. Ostend
IC	X9833/A	Crashed Rougham 29.10.41
IC	X9871	to 115 Sqn
IC	X9875	to 115 Sqn
IC	Z1069	FTR 8.11.41. Berlin ??
IC	Z1070/B	to 311 Sqn
IC	Z1101/F	to AAEE
IC	Z1103/A	Di 27.11.41
II	Z8375/Z	to 405 Sqn
II	Z8399	to 305 Sqn
II	Z8431/J	FTR 7.11.41. Berlin
II	Z8437/X	to 405 Sqn
IC	Z8781/S	FTR 4.8.41?
IC	Z8853/H	Crashed Redcar 16.11.41
IC	Z8865/O	Crashed Marham 15.10.41
IC	Z8894	to 99 Sqn
IC	Z8910/F	DBR 13.10.41
IC	Z8965/L	to 214 Sqn
IC	Z8970/W	to 214 Sqn
IC	Z8982/E	to 214 Sqn

Vickers-Armstrongs Wellington, NZ Flt

IA	P9206	to 20 OTU
IA	P9207	to 38 Sqn
IA	P9209	to 75 Sqn
IA	P9210	to RAE
IA	P9212	to 311 Sqn

Short Stirling, 218 Squadron, January – July 1942

I	N3700/O	to 1657 CU
I	N3712/Y	Blew up on landing 3/4.3.42. Paris
I	N3717/S	(Crashed 29.8.42)
I	N3718	FTR 2/3.7.42. Bremen.
I	N3720/B	to 1651 CU
I	N3721/C	to 1651 CU
I	N3722/E	Crashed King's Lynn 23.4.42
I	N3725/D	(Crashed 15.9.42)
I	N3753/U	DBR 1/2.6.42
I	N6078/P	FTR 22/23.6.42. Emden
I	N6070/A	FTR 4/5.5.42. Pilsen
I	N6071/G	FTR 17/18.5.42 minelaying
I	N6072/J	(FTR 7.8.42)
I	N6076	to 15 Sqn
I	N6077/V	(FTR 21.8.43)
I	N6089/L /Y	to 1657 CU
I	N6128/T	to 1427 Flt
I	N6129/X	(FTR 29.7.42)
I	R9311/L	DBR 30/31.5.42
I	R9313/Q	Bale-out, Norwich 4/5.5.42. Leaflets
I	R9332/G	(DBR 31.7.42)
I	R9333/F	(FTR 6.3.43)
I	R9341/N	(no serial)

I	R9357/E	(Di 11.9.42)
I	W7469/M	to 149 Sqn
I	W7473/F	Crashed 23/24.4.42. Rostock
I	W7474/O /K	FTR 3/4.6.42. Bremen
I	W7475/H	(FTR 10.11.42)
I	W7502/N	FTR 30/31.5.42. Cologne
I	W7503/R	FTR 25/26.6.42. Bremen
I	W7506/K	FTR 25/26.4.42. Pilsen
I	W7507/P	DBR 28/29.3.42. Lubeck
I	W7521/U	Crashed Norwich 4/5.5.42. Stuttgart
I	W7530/Q	FTR 20/21.6.42. Emden
I	W7535/C	FTR 29/30.5.42. Gennevilliers
I	DJ974/T	FTR 27/28.6.42. Bremen
I	DJ976/H /A	to 1657 CU
I	DJ977/F	FTR 19/20.5.42. Mannheim

De Havilland Mosquito, 105 Squadron, September 1942 – March 1944

IV	W4064	FTR 31.5.42. Cologne
IV	W4065	(missing 19.8.42?)
IV	W4069	(missing 16.7.42?)
IV	W4071	to 1655 MTU
IV	W4072	to 1655 MTU
IV	DK288	to 1655 MTU
IV	DK291	to BDU
IV	DK292	to 1655 MTU
IV	DK293	to 618 Sqn
IV	DK296	to 305 MTU
IV	DK300	to 109 Sqn
IV	DK301	Crashed Marham 8.11.42
IV	DK302	to 139 Sqn
IV	DK313	to 139 Sqn
IV	DK314	1 PRU?
IV	DK315	1 PRU?
IV	DK316	FTR 30.12.42. Lingen
IV	DK317	FTR 11.10.42. Hannover
IV	DK323	to 1655 MTU
IV	DK325	SD 26.9.42. Oslofjord
IV	DK326	FTR 19.9.42. Berlin
IV	DK328	FTR 7.11.42. R.Gironde
IV	DK330	to 139 Sqn
IV	DK333	to 109 Sqn
IV	DK336	Crashed nr Shipdham 27.1.43
IV	DK337	to 139 Sqn
IV	DK338	Crashed nr Marham 1.5.73
IV	DK339	FTR 9.10.42. Duisburg
IV	DK354	FTR 12.12.43. Essen
IV	DZ311	FTR 23.1.43. Railways
IV	DZ312	to 1655 MTU
IV	DZ313	FTR 20.10.42. Hanover
IV	DZ314	FTR 8.12.42. Den Helder
IV	DZ315	FTR 9.1.43. Rouen
IV	DZ316	to 1655 MTU
IV	DZ320	FTR 13.11.42. 'Neumark', Flushing

IV	DZ340	Crashed Marham 11.10.42	IV	DZ595	DBR 26.8.43
IV	DZ341	FTR 11.10.42. Hanover	IX	LR475	to 139 Sqn
IV	DZ343	FTR 23.10.42. Hengelo	IX	LR476	Blew up, Marham 22.3.44
IV	DZ348	to 139 Sqn	IX	LR477	Crashed Marham 23.11.43
IV	DZ349	to 305 FTU	IX	LR496	(Crashed 27.4.44)
IV	DZ351	to 139 Sqn	IX	LR497	to 637 Sqn
IV	DZ353	to 139 Sqn	IX	LR500	(SOC 26.5.45)
IV	DZ354	FTR 13.11.42. 'Neumark', Flushing	IX	LR503	to Canada
			IX	LR504	to 109 Sqn
IV	DZ355	to 618 Sqn	IX	LR506	Crashed West Raynham 29.9.43
IV	DZ360	FTR 22.12.42. Termonde	IX	LR507	(SOC 15.5.46)
IV	DZ361	FTR 13.11.42. Termonde	IX	LR508	to 109 Sqn
IV	DZ365	FTR 26.2.43. Rennes	IX	LR510	to 109 Sqn
IV	DZ367	FTR 30.1.43. Berlin	IX	LR511	to 109 Sqn
IV	DZ369	Crashed Molesworth 28.11.42	IX	LR512	to BDU
IV	DZ370	to 139 Sqn	IX	LR513	to 109 Sqn
IV	DZ371	to 139 Sqn	IX	ML896	to ME
IV	DZ372	Crashed Marham 2.3.43	IX	ML897	to 1509 Flt
IV	DZ373	to 139 Sqn	IX	ML898	to TFU
IV	DZ374	to 139 Sqn	IX	ML902	(Crashed 14.1.45)
IV	DZ378	DBR 20.2.43. To 3509M	IX	ML904	FTR 15.11.43. Dusseldorf
IV	DZ379	to 139 Sqn	IX	ML908	
IV	DZ407	FTR 27.1.43. Copenhagen	IX	ML911	(Crashed 22.12.44)
IV	DZ408	FTR 20.1.44 (crew bale out)	IX	ML913	(FTR 6.7.44)
IV	DZ413	FTR 26.2.43. Rennes	IX	ML914	to 627 Sqn
IV	DZ414	to 139 Sqn.	IX	ML915	to 109 Sqn
IV	DZ415	to 627 Sqn	IX	ML916	(Crashed 24.7.45)
IV	DZ416	FTR 28.3.43	IX	ML917	to 1409 Flt
IV	DZ420	to 139 Sqn	IX	ML919	(Crashed 15.12.44)
IV	DZ421	to 627 Sqn	IX	ML920	(SOC 17.5.46)
IV	DZ441	to 140 Wing	IX	ML921	(Crashed 9.4.44)
IV	DZ458	to 139 Sqn	IX	ML922	(FL 14.1.45)
IV	DZ460	FTR 8.3.43. Lingen	IX	ML923	(FTR 28.1.45)
IV	DZ461	to 139 Sqn	IX	ML924	(Crashed 6.3.45)
IV	DZ462	to 627 Sqn	XVI	ML934	to 139 Sqn
IV	DZ467	FTR 27.5.43. Jena	XVI	ML935	to 692 Sqn
IV	DZ468	to 139 Sqn	XVI	ML936	to 1409 Flt
IV	DZ472	FTR 11.4.43. Hengelo	XVI	ML938	to 16 OTU
IV	DZ474	Crashed Debden 19.2.43	XVI	ML958	to 109 Sqn
IV	DZ483	Crashed Marham 27.5.43	XVI	ML962	to 109 Sqn
IV	DZ489	DBR 19.11.43	XVI	ML964	(Crashed 7.7.44)
IV	DZ492	to 109 Sqn	XVI	ML967	to 109 Sqn
IV	DZ518	to 618 Sqn	XVI	ML968	to 692 Sqn
IV	DZ519	to 139 Sqn	XVI	ML970	to 692 Sqn
IV	DZ520	to 618 Sqn	XVI	ML971	to 692 Sqn
IV	DZ521	to 139 Sqn	XVI	ML974	to 16 OTU
IV	DZ522	FTR 28.3.43. Liege	XVI	ML978	(Crashed 13.5.44)
IV	DZ536	FTR 11.4.43. Hengelo.	XVI	ML982	to 109 Sqn
IV	DZ547	618 Sqn?	XVI	ML983	to 16 OTU
IV	DZ548	FTR 22.10.43. Knapsack Crashed 5.2.44 collision	XVI	ML985	to 109 Sqn
			XVI	ML986	(DBR 4.10.44)
IV	DZ550	to 1655 MTU	XVI	ML987	(Crashed 14.7.44)
IV	DZ587	Crashed nr Hardwick 5.11.43. Bochum	XVI	ML989	to 109 Sqn
			XVI	ML991	to 109 Sqn
IV	DZ589	to 1655 MTU	XVI	ML992	to 109 Sqn
IV	DZ591	FTR 23.10.43. Cologne.	XVI	ML996	(FTR 6.10.44)

XVI	ML997	to 109 Sqn
XVI	ML999	to 109 Sqn
XVI	MM112	to 109 Sqn
XVI	MM116	to 571 Sqn
XVI	MM119	to 571 Sqn
XVI	MM120	to 571 Sqn
XVI	MM121	to 571 Sqn
XVI	MM136	to 571 Sqn
XVI	MM137	to 692 Sqn
XVI	MM139	to 692 Sqn
XVI	MM154	to 109 Sqn
XVI	MM172	to 692 Sqn
XVI	MM178	to 109 Sqn
XVI	MM192	to 128 Sqn
XVI	MM199	to 128 Sqn
XVI	MM202	to 128 Sqn
XVI	MM224	to 692 Sqn
IX	MM229	to 1409 Flight
IX	MM237	(SD 7.3.45)
XVI	MM237	

De Havilland Mosquito, 109 Squadron, July 1943 – April 1944

IV	DK286	to 1655 MTU
IV	DK293	to 627 Sqn
IV	DK300	to 1655 MTU
IV	DK321	to 1655 MTU
IV	DZ317	to 1655 MTU
IV	DZ318	to 105 Sqn
IV	DZ319	to NTU
IV	DZ356	to 1655 MTU
IV	DZ414	to 105 Sqn
IV	DZ425	Crashed Marham 30.8.43
IV	DZ429	FTR 17.9.43
IV	DZ434	Crashed 22.10.43
IV	DZ436	to 1655 MTU
IV	DZ437	to 1655 MTU
IV	DZ439	to 1655 MTU
IV	DZ440	FTR 14.1.44. Essen
IV	DZ441	to 105 Sqn
IV	DZ484	to 627 Sqn
IV	DZ492	Crashed Wyton 9.11.43
IV	DZ525	to RAE
IV	DZ526	to 1655 MTU
IV	DZ550	to 105 Sqn
IV	DZ551	to 627 Sqn
IV	DZ587	to 105 Sqn
IV	DZ589	to 105 Sqn
IX	LR476	to 105 Sqn
IX	LR477	to 105 Sqn
IX	LR496	to 105 Sqn
IX	LR497	to 105 Sqn
IX	LR498	to 105 Sqn
IX	LR499	FTR Bochum 2.12.42
IX	LR500	to 105 Sqn
IX	LR501	to 1409 Flt

IX	LR502	to 1409 Flt
IX	LR503	to 105 Sqn
IX	LR504	(SOC 14.9.45)
IX	LR506	to 105 Sqn
IX	LR507	to 105 Sqn
IX	LR508	(Crashed 25.4.45)
IX	LR509	to 1409 Flt
IX	LR510	to 627 Sqn
IX	LR511	to 627 Sqn
IX	LR512	to 105 Sqn
IX	LR513	(SOC 17.5.46)
IX	ML896	to 105 Sqn
IX	ML897	to 105 Sqn
IX	ML898	to 105 Sqn
IX	ML900	(Crashed 18.6.44)
IX	ML905	(Crashed 11.5.44)
IX	ML907	(Crashed 16.11.44)
IX	ML908	to 139 Sqn
IX	ML909	to 139 Sqn
IX	ML910	to 139 Sqn
IX	ML915	(Crashed 1.2.45)
IX	ML918	to 1409 Flt
IX	ML920	to 105 Sqn
IX	ML921	to 105 Sqn
IX	ML924	to 105 Sqn
XVI	ML925	to 139 Sqn
XVI	ML927	to SFU
XVI	ML928	to 1409 Flt
XVI	ML931	(Crashed 2.7.44)
XVI	ML932	(FTR Cologne 1.9.44)
XVI	ML933	
XVI	ML938	to 105 Sqn
XVI	ML939	(Crashed 18.7.44)
XVI	ML940	to 139 Sqn
XVI	ML941	to 139 Sqn
XVI	ML956	to 105 Sqn
XVI	ML957	Crashed Bradwell Bay 9.4.44
XVI	ML958	(FTR Leverkusen 7.5.44)
XVI	ML959	to 692 Sqn
XVI	ML960	(Crashed Manston 29.6.44)
XVI	ML962	(Bale out 3.6.44)
XVI	ML963	to 692 Sqn
XVI	ML966	to 692 Sqn
XVI	ML967	(Crashed 20.7.44)
XVI	ML969	to 692 Sqn
XVI	ML972	to 692 Sqn
XVI	ML973	to 105 Sqn
XVI	ML976	to 571 Sqn
XVI	ML979	(FTR 27.11.44)
XVI	ML980	to Admiralty
XVI	ML982	(DBR 13.3.45)
XVI	ML984	to 571 Sqn
XVI	ML985	(FTR Leverkusen 1.9.44)
XVI	ML990	(Crashed 4.12.44)
XVI	ML995	to 105 Sqn
XVI	ML998	(SD 23.12.44)

XVI	MM113	to 571 Sqn
XVI	MM114	to SFU
XVI	MM117	to Admiralty
XVI	MM122	(SOC 31.7.47)
XVI	MM123	(SOC 2.4.46)
XVI	MM124	to 571 Sqn
XVI	MM141	to 692 Sqn
XVI	MM156	to 571 Sqn
XVI	MM169	to 571 Sqn
XVI	MM179	to 571 Sqn
XVI	MM181	to 692 Sqn
XVI	MM196	to 128 Sqn
XVI	MM197	to 128 Sqn
XVI	MM203	to 128 Sqn
IX	MM238	to 1409 Flt
IX	MM241	to 105 Sqn

De Havilland Mosquito, 139 Squadron, September 1942 – July 1943

IV	DK285	to 1655 MTU
IV	DK291	to 1655 MTU
IV	DK302	FTR 13.5.43. Berlin
IV	DK313	to 627 Sqn
IV	DK327	to 192 Sqn
IV	DK330	to BDU
IV	DK331	to NTU
IV	DK332	Crashed Wyton 13.1.43
IV	DK333	to 192 Sqn
IV	DK337	(FTR 31.8.43. Duisberg)
IV	DZ348	(FTR 29.8.43. Berlin)
IV	DZ351	to TFU
IV	DZ353	to 627 Sqn
IV	DZ355	to 1655 MTU
IV	DZ359	(DBR 13.3.44)
IV	DZ370	(FTR 7.4.44)
IV	DZ371	Di 6.12.42
IV	DZ373	FTR 13.3.43. Liege
IV	DZ374	(FTR 30.8.43. Duisberg)
IV	DZ379	(FTR 18.8.43. Berlin)
IV	DZ380	FTR 3.4.43. Aulnoye
IV	DZ381	Mid-air 27.5.43. Kassel
IV	DZ388	to 1655 MTU
IV	DZ414	to Swanton Morley
IV	DZ418	to 627 Sqn
IV	DZ420	FTR 18.2.43. Tours
IV	DZ421	to 627 Sqn
IV	DZ422	to 627 Sqn
IV	DZ423	to 618 Sqn
IV	DZ426	to 627 Sqn
IV	DZ458	FTR 28.7.43. Duisberg
IV	DZ461	to 692 Sqn
IV	DZ463	FTR 3.3.43. Knaben
IV	DZ464	SD 21.5.43
IV	DZ465	to 618 Sqn
IV	DZ468	to 618 Sqn
IV	DZ469	(FTR 10.3.43. Le Mans)

IV	DZ470	SD 11.4.43
IV	DZ476	(Crashed Upwood 1.1.44)
IV	DZ477	to 627 Sqn
IV	DZ478	to 627 Sqn
IV	DZ479	to 627 Sqn
IV	DZ481	FTR 26.2.43. Rennes
IV	DZ482	to 627 Sqn
IV	DZ486	to 618 Sqn
IV	DZ490	(Crashed Wyton 28.1.44)
IV	DZ491	to 192 Sqn
IV	DZ496	Crashed Martlesham Heath 21.3.43
IV	DZ497	FTR 16.3.43. Paderborn
IV	DZ515	(Bale out 15.7.43)
IV	DZ516	to 627 Sqn
IV	DZ518	to 627 Sqn
IV	DZ519	(FTR 21.10.43. Berlin)
IV	DZ593	(FTR 1.11.43. Cologne)
IV	DZ597	(FTR 21.10.43. Berlin)
IV	DZ598	(FTR 15.9.43. Berlin)
IV	DZ601	to 627 Sqn
IV	DZ602	Mid-air 27.5.43. Kassel
IV	DZ605	Crashed Coltishall 28.5.43
IV	DZ607	(Di 13.8.43)
IV	DZ609	(FTR 12.6.44. Berlin)
IV	DZ610	(FTR 27.5.44. Ludwigshafen).
IV	DZ612	to 692 Sqn
IV	DZ614	(FTR 24.11.43. Berlin)
IV	DZ615	to 627 Sqn
IV	DZ616	to 627 Sqn
IV	DZ617	to 192 Sqn
IV	DZ631	to 692 Sqn
IV	DZ632	to 1655 MTU
IV	DZ635	to 1655 MTU
IV	DZ644	(FTR 1.7.44. Homberg)
IV	DZ645	to 625 Sqn
IV	DZ646	(Crashed 5.5.44)
IX	ML908	FTR Bonn. 15.11.43
IX	ML909	(Crashed Antingham 28.6.44)
IX	ML910	to TFU
IX	ML915	to 105 Sqn
IX	ML924	to 109 Sqn

De Havilland Mosquito, 1655 MTU

IV	DK285	FTR 5.11.43
IV	DK286	(SOC 13.1.45)
IV	DK288	Crashed Bury St Edmunds 13.3.44
IV	DK291	(SOC 21.7.45)
IV	DK292	to 13 OTU
IV	DK300	Crashed 22.7.44
IV	DK313	to NTU
IV	DK321	Crashed 23.8.44
IV	DK323	Crashed Marham 8.9.43
IV	DZ312	Crashed Stradlett 26.2.44
IV	DZ317	Crashed Warboys 5.9.44

IV	DZ318	Crashed Marham 25.7.43
IV	DZ344	to 627 Sqn
IV	DZ345	to TFU
IV	DZ346	Crashed 31.10.42
IV	DZ347	Crashed Marham 28.2.43
IV	DZ348	to 105 Sqn
IV	DZ349	(SOC 10.10.46)
IV	DZ355	(SOC 21.5.46)
IV	DZ356	Blew up 8.1.44
IV	DZ361	to 105 Sqn
IV	DZ374	to 105 Sqn
IV	DZ388	Crashed Folkingham 26.3.44
IV	DZ421	Crashed 25.7.44
IV	DZ429	(Crashed Alrewas 24.11.44)
IV	DZ433	Crashed Finningley 21.8.44
IV	DZ436	DBR 2.11.44
IV	DZ437	to NTU
IV	DZ439	Crashed Little Raveley 20.4.44
IV	DZ477	Bale-out 14.8.44
IV	DZ484	(SOC 21.5.46)
IV	DZ495	Crashed 18.7.43
IV	DZ526	to NTU
IV	DZ528	Crashed Broughton 21.5.44
IV	DZ544	to 8 OTU
IV	DZ550	Crashed Chesterfield Farm 27.6.44
IV	DZ589	to NTU
IV	DZ603	Crashed St Ives 22.4.44
IV	DZ606	to 627 Sqn
IV	DZ616	to 139 Sqn
IV	DZ617	to 139 Sqn
IV	DZ630	to EANS
IV	DZ632	Crashed Lound 8.11.44
IV	DZ635	to 627 Sqn

Boeing B-29 Washington, June 1950 – February 1954

Codes:

WCU	FB
35 Sqn	FB
44 Sqn	
57 Sqn	
90 Sqn	WP
115 Sqn	KO
149 Sqn	OJ

(* = not confirmed by Marham ORB)

I	WF434/K – WCU	to 'SA'*
I	WF435/L – WCU, SF, 115	to Bristols 1.12.53
I	WF436/M – WCU	to 'SA'*
I	WF437/N – WCU, 207, 35	to USA 22.7.53
I	WF438/O – WCU	to 'SA'*
I	WF439/P – WCU	to 'SA'*
I	WF440/Q – WCU	to 'SA'*

I	WF441 – WCU	to 'SA'*
I	WF442/J /P – 115, 90	to USA 7.7.53
I	WF443/D /A – 115, 90	to USA 22.7.53
I	WF444/C – 115	to USA 25.8.53
I	WF445/F – 115	to USA 7.7.53
I	WF446/B – 115	to USA 28.7.53
I	WF447/G – 115	to 58 MU
I	WF448/A – 115	to USA 17.11.53*
I	WF490/S – 149, 35	to USA 20.10.53*
I	WF491/T – 149, 90	to USA 25.8.53
I	WF492/U – 149, 90	to USA 11.8.53
I	WF494/X – 149, 115	to USA 18.8.53
I	WF495 – 149, 115	Crashed 27.1.54
I	WF496/N – WCU	to 'SA'*
I	WF498 – 149, 35	to USA 22.7.53
I	WF499/B – 149, 115	to USA 22.2.54?
I	WF500/C – 149, 90	to USA 7.7.53
I	WF501/N – 149, 90	to USA 11.8.53
I	WF502/O	Crashed nr Mold 8/9.1.53
I	WF503/B – 90	
I	WF504	to USA 11.8.53
I	WF506	to USA 4.1.54
I	WF507	to USA 18.8.53
I	WF508 – 90	to USA 5.1.54
I	WF509 – 115	to USA 29.1.54
I	WF510	to USA 28.7.53
I	WF511	to USA 18.8.53
I	WF512	to USA 18.8.53
I	WF513 – 115	to USA 15.2.54
I	WF514/Y – 115	to USA 25.8.53
I	WF545/D – 57, 90	
I	WF546 – 149	to USA 28.7.53
I	WF548/Z – 115	to USA 28.7.53
I	WF549/M – 57, 90, 207	to USA 19.1.54
I	WF550 – 57, 90	to USA 17.11.53*
I	WF551 – 57, 90	to USA 4.1.54
I	WF552 – 57, 115	to USA 22.2.54
I	WF553 – 57	to 115
I	WF554 – 57, 90	to USA 4.1.54
I	WF555 – 57	(w/o 29.9.51)
I	WF556 – 57, 35, 90	to USA 4.1.54
I	WF557 – 57, 115	
I	WF558 – 207, 90	to USA 5.1.54
I	WF559/L – 207, WCU, 35, 115	to USA 5.1.54
I	WF560 – 207, 115	to USA 19.1.54
I	WF561 – 207	to USA .12.53
I	WF562 – 57, 115	to USA 19.1.54
I	WF563 – 57, 90	to USA 25.2.54
I	WF564 – 207	
I	WF565/B – 207	to USA 15.2.54*

I	WF566 – 207	
I	WF567 – 207	to USA 16.3.53*
I	WF568/W – 207	to USA 15.1.54
I	WF569/V – 207	to USA 15.2.54*
I	WF570/M	Crashed W. Acre 14.12.52
I	WF571/Q – WCU, 35	to USA 11.8.53
I	WF572/N – WCU, 35	to USA 22.2.54*
I	WF573/P – WCU, 35	to USA 15.1.54
I	WW342 – WCU, 35	to USA 3.11.54
I	WW343 – WCU, 35	to USA 11.8.53
I	WW344/Q – WCU, 35	to USA 22.2.54*
I	WW345/S – 35	to USA 27.2.54*
I	WW346/S – 35	to 192
I	WW347 – 90, 35	to USA 16.3.54*
I	WW348/O – 35	to USA 5.1.54
I	WW350/T – 35	to USA 22.2.54*
I	WW351 – 35	to USA 15.1.54
I	WW352/F – 207	to USA 25.2.54*

Gloster Meteor: Jet Conversion Flight/Unit

F.4	VT282	
T.7	WA653	to 231 OCU
T.7	VW420	
F.8	WA757	263 Sqn
T.7	WF843	to RAAF 21.6.55
T.7	WG942	to Upwood
T.7	WN318	to 231 OCU
F.8	WH299	263 Sqn?
T.7	WL405	to Wittering

Airspeed Oxford

I	V3404
II	BM671
I	DF256
I	HM696
I	HM954
I	HN202
I	LX431

Vickers-Armstrongs Valiant, January 1956 – May 1965

214 Sqn:	January 56–March 65
207 Sqn:	April 56–May 65
148 Sqn:	July 56–May 65
49 Sqn:	June 61–May 65
(MW = Marham Wing)	

B.1	WP206 – 49	to MoA
B.1	WP207 – 49	SOC 1.1.67
B.1	WP218 – 49, 207	SOC 1.3.65

B.1	WP211 – 214	to 232 OCU
B.1	WP212 – 214	to 199 Sqn
B.1	WP217 – 207	to 7 Sqn
B.1	WP218 – 49, MW	SOC 1.3.65
B.1	WP219 – 207	SOC 1.3.65
B.1	WP221 – 207, MW	SOC 5.3.65
B.1	WP223 – 214	to 7 Sqn
B.1	WZ361 – 207	SOC 16.6.65
B.1	WZ362 – 148	to 232 OCU
B.1	WZ363 – 148	Crashed Market Rasen 6.5.64
B.1	WZ366 – 49	to 7 Sqn
B.1	WZ367 – 148	SOC 10.6.65
B.1	WZ369 – 148	to 232 OCU
B(PR).1	WZ377 – 214, MW	SOC 1.3.65
B(PR).1	WZ378 – 49	to 7 Sqn
B(PR).1	WZ379 – 214, 148, MW	SOC 1.3.65
B(PR).1	WZ381 – 214, 49	to 7 Sqn
B(PR).1	WZ384 – 148	SOC 1.1.67
B(PR)K.1	WZ390 – 214	SOC 1.3.65
B(PR)K.1	WZ393 – 214, 90, 148	SOC 1.3.65
B(PR)K.1	WZ395 – 214, 148	SOC 1.3.65
B(PR)K.1	WZ397 – 214	to 7888M
B(PR)K.1	WZ401 – 207	SOC 5.3.65
B(PR)K.1	WZ402 – 207, MW	SOC 1.3.65
B(PR)K.1	WZ403 – 207, MW	SOC 1.3.65
B(PR)K.1	WZ404 – 207	SOC 1.3.65
B(PR)K.1	WZ405 – 207	to 138 Sqn
B(K).1	XD812	
B(K).1	XD813	
B(K).1	XD814	
B(K).1	XD815	
B(K).1	XD816	
B(K).1	XD817	
B(K).1	XD818	Gate Guard, then RAF Museum
B(K).1	XD819	
B(K).1	XD820	
B(K).1	XD821	
B(K).1	XD822	
B(K).1	XD823	
B(K).1	XD824	
B(K).1	XD825	
B(K).1	XD827	

B(K).1	XD828
B(K).1	XD858
B(K).1	XD859
B(K).1	XD860
B(K).1	XD861
B(K).1	XD869
B(K).1	XD873
B(K).1	XD874
B(K).1	XD875

De Havilland Chipmunk: Station Flight

T.10	WB733	to Hamble
T.10	WB752	to Odiham?
T.10	WB762	(no serial)
T.10	WG303	to Wittering
T.10	WG308	to RAFC?
T.10	WG364	to 1 FTS
T.10	WG477	to Hamble
T.10	WH674	(Canberra serial)
T.10	WK574	to Waddington
T.10	WK589	to Honington
T.10	WP833	to 2 FTS
T.10	WZ879	to RAFC

English Electric Canberra, January 1954 – June 1957

Squadrons are listed after each aircraft serial; the Wing concept allowed for greater sharing of airframes.

B.2	WE118 – 207	Conv to T.4
B.2	WF887 – 115	to Stn Flt Khormaksar
B.2	WF916 – 115, 207	to 44 Sqn
B.2	WH637 – 35	to 9 Sqn
B.2	WH643 – 90, 207	?
B.2	WH645 – 207, 115	to 542 Sqn
B.2	WH659 – 90	Conv to T.4
B.2	WH705 – 115	to 139 Sqn
T.4	WH848 – Stn Flt	to Stn Flt Binbrook
B.2	WH854 – 90	Conv to T.4
B.2	WH866 – 115	to Stn Flt Binbrook
B.2	WH870 – 90, 35, 207	to 32 Sqn
B.2	WH876 – 115, 207	to 73 Sqn
B.2	WH880 – 90	to 50 Sqn
B.2	WH882 – 90	to 40 Sqn
B.2	WH883 – 115	to 50 Sqn
B.2	WH885 – 115, 90	to 6 Sqn
B.2	WH904 – 207, 35	Conv to T.11
B.2	WH905 – 207, 115	to Stn Flt Binbrrok
B.2	WH906 – 207	Xxd Marham 3.12.54
B.2	WH913 – 35	to 245 Sqn
B.2	WH919 – 35	to 231 OCU

B.2	WH920 – 35	to 231 OCU
B.2	WH925 – 207	to 18 Sqn
B.2	WH944 – 35	to 231 OCU
B.2	WJ603 – 115	to 35 Sqn
B.2	WJ620 – 115	to 50 Sqn
B.2	WJ631 – 207, 115	to 9 Sqn
B.2	WJ632 – 90	to 40 Sqn
B.2	WJ637 – 35	to 231 OCU
B.2	WJ642 – 35	to 15 MU
B.2	WJ648 – 207, 35	to 45 Sqn
B.2	WJ718 – 207, 35, 115	to 61 Sqn
B.2	WJ719 – 35	to 245 Sqn
B.2	WJ731 – 90	to 50 Sqn
B.2	WJ751 – 115, 35	to 15 MU
B.2	WJ752 – 115, 35	to RN
T.4	WJ861 – 35, Stn Flt	to SF Weston Zoyland
B.2	WJ975 – 35	to to 44 Sqn
B.2	WJ978 – 207	to DH Props
B.2	WJ980 – 115	to SF Binbrook
B.2	WJ986 – 90, 115	to 542 Sqn
B.2	WJ993 – 90, 207	to 6 Sqn
B.2	WJ994 – 115	to SF Binbrook
B.2	WJ995 – 90	to RAE
B.2	WK102 – 207	to 75 Sqn RNZAF
B.2	WK104 – 90	to 32 Sqn
B.2	WK105 – 90	Crashed Wereham 25.4.54
B.2	WK106 – 90, 207	Conv to T.11
B.2	WK110 – 115	to SF Binbrook
B.2	WK114 – 35	to 76 Sqn
B.2	WK117 – 207, 90	to 18 Sqn
B.2	WK133 – 35	to 245 Sqn
B.2	WK139 – 90	to 15 MU
B.2	WK140 – 115	to 15 MU
B.2	WK142 – 115, 207, 90	to 98 Sqn?

231 OCU, February 1976 – July 1982

T.4	WE188	sold 19.11.81
T.4	WE192	sold 26.11.81
B.2	WJ637	to Cranwell 20.9.82
B.2	WJ681	AS 8735M 8.1.82
B.2	WJ731	(to Wyton)
B.2	WJ753	Crashed Marham 19.6.78
T.4	WJ869	to Zimbabwe 20.3.81
T.4	WJ870	AS 8683M 16.4.81
T.4	WJ877	(to Wyton)
T.4	WJ879	(to Wyton)
T.4	WT483	sold 11.11.81

100 Squadron, January 1976 – January 1982

B.2	WD948	to Manston
B.2	WE113	to 231 OCU
B.2	WH666	to Zimbabwe 20.3.81

B.2	WH667	Crashed Akrotiri 7.11.80
B.2	WH670	(to Wyton)
B.2	WH703	AS 8490M 29.3.76
T.4	WH848	to Luqa
T.19	WH903	AS 8584M 21.12.77
E.15	WH948	Crashed 15.8.77
E.15	WH964	(to Wyton)
E.15	WH972	(to Wyton)
E.15	WH983	(to Wyton)
B.2	WJ567	(to Wyton)
B.2	WJ640	AS 8722M 6.11.81
B.2	WJ678	(to Wyton)
B.2	WJ753	Crashed 19.6.78
E.15	WJ756	(to Wyton)
E.15	WJ975	Sold 21.5.80
T.19	WK106	SOC 16.3.76
B.2	WK116	Crashed Akrotiri 25.2.82
B.2	WK118	(to Wyton)
B.2	WK162	(to Wyton)
B.2	WK164	(to Wyton)
B.2	WP515	(to Wyton)

39 (1 PRU) Squadron, December 1993 to date

PR.9	XH131
PR.9	XH134
PR.9	XH135
PR.9	XH168
PR.9	XH169
PR.9	XH175
T.4	WJ866
T.4	
PR.7	WT509
PR.7	

Handley Page Victor, May 1965 – October 1993

55 Sqn:	May 1965–October 1993
57 Sqn:	December 1965–January 1986
214 Sqn:	July 1966–January 1977
232 OCU:	May 1970–
TTF:	1965–May 1970

(The B(K).1A aircraft are also recorded as B.1A(K2P) in the Marham ORB).

B(K).1A	XH615	scrapped
B(K).1A	XH620	scrapped
B(K).1A	XH646	w/o 8.68
B(K).1A	XH647	scrapped
B(K).1A	XH648	to Duxford
B(K).1A	XH667	
K.1A	XH587	
B.1A	XH589	conv to K.1A, scrapped
B.1A	XH591	conv to K.1A, scrapped
B.1A	XH592	to Cosford as 8429M
B.1A	XH593	to 2 SoTT as 8428M
B.1A	XH594	scrapped
B.1A	XH614	conv to K.1A, scrapped

B.1A	XH616	conv to K.1A, Manston Fire training
B.1A	XH617	w/o 19.7.60
K.1A	XH619	scrapped
K.1A	XH621	scrapped
K.1A	XH645	scrapped
K.1A	XH649	scrapped
K.1A	XH650	Manston dump
K.1A	XH651	scrapped
K.1	XA926	scrapped
K.1	XA927	scrapped
K.1	XA928	to Farnborough
B.1	XA930	conv to K.1
K.1	XA932	scrapped
B.1	XA933	scrapped
K.1	XA936	to 8911M at Marham
K.1	XA937	PEE Foulness
K.1	XA938	scrapped
K.1	XA939	to Catterick
B.1	XA940	scrapped
K.1	XA941	scrapped
B(K).1	XA937	PEE Foulness
B(K).1A	XH618	w/o 24.3.75
K.2	XH671	
K.2	XH672	
K.2	XH673	
K.2	XH675	to Marham fire dump
K.2	XL158	
K.2	XL160	DBR Marham
K.2	XL161	
K.2	XL162	to Manston FSCTE
K.2	XL163	to St Athan
K.2	XL164	
K.2	XL188	to Kinloss fire dump
K.2	XL190	
K.2	XL192	to Marham fire dump
K.2	XL231	
K.2	XL511	
K.2	XL512	
K.2	XL513	
K.2	XM715	
K.2	XM717	

Panavia Tornado, January 1983 to date

It must be stressed that, in the case of Tornado units, it is only possible to list the aircraft that are on the notional establishment of a given squadron. Within the Tornado force a great deal of aircraft 'borrowing' goes on; this is especially true with regard to exercises and detachments. If a squadron is in Goose Bay, Canada, it will make use of the 'North American' fleet (comprising aircraft loaned by various units for a certain number of months), and its own aircraft may well be loaned to another unit. Thus a photograph of 12 Squadron Tornadoes at low level over Alaska in mid-1994 would feature II Squadron crew on a II Squadron deployment.

Panavia Tornado, II Squadron, December 1991 to date

The aircraft tail-letters of II (AC) Squadron traditionally make up the words SHINEY TWO AC. Extra aircraft are given codes as appropriate, the two trainers, for example, being coded X and Z.

GR.1A	ZA369/II	
GR.1A	ZA370/A	
GR.1A	ZA371/C	
GR.1A	ZA372/E	
GR.1A	ZA373/H	
GR.1A	ZA395/N	
GR.1A	ZA397/O	Crashed Canada 1.8.94
GR.1A	ZA398/S	
GR.1A	ZA400/T	
GR.1A	ZA401/R	
GR.1A	ZA404/W	
GR.1A	ZA405/Y	
GR.1T	ZA411/Z	
GR.1T	ZA552/X	
GR.1A	ZA559/L	
GR.1A	ZD996/I	

Panavia Tornado, XIII Squadron, February 1994 to date

GR.1A	ZG705/A	
GR.1A	ZG707/B	
GR.1A	ZG708/C	Crashed Scotland 1.9.94
GR.1A	ZG709/I	
GR.1A	ZG710/D	
GR.1A	ZG711/E	
GR.1A	ZG712/F	
GR.1A	ZG713/G	
GR.1A	ZG714/H	
GR.1A	ZG725/J	Crashed Sardinia 19.9.94
GR.1A	ZG726/K	
GR.1A	ZG727/L	
GR.1T	ZG750/Y	
GR.1T	ZG752/Z	

Panavia Tornado, 27 Squadron, May 1983 – renumbered as 12 Squadron, October 1993

GR.1	ZA365
GR.1	ZA375
GR.1	ZA376/JL
GR.1T	ZA409
GR.1T	ZA410
GR.1	ZA447
GR.1	ZA450
GR.1	ZA452
GR.1	ZA453
GR.1	ZA455
GR.1	ZA473
GR.1	ZA474
GR.1	ZA475

GR.1	ZA490	
GR.1	ZA491	
GR.1	ZA492	
GR.1	ZA494	Crashed Goose Bay 7.84
GR.1T	ZA540/JQ	
GR.1	ZA542/JA	
GR.1	ZA546/JB	
GR.1	ZA547/JC	
GR.1T	ZA549	
GR.1	ZA550/JD	
GR.1	ZA553/JE	
GR.1	ZA557	
GR.1	ZA561/JH	
GR.1T	ZA562/JT	
GR.1	ZA563	
GR.1	ZA564/JK	
GR.1	ZA591/JH	
GR.1	ZA601/JG	
GR.1	ZA603	Crashed Germany 11.84
GR.1	ZA604	
GR.1	ZA609	
GR.1	ZA613	

Panavia Tornado, 617 Squadron, January 1983 – April 1994

The squadron adopted its Second World War Lancaster codes of 'AJ' to add to the more normal single-letter identification.

GR.1T	ZA367/AJ-Y
GR.1T	ZA368/AJ-P
GR.1	ZA392
GR.1	ZA393/AJ-T
GR.1	ZA399/AJ-G
GR.1	ZA411/AJ-S
GR.1	ZA446/AJ-H
GR.1	ZA456/AJ-Q
GR.1	ZA457/AJ-J
GR.1	ZA458/AJ-A
GR.1	ZA459/AJ-B
GR.1	ZA460/AJ-A
GR.1	ZA461/AJ-M
GR.1	ZA462/AJ-J -M?
GR.1	ZA465/AJ-F
GR.1	ZA469/AJ-O
GR.1	ZA470/AJ-L
GR.1	ZA472
GR.1	ZA473/AJ-K
GR.1	ZA546/AJ-C
GR.1	ZA547
GR.1	ZA554
GR.1	ZA558/F
GR.1	ZA560/C
GR.1	ZA561
GR.1	ZA563
GR.1	ZA585/G

GR.1	ZA592/B
GR.1	ZA593
GR.1T	ZA598/S
GR.1T	ZA599/P
GR.1	ZA600
GR.1	ZA601
GR.1	ZA603
GR.1	ZA604
GR.1	ZA605/G
GR.1	ZA606
GR.1	ZA608/A
GR.1	ZA609/J
GR.1	ZA610
GR.1	ZA611
GR.1T	ZA612
GR.1	ZA613/N
GR.1	ZA614/E
GR.1T	ZD713/P
GR.1	ZD793
GR.1	ZD849/AJ-F

Other Types

In common with most stations, Marham has operated a variety of aircraft other than its major types. These have either served on the Station Flight, or as add-ons to the individual squadrons. They are among the hardest to identify, usually appearing in the ORBs only in the event of a crash. Most units had a variety of light types such as Magisters, Tiger Moths, Oxfords, Ansons, and Proctors as communication and liaison aircraft. The details of known examples that have not already featured in one of the main sections above are given here.

Anson C.19	VV964	
Anson C.19	TX155	
Anson C.19	TX196	
Anson C.19	VM409	
Anson C.21	VV964	
Oxford I	NM510	Crashed 1.4.51

APPENDIX C

MARHAM BURIALS

Over the years that Marham has been an RAF station, the burial grounds in the village have been used as the last resting place for a number of Marham personnel. The following lists give the basic headstone details. All headstones are in the standard Commonwealth War Graves style. The entries are in chronological order.

The major collection is in the village cemetery.

Plt Off J. Maxwell RCAF	3.8.41
Sgt P. Docking RCAF	17.6.41
Plt Off A. Brown	17.6.41
Plt Off A. Evans	17.6.41
Sgt W. Blades RCAF	30.8.41
Sgt R. Newbury	11.11.41
Flt Sgt H. Mellows	11.11.41
Sgt L. Pitt RCAF	11.11.41
Sgt J. Dix	7.11.41
Sgt E. Lawrence	24.11.41
Sgt P. Crosbie	24.11.41
Sgt M. Constable RCAF	7.9.42
Sgt S. Scott RCAF	7.9.42
Flt Lt L. Colbran RCAF	7.9.42
Flt Sgt C. Langeley RCAF	8.9.42
Sgt S. Orford	15.1.42
Sgt R. Shaw	15.1.42
Sgt D. Maskill RCAF	15.1.42
Sgt D. Faith	15.1.42
Sgt A. Thorburn	23.4.42
Sgt J. Reynolds	11.5.42
Sgt K. Jones	11.5.42
Sgt R. Batchen	11.5.42
Sgt C. Jones	12.6.42
Flt Sgt W. McCann RCAF	28.6.42
Fg Off J. Frankcomb RNZAF	14.9.42
Sgt E. Pellow	14.9.42
Sgt S. Ives	14.9.42
Sgt E. Recchia ??RCAF	29.10.42
Sgt R. Ponting	29.10.42
Sgt W. Hood RNZAF	29.10.42

Sgt P. Head	29.10.42
Sgt A. McIntosh	29.10.42
Sgt R. Clare	27.1.43
Fg Off E. Doyle	27.1.43
Fg Off G. McCormick RAAF	27.2.43
Flt Sgt K. Newland RNZAF	30.3.43
Flt Sgt B. Harvey RCAF	30.3.43
Sgt M. Langdale-Hunt RNZAF	30.3.43
Fg Off B. Neal RNZAF	30.3.43
Fg Off O. Thompson	1.5.43
Fg Off A. Rea	27/28.5.43
Fg Off S. Abbott RAAF	9.8.43
Cpl F. Magson	9.8.43
Sqn Ldr E. Costello-Bowen	9.8.43
Flt Lt B. MacDonald RCAF	11.8.43
Plt Off D. Ballard	14.12.52
Sgt A. Cameron	10.12.54
Flt Lt C. Moore	25.4.54
Fg Off C. Hasler	3.12.54
Fg Off G. Hayes	3.12.54
SAC D. Farmer	14.5.59
Flt Lt D. Howard	11.9.59
Fg Off P. Wormall	11.9.59
Fg Off C. Candy	11.9.59
C/T R. Sewell	11.9.59
Flt Sgt E. Barber	27.11.61
SAC A. Muir	9.5.62
Sgt R. Noble	6.5.64
Flt Lt L. Hawkins	6.5.64
Flt Lt F. Welles	6.5.54
Flt Lt W. Brownlie	7.5.64
SAC W. Whiteside	28.11.67
Flt Lt W. Gallienne	19.8.68
SAC P. Jones	28.5.70
WO B. Dove	11.8.75
Sgt K. Williamson	7.12.77
WO W. Watt	25.1.83
SAC P. Linning	12.2.83
Flt Lt J. Sheen	12.11.85
WO J. Harriman	13.6.86
Flt Lt C. Oliver	9.8.88

The two Marham burial plots reflect the losses in two world wars and the post-1945 period.

Flt Lt M. Collier	17.1.91		Sgt J. Eades	23.2.41
Sqn Ldr K. Weeks	22.1.91		Plt Off S. Barnett	4.4.41
J/Y K. Woffinden	31.10.91		Sgt H. Chard	4.4.41
			Fg Off F. Holmes	30.4.41
			Sgt K. Martin	12.5.41

There is also a plot in the churchyard containing a further 16 Second World War and two First World War graves.

			Plt Off B. Lymbery	18.5.41
			Sgt W. Webber RCAF	18.5.41
			Sgt G. Aikenhead	15.6.41
2nd Lt A. Hodges RFC	20.3.18			
Flt Cadet W. Barker	13.6.18		German graves, located in the main plot	
LAC D. George	5.11.39			
Sgt E. Summers	5.11.39		J. Reisenger	14.6.41
LAC G. Carter	14.4.40		T. Romelt	23.8.42
Plt Off J. Marshman	1.5.40		G. Rockstrok	23.8.42
Plt Off P. Leach	21.7.40		R. Hellmann	23.8.42
Sgt J. Myers	9.12.40		R. Bodenhagen	23.8.42
Sgt D. Thomas	23.2.41		F. Schiller	13.1.47
Fg Off P. Maclaren	15.1.41			

APPENDIX D

AIRFIELD PLANS

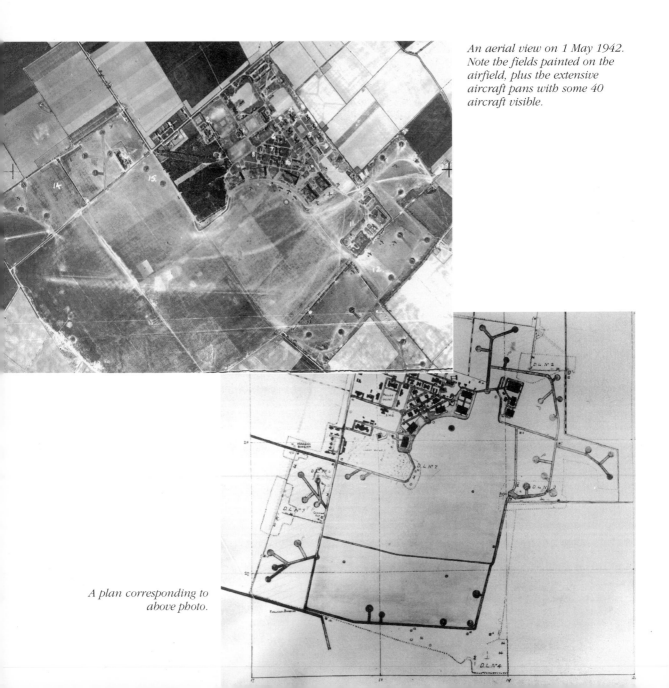

An aerial view on 1 May 1942. Note the fields painted on the airfield, plus the extensive aircraft pans with some 40 aircraft visible.

A plan corresponding to above photo.

A site plan for Marham, 1935.

A site plan showing planned runway layout.

Extracts from the Luftwaffe target folder.

Marham Home Defence landing ground 1917, plus a description of the facilities.

MARHAM SQUADRON STATION 6TH BRIGADE.

MARHAM.
6th Brigade Flight Station (Midland Area ; H.D. Group, 47th Wing).

LOCATION.—England, Norfolk, 6 miles from Swaffham (pop., 3,200). · Narboroug Aerodrome is 1 mile to the north-east.
Railway Stations :—Narborough (G.E. Rly.), 4 miles. Swaffham (G.E. Rly.), 6 miles.
Road :—Fair approach road from the main road.

FUNCTION.—Home Defence Station for Headquarters and "C" Flight of No. 9. Squadron (6th Brigade).

ESTABLISHMENT.

Personnel.

			Transport.			
Officers	..	.. 14	Motor Cars	..	..	1
W.O.'s and N.C.O.'s above			Light Tenders	..	..	4
the rank of Corporal	..	15	Heavy Tenders	..	..	6
Corporals	..	.. 14	Motor Cycles	..	..	8
Rank and File	..	.. 113	Sidecars	..	..	4
Women	..	.. 3	Trailers (Mark I.)	..	..	3
Women (Household)	..	12	Repair Trailers	..	..	4
			Ambulances	..	..	3
TOTAL (*exclusive of Hotel Staff*)		171	Total			

Portions of the above transport are allotted to the Flights at Mattishall and ?. St. Mary.

Machines.— F. 2b (changing to Avro) 8

AERODROME.—Maximum dimensions in yards, 740×550. Area, 80 acres, of which 10 acres are occupied by the Station Buildings. Height above sea level, 75 feet. Soil, light loam on chalk. Surface, good, level. General surroundings, open and flat with large field?

METEOROLOGICAL.—The reports for the winter months, October, 1917, to March 1918, inclusive, for 1,926 daylight hours observed are as follows :—

Low Clouds Hours.	Rainfall Hours.	Snow Hours.	Mist Hours.	Fog Hours.	Possible Flying Hours.	Total Hours of Daylight observed.	Ratio of Possible Flying to Daylight Hours % .	Gales
117·5	309	570	100·5	—	1,100	1,926	57·12	2

TENURE POLICY.—Not at present on the list of permanent stations.

ACCOMMODATION.

Technical Buildings.	*Map Reference.*	*Regimental Buildings.*	*Map Reference.*
2 Aeroplane Sheds—		Officers' Mess	3
Each 130′×60′	1	3 Officers' Quarters ..	—
M.T. Shed, 120′×80′ ..	—	Officers' Baths	—
M.T. Repair Shed	—	Officers' Latrines ..	—
General Workshop,		Sergeants' Mess	—
115′×15′	—	Regimental Institute ..	4
Smiths' Shop, 20′×16′ ..	—	Regimental Store	—
Technical Store and Office ..	—	5 Men's Huts	—
Technical Store	—	Men's Baths	—
Oil Store	—	Men's Latrines and Ablu-	
Petrol Store	—	tion	—
Offices	—	Coal Yard	—
Guard House	—		
Machine Gun Store ..	—		
Bomb Store	—		
Wireless Telegraphy Hut ..	—		

MARHAM

Lat. 52° 39′ 10″ N. Long. 00° 33′ 30″ E. 70 FT. A.S.L.

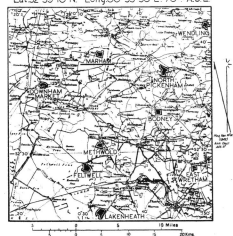

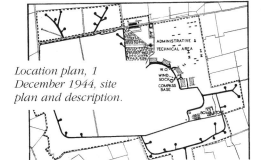

Location plan, 1 December 1944, site plan and description.

ADMINISTRATIVE & TECHNICAL AREA

W.O. WIND SOCK COMPASS BASE BOMB STORE

DESCRIPTION OF MARHAM AIRFIELD

As at 1st December, 1944.

Grid Reference : G.S.G.S. No. 3907. (1-in. Map.) G.186280. Sheet 66.

Graticule : Latitude : 52° 39′ 08″ N.   *Height A.S.L. :* 80 ft.
Longitude : 00° 33′ 00″ E.   *COUNTY :* Norfolk.
Locality : 10 miles S.E. King's Lynn.

COMMAND : Bomber (R.A.F.).   *Nearest Railway Station :*
Narborough and Pentney, L.N.E.R. (3 miles).

FUNCTION : Operational Base.

AFFILIATED AIRFIELDS : Downham Market (Sub-station).

LANDING AREA :

Runways		Extensibility		
Q.D.M.	Dimensions	Dimensions	Remarks	
245°	3,000 × 100 yds.	4,000 yds.	Entails diversions of	
293°	2,000 × 100 yds.	2,000 yds.	main road and demo-	
335°	2,000 × 100 yds.	2,000 yds.	lition of 2 farms and R.A.F. buildings.	

Type of Surface : Concrete, ~~estimated date of completion 9/45~~

PERMANENT LANDMARKS :
(i) By Day.. .. .. .. Lady's wood.
(ii) By Night .. .. .. Nil.

PERMANENT OBSTRUCTIONS .. Lady's wood in N.W. corner of airfield.

FACILITIES :
Airfield Lighting .. .. .. Mark I.
Beam Approach .. .. ..
Radio .. .. .. Q.D.M. :
Flying Control .. .. .. Yes.

ACCOMMODATION .. .. .. Permanent technical and domestic accommodation.

Technical :

	Hangars		Hardstandings	
Type		No.	Type	No.
C.		5	~~Heavy Bomber~~ Very Heavy Bomber	~~36~~ 10.

Domestic :

		Officers	S.N.C.O's	O.R's	Total
R.A.F.	.. .. ..	139	296	1,893	2,328
W.A.A.F.	.. .. ..	10	16	318	344

REMARKS :

23

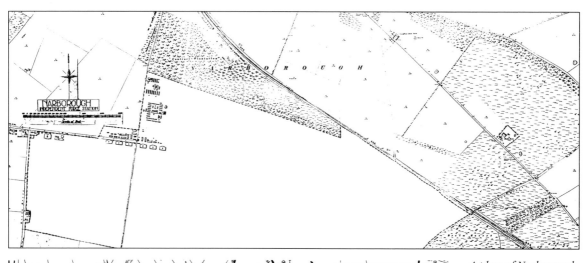

A plan of Narborough.

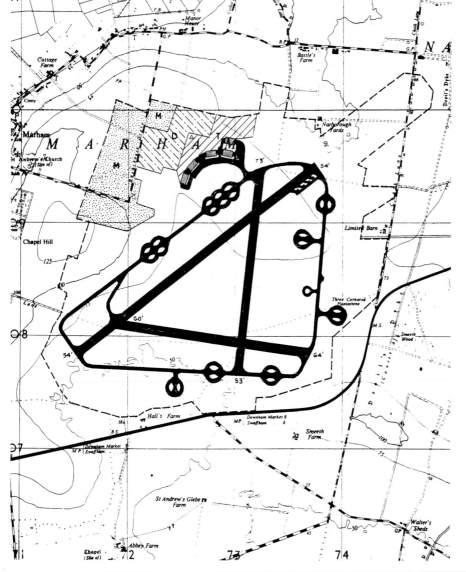

Marham, June 1965.

INDEX